MANAGING COMMUNITY PRACTICE

Principles, policies and programmes

Second edition

Edited by Sarah Banks, Hugh Butcher,
Andrew Orton and Jim Robertson

First published in 2003
Second edition published in Great Britain in 2013 by

The Policy Press
University of Bristol
Fourth Floor
Beacon House
Queen's Road
Bristol BS8 1QU
UK
Tel +44 (0)117 331 4054
Fax +44 (0)117 331 4093
e-mail tpp-info@bristol.ac.uk
www.policypress.co.uk

North American office:
The Policy Press
c/o The University of Chicago Press
1427 East 60th Street
Chicago, IL 60637, USA
t: +1 773 702 7700
f: +1 773-702-9756
e:sales@press.uchicago.edu
www.press.uchicago.edu

British Library Cataloguing in Publication Data
A catalogue record for this book is available from the British Library.

Library of Congress Cataloging-in-Publication Data
A catalog record for this book has been requested.

ISBN 978 1 44730 124 0 paperback
ISBN 978 1 44730 125 7 hardcover

Cover design by Qube Design Associates
Front cover: image kindly supplied by istock.com
Printed and bound in Great Britain by Hobbs, Southampton
The Policy Press uses environmentally responsible print partners

Contents

List of figures, tables and boxes

List of figures

List of tables

List of boxes

Preface to the second edition

Preparing a new edition of a book offers a timely opportunity to reflect on how the world has changed since the previous version, and how the authors' and editors' ideas have (or have not) moved on and developed. Working on the second edition of *Managing community practice* has been particularly interesting, as it is part of an ongoing project on the theme of 'community practice', which began in the early 1990s, leading to the publication of *Community and public policy* (Butcher et al, 1993). That book used the concept of 'community practice' to explore the impact of what we might now call 'the community turn' in public policy on the work of practitioners in fields ranging from the arts to criminal justice. *Community and public policy* described and debated the focus on 'community' as both a source of and solution to social and economic problems through exploring the practice of community arts, community health, community policing and a range of other fields. Following the launch conference for that book in 1993, a need for further work on the management of community practice was identified and a working group was established to explore this theme. A small research project was undertaken (Thornton, 1996) and a book planned, which was finally published many meetings later as the first edition of *Managing community practice* (Banks et al, 2003).

Aware of the growing focus on 'community' in the middle part of the 'New Labour era' (1997–2010) in the UK, and perhaps reluctant to give up our regular meetings in York, the editors of *Managing community practice* (Banks, Butcher, Henderson and Robertson) devised a plan for a new co-authored book on *Critical community practice*. This book (Butcher et al, 2007) developed a particular model of community practice that took an overtly radical approach to working in and with communities – stressing the importance of understanding and working with the political context, challenging power structures and promoting social justice.

In compiling the second edition of *Managing community practice*, we are very much aware of the constantly changing political, economic and social context and the impact this has on community practice and the management of community practice both in the UK and worldwide. While the focus on 'community' in public policy is still evident, it is important to be aware of the many and changing meanings of 'community' and different rationales for community practice, particularly in a climate of economic austerity and cuts in social welfare provision. We also need to take into account the changes in our own thinking, theorising and understanding of community practice and make clear the differences between the generic, more descriptive concept of 'community practice' and the more specific and value-laden idea of 'critical community practice'.

While the majority of the editorial team and authors remain the same, several have changed, providing an opportunity to bring new ideas and interpretations into the collection. Andrew Orton has joined the editorial team and contributed the final chapter. Paul Henderson, whose major contribution to the thinking behind the book and the community practice project as a whole is still very evident, has left. Murray Hawtin and Tony Herrmann have contributed a new chapter on community research, replacing chapters on auditing and sustaining community involvement in the first edition. All the other chapters have been revised and updated. We hope, therefore, that this new edition will be a useful source of ideas, conceptual frameworks and practice wisdom for all those who are involved in, or who are studying, the challenging role of managing community practice.

References

Banks, S., Butcher, H., Henderson, P. and Robertson, J. (eds) (2003) *Managing community practice: principles, policies and programmes*, Bristol: The Policy Press.

Butcher, H., Glen, A., Henderson, P. and Smith, J. (eds) (1993) *Community and public policy*, London: Pluto Press.

Butcher, H., Banks, S. and Henderson, P., with Robertson, J. (2007) *Critical community practice*, London: The Policy Press.

Thornton, P. (1996) *Management development for community practice*, Leeds: CDF, Northern Office.

Acknowledgements

All those whom we acknowledged and thanked in connection with their contribution to the first edition deserve to be thanked again, because without their support and encouragement, the first edition, upon which this book builds, would never have been possible. We are especially grateful to Paul Henderson, whose thinking contributed greatly to the earlier book, and to the Community Development Foundation (CDF), where Paul worked, for financial and moral support for the first edition. We benefited greatly from the contributions of a range of academics, managers, practitioners and representatives of professional bodies who attended conferences, seminars and meetings on the theme of management for community practice during the 1990s and early 2000s. The list is too long to name everyone individually, but we would particularly like to acknowledge the contribution of Paul Thornton, who undertook the feasibility study on management development for community practice, and Charlie McConnell, formerly Chief Executive of Community Learning Scotland, who worked with us to develop guidelines for post-qualifying training in community practice during 1997–98.

Most importantly, in relation to this new edition, we are very grateful to all the contributors, who have been prepared to work with us in revising their earlier chapters or, in some cases, writing new chapters from scratch.

Finally, we would like to thank Emily Watt, our editor at The Policy Press, and the anonymous referees whom she engaged, for their helpful advice and encouraging enthusiasm for this project.

Sarah Banks, Hugh Butcher, Andrew Orton and Jim Robertson
September 2012

Notes on contributors

Sarah Banks is Professor in the School of Applied Social Sciences and co-director of the Centre for Social Justice and Community Action at Durham University, UK. She researches and teaches in the fields of community development and professional ethics, and has a particular interest in community-based participatory research. Her publications include *Ethics and values in social work* (4th edn, 2012) and edited collections on *Ethical issues in youth work* (2nd edn, 2010) and, with K. Nøhr, *Practising social work ethics around the world: cases and commentaries* (2012).

Alan Barr was formerly based at Glasgow and Strathclyde Universities and Co-Director of the Scottish Community Development Centre. He is the author of many publications on community work and community development and has been particularly involved in developing pioneering approaches to planning and evaluating community development, including: 'Achieving Better Community Development' and 'LEAP – Learning Evaluation and Planning'.

Hugh Butcher has been actively engaged in community practice since the publication of the first edition of this book, participating extensively in user involvement in cancer care in the NHS and voluntary organisations, locally and nationally. In 2010, as a member of the National User Steering Group for NHS Cancer Peer Review, he published *Service user involvement in cancer care: policy, principles and practice*. With prior experience as Head of Department of Applied Social Science and Humanities at Bradford College, a field social worker and a community worker, he has published extensively in the fields of community practice and community development.

Alison Gilchrist is an independent consultant (alisongilchrist. co.uk). She has a particular interest in promoting genuine community involvement in cross-sectoral partnerships and equalities strategies, and has published on the value of networking for community development. Previously, she worked as a community development worker in inner-city neighbourhoods in Bristol, before moving on to teach community and youth work at the University of the West of England and to work in policy and practice development for the Community Development Foundation.

Murray Hawtin was a Community Development Officer in Aberdeen and Leeds for a number of years before becoming a Housing Project Officer. After completing an MA in Housing at York University, he joined the Policy Research Institute (Leeds Metropolitan University), where he was a Senior Researcher for 18 years. Murray left the University to become a Director of COGS (Communities and Organisations: Growth and Support) in 2010. He still teaches and is an external examiner on a number of Community and Youth Work courses.

Tony Herrmann has worked for over 17 years in a range of neighbourhoods in Leeds as a community development worker for community, voluntary and statutory organisations, including a three-year secondment to the University of Leeds to develop community-based learning programmes. He managed the Community Work Training Co, a West Yorkshire Infrastructure organisation, for eight years before becoming a director at COGS in 2007.

Marjorie Mayo is Emeritus Professor of Community Development at Goldsmiths, University of London. She has taught, researched and practised in a variety of settings, across statutory, voluntary and community sectors. Her publications include *Communities and caring: the mixed economy of welfare* (1994), *Imagining tomorrow: adult education for transformation* (1997), *Cultures, communities. Identities: cultural strategies for participation and empowerment* (2000) and, with Gary Craig, *Community empowerment: a reader in participation and development* (1995).

Andrew Orton is Lecturer in Community and Youth Work at Durham University, with experience of working in a wide range of practice settings and roles as a practitioner, manager, volunteer, trustee and consultant. Recent research includes work on enabling cross-community interactions (with the Department for Communities and Local Government) and supporting migrant integration (with the Council of Europe). He has a particular interest in faith-based community development work, and recently completed a study into good practice in diaconal ministry in the Methodist Church in Britain.

Jim Robertson is currently Chair of the Churches Community Work Alliance. He is co-coordinator of the community resilience project and is currently a project tutor on the Faith in Community Project. Formerly Senior Lecturer, Faculty of Health, Social Work and Education, University of Northumbria, he is co-author of *Challenging* *communities* (2001) and *Acting in good faith* (2004) and is concerned with church-related community development and neighbourhood renewal.

Introduction

Sarah Banks, Hugh Butcher, Andrew Orton and Jim Robertson

Managing community practice

This book is about the management of community practice. By *community practice* we mean the work done by paid and voluntary workers that is based in and/or concerned to stimulate or develop communities of place, interest or identity. 'Community practice' is an umbrella term that encompasses the work of volunteers and community activists, specialist community workers/community development workers (who have a main focus on work in/with communities), as well as the work of other professionals (who may take a community-oriented approach to their work and for whom stimulating and supporting 'community' is part of their work). The purposes of such work may be, for example, to gain rights for oppressed groups, achieve better-quality community services, enhance community governance, develop or support community capacity for self-help and social enterprise. The role of community practitioners is to ensure effective engagement of community members in the identification and realisation of such goals, based on values that emphasise 'active' and 'empowered' citizens, collectively and democratically working to change the conditions that affect people's lives in their communities. Their role is also to work with the conflicts that inevitably emerge between individuals, groups and communities and to identify and challenge discriminatory attitudes and actions.

To talk about *managing* community practice may seem like a contradiction in terms. Community practice is about promoting the self-determination and empowerment of communities and their members, while managing has connotations of control and 'top-down' leadership. However, just as there are many approaches to community practice, some of which are more empowering than others, so there are many approaches to management. In so far as 'management' is about enabling and supporting good practice, as well as ensuring accountability to stakeholders and meeting predetermined targets, it can be regarded as positive and an essential component of community practice. In this book, we are concerned to promote and develop an approach to managing community practice that works in the spirit, and according to the values, of community practice itself – that is, it is about creating learning spaces and learning organisations, promoting democracy in decision-making, and encouraging as well as ensuring practice that is both critical and ethical. The tensions and contradictions that lie in community practice itself – between liberation and control, exclusivity and inclusivity, strong leadership and participatory decision-making – are also present in the process of managing that practice. Managers of community practice have to negotiate tensions between different interest and identity groups, battles for power and control, the dangers of community co-option by government or business interests, and the oppressive attitudes and behaviours that may exist within and between communities. This work is not easy, and the challenges faced by its practitioners and managers change as new contexts for the work emerge.

The changing context for community practice

In 2003, when the first edition of the book was published, the UK was six years into a Labour government that had made a strong commitment to tackling social exclusion and inequality. Large-scale national state-funded programmes such as Sure Start (neighbourhood-based centres working with the poorest children and families) and New Deal for Communities (a 10-year regeneration programme in 39 'deprived' areas) were in progress (Lawless, 2006; Belsky et al, 2007; Batty et al, 2010; Eisenstadt, 2011). There was a focus on 'joined-up' working (inter-departmental and inter-professional) and neighbourhood-based, community-engaged and community-led programmes. Many policymakers, professionals and volunteers were doing 'community' – whether in the sense of policies and practices being based in or focused on communities of place, identity or interest as sites where social problems could be tackled, or in the sense of creating and strengthening 'communities' of active citizens involved in generating solutions. Community (development) work as a specialist occupation, always small and relatively marginal, was expanding its influence and defining its role, values and skills as part of mainstream policy and practice to tackle social exclusion and promote community engagement and empowerment – as later outlined in *The community development challenge* (Communities and Local Government, 2007). In addition to debates about whether 'community-based' policies could, in fact, make a significant contribution to tackling disadvantage and promoting social inclusion, critiques were also emerging of what were perceived as 'managerialist', 'top-down' and target-driven approaches to promoting and managing community engagement, with the imposition of performance measures and sometimes tokenistic partnerships (Hodgson, 2004; Shaw, 2008; Dargan, 2009; Banks, 2011).

Since the publication of the first edition, however, the political, economic and social climate in the UK and globally has changed significantly. Following the financial crisis starting in 2007/08 and the election of a Conservative–Liberal Democrat Coalition government in the UK in 2010, the ambitious national state-funded programmes have ended or been absorbed into mainstream local authority services, many third-sector organisations are facing financial difficulties, and the profile of professional community (development) work is in decline. Yet, 'community' as a focus of public policy is still very much in evidence – albeit in different guises and with changed emphases. In times of economic austerity and Conservative-led government, the turn to 'community' focuses inevitably on self-help, volunteering, social enterprise and community organising as a challenge and alternative to state provision of welfare. Following the election of the Coalition government in 2010, for example, small-scale national programmes of youth volunteering (the National Citizen Service, see: https://nationalcitizenservice.direct.gov.uk) and training of community organisers (see: www.cocollaborative.org.uk/) have been introduced to stimulate citizen responsibility and locally based action, alongside the promotion of a 'new localism', with greater rights and powers for local governments and communities (www.urbanforum.org.uk/briefings/localism-act-briefing). Debates are now beginning to focus on the 'responsibilisation' of communities in the context of withdrawal or reduction of state services, and the capacity for 'communities' and volunteers to survive, let alone engage, in community-led service delivery and community enterprise (Scott, 2011).

Yet, while the context in which 'community practice' takes place and some aspects of its rationale have changed, the centrality of community practice remains and its role is as contested as ever – as are the challenges for those who play a role in its management.

Outline of the book

In this book, we aim to offer conceptual and practical frameworks and ideas that will be of use to those who have responsibility for managing community practice – helping them face the challenges presented by the continuing development of a community focus in public policy.

The first two chapters outline the nature of community practice and the context in which it has developed and is currently taking place. In Chapter One, Banks and Butcher explore the nature of community practice, examining meanings of 'community' and offering illustrations of different approaches to community practice (from self-organised community groups to the co-production of services). A set of values and principles for community practice is outlined and discussed, along with the relationship between community practice and critical community practice. In Chapter Two, Mayo and Robertson locate the development of community practice in a historical and policy context, charting the 'rediscovery of community' and the development of community-based social policies in the 1960s and 1970s, through the New Labour project at the turn of the century in the UK, with its focus on neighbourhood renewal and community participation, to the focus on the 'Big Society' and its implications for community practice post-2010.

The next three chapters move into a closer examination of the role of management in community practice. Chapter Three, by Butcher, explores the nature of the roles of managing and organising, focusing particularly on those aspects that are distinctive for community practice. Butcher then continues in Chapter Four to pursue in more detail the types of staff and organisational development that can best enable community practice to flourish. He articulates an experiential learning approach, based on theories of individual and organisational learning cycles, drawing on the work of Kolb and others.

In Chapter Five, Banks explores some of the ethical conflicts and dilemmas that arise for managers of community practice, particularly in relation to issues of power and responsibility. She uses two case studies relating to the work of a UK neighbourhood regeneration programme and a non-governmental organisation working in conflict-ridden areas of Pakistan to illustrate how managers conceptualise and handle ethical dilemmas, and demonstrates how their practice embodies certain core values or principles.

The book then moves on to cover the management of specific aspects of community practice, focusing particularly on the approaches that can be taken and the skills required of practitioners and managers. In Chapter Six, Gilchrist offers a critical analysis of the concepts and practice of partnership-working and networking, particularly as these apply to community and voluntary-sector organisations. She highlights some of the complexities and difficulties of partnership-working, and suggests ways in which work in this area can be developed by both practitioners and managers. In Chapter Seven, Hawtin and Herrmann take account of the increasing trend towards community-based research and outline the role of managers in supporting community groups and organisations in conducting their own research. They offer three examples from practice, outlining the complex processes and achievements of research that is 'community-led' (when community groups themselves own and undertake research in collaboration with others). Barr (Chapter Eight) emphasises the importance of evaluation in developing good community practice, and draws on three participative models – Achieving Better Community Development (ABCD), Learning Evaluation and Planning (LEAP) and Visioning Outcomes in Community Engagement (VOiCE) – which can be applied to both the planning and evaluation stages of programmes or projects. He outlines the importance of involving relevant stakeholders in designing and implementing evaluation.

The book concludes with a chapter by Orton, which draws together the earlier chapters of the book and identifies some of the challenges to the sustainability of community practice. He identifies three areas for further research and development: the interplay between individual and organisational learning, organisational design and management within changing socio-political contexts; the relationship between localism and community empowerment; and developing strengthened communities of practice, the members of which are able to reflect and learn together.

References

Banks, S. (2011) 'Re-gilding the ghetto: community work and community development in twenty-first century Britain', in Lavalette, M. (ed) *Radical social work today: social work at the crossroads*, Bristol: The Policy Press, pp 165–85.

Batty, E., Beatty, C., Foden, M., Lawless, P., Pearson, S. and Wilson, I. (2010) *The New Deal for Communities experience: a final assessment*, London: Communities and Local Government.

Belsky, J., Barnes, J. and Melhuish, E.C. (eds) (2007) *The national evaluation of Sure Start: does area-based early intervention work?*, Bristol: The Policy Press.

Communities and Local Government (2007) *The community development challenge*, London: Communities and Local Government.

Dargan, L. (2009) 'Participation and local urban regeneration: the case of the New Deal for Communities (NDC) in the UK', *Regional Studies*, vol 43, no 2, pp 305–17.

Eisenstadt, N. (2011) *Providing a sure start: how government discovered early childhood*, Bristol: The Policy Press.

Hodgson, L. (2004) 'Manufactured civil society: counting the cost', *Critical Social Policy*, vol 24, no 2, pp 139–64.

Lawless, P. (2006) 'Area-based interventions: rationale and outcomes: the New Deal for Communities programme in England', *Urban Studies*, vol 43, no 11, pp 1991–2011.

Scott, M. (2011) 'Reflections on the "Big Society"', *Community Development Journal*, vol 46, no 1, pp 132–7.

Shaw, M. (2008) 'Community development and the politics of community', *Community Development Journal*, vol 43, no 1, pp 24–36.

ONE

What is community practice?

Sarah Banks and Hugh Butcher

Introduction

This chapter outlines the nature of community practice – defined as work that stimulates, supports and engages 'active communities'. Along with Chapter Two on historical and recent policy developments, it sets the scene for the rest of the book, which focuses on issues relating to the management of community practice. In this chapter, we briefly discuss the 'community turn' in public policy and the growth of work with a community focus. We then explore the contested concept of 'community', leading to a discussion of the nature of 'community practice'. We examine the nature of community practice by first considering who its practitioners are, and then discussing how the power and goals of institutions and practitioners interact to create the complex field of community practice. Next, we describe and illustrate a range of different approaches to community practice, outline the underpinning values and principles of action, and discuss the nature and role of critical community practice. While acknowledging the challenges of implementing a critical community practice model in a climate of austerity, we argue that it is more important than ever to take a critical stance in relation to this kind of work, in order to resist and move beyond some of the more regressive political and policy trends that are outlined in Chapter Two.

The 'community turn' in public policy

As noted in the Preface, it is now 20 years since the publication of *Community and public policy* (Butcher et al, 1993). That book introduced the concept of 'community practice' and examined a range of public policy initiatives that had resulted in the growth of work with a community focus on the part of a growing number of practitioners (including paid community development workers). Chapters covered a range of areas, including: community care, community arts, community youth work, community enterprise, community government and community policing. Contributors noted the trends towards developing and delivering services at the level of both neighbourhood and interest/ identity communities, and engaging members of such communities in consultation about their needs and involving them in service planning and delivery.

During the last 20 years, there has been a continuing, if sometimes uneven, trend towards community-oriented policies and associated professional practices. This has been based on an ambition to make institutions and organisations that serve the public more 'community responsive' and to stimulate community-led services and activities. In the UK, for example, until 2010, when a change of government coupled with a policy of financial austerity began to make an impact on public sector and social welfare spending, there was a growth in the number of posts at professional, policymaking and managerial levels with a brief to develop and implement community policies. While the growth of paid posts in public- and third-sector organisations for community development workers has come to a halt, and some of the community practitioners in other professions (such as health or policing) may be losing their jobs as a result of public-sector cutbacks, nevertheless, the importance of community-based activities (self-help, community enterprise, community surveillance) is increasingly stressed in public policy and government responses. Indeed, there is positive encouragement of organic, 'autonomous' community activities (unfettered by state support or direction), which are seen as a good in themselves as well as a way of replacing the state as a provider of social welfare. The concept of community practice, therefore, is of continuing relevance and importance, and must be understood in relation to changing political and policy contexts and understandings of 'community'.

'Community' in relation to 'community practice'

There is no shortage of discussions of the various meanings of 'community' and the contested nature of the concept (eg Bauman, 2001; Little, 2002; Somerville, 2011). Indeed, most books on work in or with 'communities' have a section on this topic, and we hesitate to add yet another variation on this well-trodden theme (see, eg, Willmott, 1989; Mayo, 1994, 2000; Popple, 1995; Hoggett, 1997; Gilchrist and Taylor, 2011). Yet, it is impossible to develop an account of the nature of community practice without discussing the nature of 'community'.

One of the difficulties with 'community' is that it falls into the category of what Plant (1974) calls an 'essentially contested concept'. As Plant points out, 'community' has both a descriptive and an evaluative meaning. The descriptive meaning refers to features of the world that describe what being a 'community' is – for example, 'a group of people with something in common'. Community has many descriptive meanings – indeed, as long ago as 1955, Hillery noted 94 definitions (Hillery, 1955, quoted in Clarke, 1981). The evaluative meaning comprises the value connotations that attach to the term – that is, 'community' is still generally seen in positive terms, conjuring up images of warmth, friendliness, collaboration and, sometimes, joint action. These positive value connotations ignore the possibility of 'community' also entailing stifling conformity, exclusiveness and resistance to innovation and change.

In what follows, we draw on our earlier work (Butcher, 1993), where we identified three senses of the term 'community': 'descriptive', 'value' and 'active'. The first two senses build on Plant's distinction between descriptive and evaluative meanings. The third meaning is developed from the other two, and has particular relevance to community practice in that it refers to groups of people with something in common who act in concert to influence policy or work towards change within their neighbourhoods or communities of interest or identity. The three senses of community adapted from Butcher (1993, pp 11–18) are summarised as follows.

Descriptive community

Descriptive community refers to social scientists' use of the term to describe a group or network of people who share something in common. This generally involves both social interaction within the group or network, along with a sense of attachment, identification or belonging. A distinction is often made between three types of communities: territorial communities, communities of interest and communities of identity. In territorial communities, what people have in common is their attachment, identification or sense of belonging to a geographical location – their neighbourhood, village or town – whereas communities of identity or interest are based on identities or shared interests other than physical proximity, such as ethnicity, (dis)ability, occupation, life-threatening illness, faith, sexual orientation, sport or hobbies. These categories are not mutually exclusive, as some communities, such as mining villages, for example, may be rooted in both shared locality and common identities and interests.

It is important to note that 'community' is very often used in the context of policy and practice simply to refer to a geographical neighbourhood (eg 'the Victoria Road community') or set of individuals (eg 'the black community') who may not actually feel any sense of attachment to or identity with the area or group referred to. Strictly speaking, this is a misuse of the term. In this book, we generally use descriptive community in its 'strong' sense because having a common attachment or sense of belonging is one of the prerequisites of 'active community'. Descriptive communities tend to vary with respect to a number of attributes, for example: members may have a strong or weak identification with the group or ties to each other; membership may be more or less homogeneous or heterogeneous; boundaries may be relatively open or closed; or the group may be relatively united or divided (Somerville, 2011, pp 10–28). The profile of a 'community' in these respects will be important in understanding the likely effectiveness of particular forms of community practice.

Community as value

As already noted, 'community' not only has several different descriptive meanings, but also has evaluative meanings with positive or negative connotations. However, precisely what values are embodied by the concept of community will vary according to the ideological position held by members of that community. We identify three general types of 'community values' – solidarity, participation and coherence – which may, taken together in their strongest forms, be associated (positively or negatively) with communitarian values and beliefs. Although there are many different versions of communitarianism, broadly speaking they all hold to a view of the individual as constituted by society (Sandel, 1982; Kymlicka, 1990; Etzioni, 1995; Tam, 1998). What people are, and what they can become, is profoundly affected by their inherent disposition and need to associate and to live a life with others in society. The three community values can be described as follows:

- *Solidarity* – the relationships that sustain community members at an emotional level. Solidarity is what inspires affection, even loyalty, of an individual member towards the group.
- *Participation* – shared activities with others, through which individuals are involved in realising common goals and playing a part in the collective life and aspirations of the group.
- *Coherence* – the embracing by individuals of a shared framework of meanings and values that provide some overall sense of their world.

Together, these influence the 'social capital' (Putnam, 2000) of communities – the strength and quality of relationships, norms and trust – which is believed to affect the form and robustness of the ability and capacity of community members to act together in pursuit of common interests and purposes.

Active community

This meaning of community builds on and encompasses the descriptive and value meanings identified earlier. It refers to collective action, by members of territorial, interest or identity communities, that embraces one or more of the communal values of solidarity, participation and coherence. This is the idea of community that public policymakers often have in mind when they seek to promote initiatives drawing upon community strengths and capacities. It is also an essential element of community practice, the role of which is to stimulate and support the active community.

What is 'community practice'?

We are using the term 'community practice' to refer to work (paid or unpaid) that stimulates, supports or engages with 'active communities'. This covers a broad range of types of activity carried out for many different purposes by various types of people – from community-based initiatives by volunteers and activists with a view to providing their own services or challenging a policy, to community consultation exercises by service providers to gain the views of local residents/service users/ other stakeholders about how to make improvements in services.

Before exploring in more depth the key features of community practice, we will briefly outline what kinds of people, in what kinds of positions and with what kinds of roles we would categorise as community practitioners, since it is the positions and roles occupied by people doing community practice, and the power and goals that they have in those roles, that partly influence the character of community practice and its management.

Who are the community practitioners?

The following is a list of people in particular types of roles who commonly engage in community practice:

- *Members of self-organised community action groups and associations.* There exists a wide variety of community groups and associations working for change in their neighbourhoods, or in their communities of identity or interest. Members may come together voluntarily to take action on the basis of a shared concern or interest. These range from babysitting circles and residents' associations to campaigns for local traffic-calming measures (Williams et al, 2004; also, for a range of examples of local and global campaigning and self-help groups, see Mayo, 2005).

• *Community (development) workers.* There are substantial numbers of workers employed by charitable, local government, faith-based and social enterprise organisations operating with a brief to undertake community work of some kind, for example: community development workers, community educators and community organisers, as well as workers employed to focus on issues identified by communities themselves. Such workers may or may not be professionally qualified in community development work or a related field, and they may be employed to work either generically in a neighbourhood, or in a specialist field such as tenant participation, environmental action, social inclusion and cohesion or health promotion (see Glen et al, 2004). In the UK, in so far as these workers identify with an occupational group, there are specific occupational standards for community development work that outline the key purposes, knowledge, values and skills of the work (Lifelong Learning UK, 2009).

• *Other professionals with a community focus.* This category of practitioners includes a range of professionals whose main role would not be described as community work per se, but who may use some of community work methods and approaches in their practice alongside other more specialist approaches to developing and supporting communities. These professionals include service-user involvement facilitators, neighbourhood regeneration officers, social workers, police officers, architects and planners who may have a community brief; for example, a police community liaison officer may be employed to encourage community participation in matters of community safety and the diversion of youth offenders.

• *Managers of organisations with a community practice remit.* Some managers carry a brief to promote and support community practice; for example, those who manage community regeneration or community development programmes would fit this description. Others in the fields of youth work, health promotion or housing, for example, can carry a responsibility for community engagement within their wider remit. Such managers, who are employed by organisations that relate in one way or another to communities, are well positioned to promote and resource aspects of community practice by virtue of their access to organisational decision-making, training and other resources. The argument throughout this book is that managers have the potential to advance the cause of community practice in important ways.

• *Politicians and policymakers.* Similarly, senior executives, policymakers and politicians in local and central government or other public-, voluntary- and private-sector agencies may be involved in the development of community policies, partnership-working or encouraging cultural change to make organisations more community-oriented. This means that they have the potential to promote a wide range of work with a community focus. We also include here the 'opinion-shapers' (both individuals and organisations) who have gained increasing prominence in public affairs in recent years. In a UK context, this would include think tanks such as the Institute for Public Policy Research and Demos, as well as charitable bodies such as the Community Development Foundation and the Joseph Rowntree Foundation. These bodies have, through provision of evidence and ideas, promoted active citizenship, neighbourhood development and community resilience.

If we consider this list of the variety of people who may undertake community practice, it is immediately apparent that they occupy very different positions in society, may wield different degrees of power in relation to the positions they hold and may have different goals linked to their positions and roles. In mapping the terrain of community practice, there are several features in relation to which the practice can be categorised, linked with who the community practitioners are. One important feature relates to where power and control lies; the other relates to the goals of the practice. We will discuss each of these in turn.

Power and control in community practice

Analysis of power is a complex matter, as power has a number of dimensions or 'faces' (Lukes, 2004). To analyse power entails looking at: who frames the overarching discourse in which the activities that constitute 'community practice' take place and are understood; who controls the agenda; and who influences and controls the decision-making and actions. Power may be hidden, it may shift and power-holders may interact in dynamic ways. Gaventa (2006), in his analysis of the many dimensions of power, offers a useful distinction between three types of 'spaces' in which power is framed and exercised (closed, invited and claimed/created). The distinction between 'invited spaces'

(spaces owned and controlled by others into which communities are invited) and 'claimed spaces' (community-owned spaces) is a useful one in considering power and control in community practice.

While acknowledging the multidimensional and complex nature of power in community practice (for a useful discussion, see Taylor, 2011), it is possible to identify a simplified continuum representing the balance of power between community participants and 'outside agencies' (public- or larger voluntary- and private-sector organisations) in respect of policymaking and service delivery. Clearly, in practice, the situation is never simple, as the overarching agendas and discourses that frame the way policies are made and services delivered are influenced and often controlled by national governments, business interests or global trends. Furthermore, some 'community participants' may also be professional workers in agencies and organisations, while others may be both community participants and elected members of local authorities or members of boards of large organisations. So, a clear distinction between 'community' and 'outside agencies' is not possible – and, indeed, as Gilchrist (Chapter Six, this volume) suggests, many individuals play important roles as 'boundary-spanners'. Nevertheless, the following simplified categorisation of three 'ideal types' may be helpful – acknowledging that there is overlap and movement between points on a continuum:

1. *Community control* – self-help, campaigning and other plans, policies and activities organised and delivered by volunteers and activists who set the agenda and decide on what action to take. Activity is often undertaken and 'managed' by self-starting, autonomous community groups. Sometimes, community groups may employ workers, and sometimes professionals may give support and advice; sometimes, such groups gain funding that has strings attached. So, there is always an issue about how 'autonomous' a group can be and it may make more sense to think in terms of relative autonomy, with the balance of control lying with the community group. However, the spaces in which the activities and decisions take place could be regarded as created by the community participants themselves.
2. *Joint control* – a partnership that is as equal as possible between community participants and public- or larger voluntary- or private-sector agencies in developing policies or delivering services. While 'co-production' is much promoted and talked about, and it is an ideal to work towards, genuine 'equality' of status and power (recognising and valuing the different contributions each party brings) is rarely

achieved in practice. For this to happen, the spaces for action and decision-making should ideally be jointly created.

3. *Outside agencies in control* – community-engaged policymaking and activities are initiated and managed by public- or larger voluntary- or private-sector organisations. Outside control may be relatively high (such as in the form of consultations) or low (as in deliberative and participatory processes of policymaking or decision-making), but such spaces could be characterised as ones where the outside agencies invite in the community participants.

Goals of community practice

Another feature that can be used to categorise different types of community practice relates to the goals for which community practice is pursued. While communities comprise individuals, who may work towards various goals, not all of which are shared, it is possible to identify some ideal types of community practice classified according to underlying goals. The following list is not exhaustive, but offers examples of some of the main goals underlying community practice:

- *Radical change in the distribution of power and resources* – such goals are often associated with campaigning on specific issues by community groups (community action), and broad-based community organising designed to build a power base through developing and mobilising coalitions of organisations and groups to challenge established public- and private-sector bodies.
- *Development of communities* – these goals are typified by what is often termed a 'community development approach', designed to build community spirit, cohesion, skills and capacity in order to engage in self-help activities and encourage greater control over future planning and decision-making.
- *Improvement of community-based policy, planning and service delivery* – these goals are linked with a community planning and service development approach associated with community organisations, policy-making and service delivery agencies working towards opening up their decision-making processes to allow for influence and voices to be heard. This may be achieved through community consultations or deliberative processes for allocating resources to community projects. These processes contribute towards 'democratic renewal' (engaging citizens in political deliberation and decision-making) – which might be regarded as a goal in its own right.

Power and goals

The preceding discussion suggests that community practice may be more or less radical in its goals – which range from challenging and changing existing power structures to ameliorating some inequalities or gaps in services. Communities may be more or less in control – ranging from situations where outside agencies play no role to situations where outside agencies provide support and facilitation or control the agenda. Putting these together, then, produces a two-dimensional matrix that maps power against purposes, as shown in Table 1.1, which also offers some examples in each category.

Table 1.1: Power and goals in community practice

Goals	Control		
	Community control	*Joint control*	*Outside agencies in control*
Radical change in power structures	Self-organised community campaigns (eg against road-building or for a living wage)	Coalitions between community groups and other agencies/ bodies for policy change (eg local residents work with national trades unions on nuclear power plant safety issues)	Outside organisations plan and mount action and mobilise support at the community level (eg national campaigning organisation plans local actions for asylum seekers' rights)
Development of communities	Community-led strategic planning and development of alternative facilities and services (eg a community-run post office)	Partnership-working between community groups and agencies to develop community cohesion and capacity (eg community development training programme)	Outside agencies control plans for development of the community (eg government or other agencies plan for physical and social renewal of an area, or development of facilities for a group, with some consultation)
Improved policies and services	Self-help groups, informal caring, community contracting for service delivery (eg volunteer driving service)	Co-production or partnership between communities and agencies for planning and service delivery (eg jointly produced community health strategy)	Agencies plan and deliver community-responsive services with community consultation or deliberation (eg local emergency response plan developed by statutory agencies with input from community groups)

Approaches to community practice

Having considered who drives forward community practice, we now turn to consider a range of different approaches that can be taken. We are using the term 'approach' to summarise a complex interplay of methods, processes and goals. The choice of approach will vary according to who is in control/where the power lies and the goals to be achieved. In Box 1.1, we offer illustrative examples of six approaches. The list is not exhaustive, and neither are the approaches mutually exclusive. We are presenting these as approaches to community practice as they all entail stimulating, supporting or engaging the 'active community' in a variety of ways and to a greater or lesser extent. They represent contemporary approaches, accounting for much 'everyday' and leading-edge community practice; they also frame contemporary management debates.

Box 1.1: Approaches to community practice

1. **Community self-help activities, projects and delivery of services.** Members of a community (place, identity, interest) join together on a voluntary basis to develop their own autonomously run services, projects or informal networks for caring and leisure activities (see Williams et al, 2004; Richardson, 2008). Examples include: reading groups; pub-quiz teams; senior citizens' clubs; women's groups; disability rights groups; community associations; time-banking schemes; and community carnivals.

2. **Community organising.** Identified and trained community leaders mobilise and organise communities in order to ensure that public authorities and businesses respond to the needs of ordinary people, or mobilise community members to help to meet those needs themselves (see Alinsky, 1989; Pyles, 2009; Bunyan, 2010; see also www.citizensuk.org). Examples include campaigns to ensure that local businesses pay a living wage and the development of Credit Unions based on the common bond of local community membership.

3. **Community capacity-building and development.** Development of the skills, knowledge and confidence of community members to assess their own needs, develop plans to meet them and carry through those plans in groups and organisations controlled by, and accountable to, the community (see Banks and Shenton, 2001; Craig, 2011). Examples include training programmes for faith leaders on developing community cohesion in local neighbourhoods and a regional network of black and minority ethnic groups offering information exchange and skills workshops.

---

4. **Co-production of services/policies.** Joint planning and/or delivery of public- or private-sector services through partnership-working by service users and providers/decision-makers (see Boyle and Harris, 2009; Khan, 2010). Examples include a service-user partnership in a hospital trust working with clinicians and managers to reform the system of patient follow-up care and participatory budgeting via partnership-working between citizens and local politicians.

5. **Deliberative community engagement.** Developing and sustaining collaborative/partnership relationships between public bodies, social enterprises, businesses and other agencies with community groups, projects and organisations in order to ensure the development of plans and services that are responsive to community needs and preferences (see Kelly, 2010). Examples include: a partnership-based local health campaign on breast-screening for Asian women; participatory budgeting; community and area forums run by local authorities; and participatory appraisal.

6. **Consultative community engagement.** Planning and service delivery approaches to informing, consulting, listening to and receiving information from communities, in order to respond to stakeholder needs and preferences (see Jones and Gammell, 2009). Examples include community service providers (police, health, housing) consulting about needs and issues, using the media, community meetings, presentations or websites to keep community members informed.

7. **Community management.** Managers work to ensure a good 'fit' between key features of community practice (as a set of work processes to be managed) and their organisational responsibilities for effective coordination and control, quality enhancement, strategic direction, and resource allocation. They embrace new models of (democratic) professional working that rest on values of partnership, negotiation and power-sharing. Examples include: managers promoting open communication; participative and inclusive approaches to decision-making; and encouraging team-based forms of organisation.

Boxes 1.2 and 1.3 give examples of these approaches in the fields of health and neighbourhood regeneration, respectively. The examples are drawn from real projects and programmes in two specific fields of practice, with the aim of enabling the reader to see how each approach might engage differently with the active community (for further information on community practice approaches in the health field, see Andersson et al, 2008; Butcher, 2009; and for the neighbourhood regeneration field, see Somerville, 2011, chs 5, 8; Chanan and Miller, 2013).

Box 1.2: Community practice in the prevention and treatment of cancer

1. **Community self-help activities, projects and delivery of services.** A voluntary local cancer support group, established by and for those with colon cancer, sets up a 'buddy' scheme for new members and for those newly diagnosed with the disease.

2. **Community organising.** A number of residents become concerned that several streets in their neighbourhood are being increasingly used as a short cut by heavy diesel lorries. Exhaust emissions are affecting people's health (respiratory problems) and there is growing alarm about the possible carcinogenic effects of exhaust fumes. A local community group, some of whose members have undertaken training in community organising, decide to build a coalition of individuals and groups – including the local school, churches, GP practices and a local playgroup. A meeting is called, an action group is formed and petitions, rallies and a traffic blockade are used to campaign for change.

3. **Community capacity-building and development.** A team of health development workers (employed by a third-sector organisation with a brief to promote community health) is working on a rural health project. This involves training a county-wide network of 'village agents'– some with a specific 'cancer support' brief. Cancer patients and their families can contact the scheme representative in their community to obtain information about services (eg finance, transport) and to get practical support (help with shopping, getting to the hospital) and emotional support.

4. **Co-production of services/policies.** Cancer service users work collaboratively with medical professionals, within a close partnership group, to design and then launch an information and support website for local people facing both active and follow-up treatment. A successful joint bid is made to Macmillan Cancer Support for funding to secure technical support.

5. **Deliberative community engagement.** Members of a service-user partnership group of a local Cancer Network (a standing network group responsible for spearheading user involvement) have a role as user representatives on the Clinical Quality Assurance Committees in the Network (for breast, urological, head and neck cancers). A user involvement facilitator, employed by a hospital trust, offers training and support (ie capacity-building) to enable the service users to engage in deliberations on the committees.

6. **Consultative community engagement.** Members of a service-user involvement group of a hospital trust are invited to respond to a consultation exercise about service reconfiguration initiated by the hospital's Cancer Directorate.

7. **Community management.** A hospital's management team successfully makes a case for additional service-user facilitator support, plus part-time administrative back-up, in order to strengthen service-user involvement in service planning and delivery.

Box 1.3: Community practice in securing housing, jobs and services

1. **Community self-help activities, projects and delivery of services.** A neighbourhood action group, established 20 years ago, in what was then a very rundown inner-city district, has continued to work in a highly democratic and fully participative way with its local community, and has had considerable success in turning the neighbourhood around. The group currently employs 20 people who work with scores of volunteers, on seven areas (including 'Environment', 'Business', 'Safety' and 'Health'). The group runs a Healthy Living Centre, Good Neighbour Schemes and community newspaper, and employs five community safety workers, coordinates 70 volunteer street wardens, organises an annual carnival and lots more.

2. **Community organising.** A coalition of groups in an inner-city neighbourhood has run a lengthy campaign against a large-scale commercial development of a 13-acre site in the area. Forming themselves into a not-for-profit social enterprise (with a board comprised solely of local residents), funding was secured from a government-funded Enterprise Board to buy the land, and over the last 20 years, the organisation has promoted the establishment of a range of housing cooperatives ('affordable housing', shops, a nursery, galleries, restaurants and cafes, and gardens).

3. **Community capacity-building.** 'Community Futures' is a community development workshop process that offers a series of highly structured action-learning workshops to help attendees to create a community-led vision for achieving local economic development through partnership-working (between residents, local businesses and public, church and voluntary organisations), starting in the first workshop with creating a clear common understanding of the community and its problems, and ending with a clear vision of what needs to change, along with a practical plan for action.

4. **Co-production of services/policies.** A local housing authority uses a co-production model of working with members of established local disability groups to develop fully inclusive housing policies and plans. A partnership agreement is put in place, the partnership is co-chaired by a local councillor and the chair of one of the disability groups, and the community partners are paid a daily rate for their time.

5. **Deliberative community engagement.** A large third-sector community project initiates an in-depth consultation process within its area – using participatory planning techniques – in order to maximise proactive, democratic and creative ideas for distillation into community-led and agreed aims and priorities for future work.
6. **Consultative community engagement.** Tenants of a housing association are sent a postal questionnaire about their level of satisfaction with the service they receive from their landlord. This is followed by an open meeting seeking views on priorities for improvements/changes.
7. **Community management.** Managers demonstrate and support paid professional staff to use facilitative models of working and joint/partnership decision-making, rather than reward short-term 'problem-fixing' and bureaucratic/hierarchical compliance models.

It is important to stress that the boundaries between the different approaches are not clear-cut, and neither are the approaches mutually exclusive. A particular project or group might engage in both community delivery of services and community organising, for example; while a service provider might initiate both consultative and deliberative community engagement with service users, which might lead later to the co-production of plans and services by various providers in partnership with service users. However, while these approaches do overlap, it is important that those involved are clear about what they are doing and why, where the main initiative for the practice comes from, and where power lies. In the case of community delivery of services, and sometimes community organising and community capacity-building and development, members of community groups may be the ones taking a lead. Sometimes, community organising may be led by organisers trained and supported by bodies outside the communities where they work, and community capacity-building may very often be supported or facilitated by community development workers or other specialist professionals. As noted, while the ideal of co-production is an equal partnership between service providers/decision-makers and service users or other community groups, this ideal is not easily achievable in practice and it needs considerable work to achieve genuine power-sharing. In participatory or deliberative community engagement, it is usually the service providers or policymakers who initiate and facilitate the intervention, but community participants may have control over certain aspects of the process and outcomes as a result of their deliberations – exemplified by the work of the facilitator with the Cancer Network Service User Partnership Group in Box 1.2. However, consultation may be less participatory, as the example in Box 1.3 relating to questionnaires to housing association tenants indicates. The results of consultations may or may not inform future action directly, and sometimes community engagement exercises may be deliberately and cynically established in a tokenistic fashion to garner public acceptance for decisions about courses of action that have already been determined. Arnstein, in her famous 'ladder' of citizen involvement, referred to 'rubberstamp' advisory committees and consultation exercises set up with the express purpose of engineering support or 'educating' the public (Arnstein, 1969).

Underpinning values and principles of action

So far, we have touched on *where* community practice is located, *who* undertakes it and *what* such work involves in practice. We now turn to a final, and fundamental, aspect of community practice that managers have to take into account when thinking about and undertaking their role – the values and principles that underpin such work.

It is common for occupational groups or professions to develop and promote lists of values (fundamental beliefs about what is worthy or valuable) and principles (how the values are put into practice) in relation to their work. These are often encapsulated in codes of ethics, occupational standards or statements of purpose. While community practice is not a distinct occupation as such, arguably, it is important that practitioners recognise and hold to a set of values and principles that define the overall rationale for the work and the ways in which they should treat the people and groups with whom they work. The list that follows is a development and updating of the values identified in the first edition of the book, which was based on a set of standards developed for community practice and development (Scottish Community Education Council, 1998; Banks, 2003). It also draws upon the values identified for community development work in the UK, which are now being promoted as applying not just to professionally qualified community development workers, but also to volunteers, practitioners in other professions who take a community development approach and managers of community development practice (Lifelong Learning UK, 2009). The major change from the 2003 list is the addition of 'social justice' as the sixth value and the inclusion of examples of 'principles of action' underneath each of the values, which illustrate how they might be put into practice:

1. *Equality and diversity* – this value is based on the recognition that all human beings are inherently valuable and worthy of respect, regardless of who they are or what they have done. People may come from diverse cultural, faith or ethnic backgrounds and have more or less wealth and status, for example, but they should not be negatively discriminated against or accorded less respect or fewer opportunities on these grounds. Indeed, taking the promotion of equality one step further (from equality of opportunity to equality of result) entails a call for active steps to be taken to redress these inequalities.
   Principles of action include:
   - recognising and valuing diverse individuals, groups and communities – for example, ethnic, faith or disability communities or poor neighbourhoods; and
   - raising awareness of and counteracting discriminatory and oppressive attitudes and actions within and between communities and in society more generally.

2. *Empowerment* – this value, like equality, is a contested and complex value that applies at the individual and group/community levels. While the term 'empowerment' has connotations of professionals or other power-holders 'giving power' to communities or their members, we prefer to see it in terms of people themselves mobilising, creating or drawing out their own inherent power to decide and act – sometimes with outside assistance; sometimes without. This value is a counterweight to the 'parentalism' (a gender-free term for 'paternalism') of professionals or dominant community leaders and activists, who are often accused of 'knowing what is best' or deciding for people.
   Principles of action include:
   - engaging in a critical examination of how power operates in communities; and
   - facilitating and supporting individuals and groups to take more control over their lives, their communities and their environments.

3. *Participation* – this value is about ensuring that individuals and community groups are encouraged and enabled to take an active part in determining needs, developing policies and planning and implementing services. It follows on from the promotion of empowerment and is grounded in principles of participatory democracy, and the rights of citizens to play a part in decision-making in society. It is linked to the value of equality, in that unless attention is paid to making groups accessible to people who are

often excluded and opportunities made for a range of voices to be heard, then genuine participation cannot be achieved.

Principles of action include:

- promoting and respecting the rights of individuals and groups to take an active part in decision-making and action relating to issues that affect their lives; and
- ensuring opportunities for decision-making and action are accessible in terms of language, physical space and ethos to a diverse range of people, including those who might not usually take part.

4. *Partnership and collaboration* – this further builds on the notion of participation, to involve individuals and groups not just as participants in the process of community practice, but also as partners in a joint enterprise with a recognised and valuable contribution to make. Collaborative methods of working emphasise this principle of sharing responsibility and power. As discussed earlier, genuine 'partnership' or 'co-production' between community groups and outside agencies is challenging to achieve, and in many cases it is not the purpose of community practice. However, a spirit of partnership and collaborative working is essential for groups of community participants themselves to function well as 'active communities', and this is a key value for community practitioners to promote and put into practice.

Principles of action include:

- recognising and valuing the contribution of a range of skills and expertise offered by different people to joint-working; and
- developing transparent agreements between all parties about how to work together – including sharing responsibility and power.

5. *Learning* – this refers to the process of community practice as being about both developing the knowledge, confidence and skills of individuals and groups, and promoting 'organisational learning' and a learning culture in the agencies and groups involved in community practice. This is a reminder that the process of community practice (how outcomes are achieved) is as important as the actual achievements, and that the relationships between those involved in community practice should be about mutual learning and growth.

Principles of action include:

- creating spaces and organisational climates that are conducive to mutual learning, including encouraging individual and collective reflection on attitudes and actions; and

- using the results of reflections and evaluations to inform future practice, and sharing the learning with other groups and communities.
6. *Social justice* – the promotion of social justice is about working for a fair distribution of 'goods' in society and the removal of oppressive power structures. Hence, it is very closely linked with equality of outcome. 'Social justice' can be understood and implemented in many different ways. A reformist interpretation of social justice would entail improving or developing the status quo. In its more radical version, it is premised on a structural analysis of society and a recognition that institutional power structures need to change drastically if social justice is to be achieved. This radical version of social justice is a core value in our model of critical community practice (Butcher et al, 2007) discussed in the next section.
   Principles of action include:
   - identifying and challenging the underlying causes and effects of structural power imbalances – including making links between local, societal and global contexts; and
   - working towards a more equal distribution of power, status, wealth and opportunities between individuals, groups, communities and nations.

Critical community practice

As mentioned earlier, we have developed a model of critical community practice, which is based around a critical analysis of political and economic power in society and the promotion of outcomes linked to the first purpose identified in Table 1.1 – radical change in power structures. Part of the rationale for this was a growing concern about the tendency for communities to be co-opted to the agendas of governments and other agencies, alongside growing inequalities and a shifting of collective responsibilities at the societal level onto families, neighbours, groups and communities. While we would actively advocate the adoption of a critical community practice model as outlined in Butcher et al (2007), we recognise that this approach is difficult to achieve in practice for workers based in institutional contexts, and, indeed, for many community groups whose members are not interested in emancipatory or transformatory practice. However, this does not mean that a critical approach to community practice should be sidelined or abandoned. On the contrary, it is more important than ever for community practitioners to develop and maintain a critical approach to their practice, and the critical community practice model is helpful in this respect.

According to this model, a key role of critical community practitioners is to work with others in community settings to raise awareness and develop critical consciousness of the political, economic and social contexts within which they work and subject the attitudes and behaviours of themselves and others to critical scrutiny. Following the terminology of Freire (1993), this process can be described as 'conscientisation'. Here, the role of managers, and others that supervise and support community practitioners, can be very important and influential in encouraging critical reflection on the role of community practitioners and the purposes of their work. Managers can also offer support in finding 'spaces', and the courage, to speak out more strongly against injustice and consider broader and longer-term tactics and strategies to achieve transformatory change. Critical community practice provides a model to enable practitioners to adopt a different approach, and, at the very least, it can be used as an ideal type or exemplar against which to evaluate other forms of community practice. As already indicated, social justice is a key value and guiding ideal of critical community practice, which is reflected in the underlying principles of action, outlined as follows (Butcher et al, 2007, p 57):

- *Conscientisation* – the development, through action for change, of a particular form of critical consciousness, one that generates the hope, energy and know-how necessary to achieve 'action for liberation'.
- *Empowerment* – the effective mobilisation of power to shape decisions, influence agendas and effectively challenge hegemonic ideologies and oppressive discourses.
- *Collective action* – the development of the motivation, skills and capacities to work cooperatively with others to effect change through active citizenship.

Conclusions

What we have called 'active communities' are at the heart of community practice, with the essential role of community practitioners being to engage with individuals and groups that could contribute to developing communities. As will be outlined in the Chapter Two, the promotion of community practice can be linked very closely to government policies – whether these focus on poverty reduction, area-based regeneration, social inclusion, democratic renewal or the stimulation of voluntary action and community-based service delivery. Community practitioners and their managers face considerable challenges in holding on to the values of promoting equality and social justice, and working towards a model of critical community practice, while operating in a climate of austerity and welfare reform. How community practice is being managed and could be managed will be the theme of the rest of this book. After Chapter Two, which looks at the historical and policy context for the growth of community practice, the following chapters will explore the management of community practice at two levels: managing systems and people involved in working for active community at the level of neighbourhoods or local interest or identity communities (eg through community-led service delivery, capacity-building or grass-roots campaigning); and managing people involved in seeking to ensure organisations are community-responsive in their policies and practices.

References

Alinsky, S. (1989) *Rules for radicals*, New York, NY: Vintage Books (1st published in 1971 by Random House).

Andersson, E., Tritter, J. and Wilson, R. (2008) *Healthy democracy: the future of involvement in health and social care*, London: Involve and The National Centre for Involvement.

Arnstein, S. (1969) 'A ladder of citizen participation', *Journal of American Planning Association*, vol 35, no 4, pp 216–24.

Banks, S. (2003) 'What is community practice?', in S. Banks, H. Butcher, P. Henderson and J. Robertson (eds) *Managing community practice: principles, policies and programmes*, Bristol: The Policy Press, pp 9–22.

Banks, S. and Shenton, F. (2001) 'Regenerating neighbourhoods: a critical look at the role of community capacity building', *Local Economy*, vol 16, no 4, pp 286–98.

Bauman, Z. (2001) *Community: seeking safety in an insecure world*, Cambridge: Polity Press.

Boyle, D. and Harris, M. (2009) *The challenge of co-production: how equal partnerships between professionsals and the public are crucial to improving public services*, London: National Endowment for Science, Technology and the Arts (NESTA).

Bunyan, P. (2010) 'Broad-based organizing in the UK: reasserting the centrality of political activity in community development', *Community Development Journal*, vol 45, no 1, pp 111–27.

Butcher, H. (1993) 'Introduction: some examples and definitions', in H. Butcher, A. Glen, J. Smith and P. Henderson (eds) *Community and public policy*, London: Pluto Press, pp 3–21.

Butcher, H. (2009) 'Service user involvement in cancer care – policy, principles, practice'. Available at: www.dh.gov.uk/en/Publicationsandstatistics/Publications/PublicationsPolicyAndGuidance/DH_114581 (accessed August 2012).

Butcher, H., Glen, A., Henderson, P. and Smith, J. (eds) (1993) *Community and public policy*, London: Pluto Press.

Butcher, H., Banks, S. and Henderson, P., with Robertson, J. (2007) *Critical community practice*, London: The Policy Press.

Chanan, G. and Miller, C. (2013) *Rethinking community practice: developing transformative neighbourhoods*, Bristol: The Policy Press.

Clarke, J. (1981) 'The concept of community', in P. Henderson and D. Thomas (ed) *Readings in community work*, London: Macmillan, pp 32–8.

Craig, G. (2011) 'Community capacity building: critiquing the concept in different policy contexts', in S. Kenny and M. Clarke (eds) *Challenging capacity building*, Basingstoke: Palgrave, pp 41–66.

Etzioni, A. (ed) (1995) *New communitarian thinking: persons, virtues, institutions, and communities*, Charlottesville, VA: University Press of Virginia.

Freire, P. (1993) *Education for critical consciousness*, New York, NY: Continuum.

Gaventa, J. (2006) 'Finding the spaces for change: a power analysis', *IDS Bulletin*, vol 37, no 6, pp 23–33.

Gilchrist, A. and Taylor, M. (2011) *The short guide to community development*, Bristol: The Policy Press.

Glen, A., Henderson, P., Humm, J., Meszaros, H. and Gaffney, M. (2004) *Survey of community development workers in the UK*, London: Community Development Foundation/Community Development Exchange.

Hillery, G.A. (1955) 'Definitions of community: areas of agreement', *Rural Sociology*, vol 20, pp 111–23.

Hoggett, P. (1997) 'Contested communities', in P. Hoggett (ed) *Contested communities: experiences, struggles, policies*, Bristol: The Policy Press, pp 3–16.

Jones, R. and Gammell, E. (2009) *The art of consultation*, London: Biteback Publishing.

Kelly, U., with Cumming, L. (2010) *Civil society supporting dialogue and deliberation*, Dunfermline and London: Carnegie UK Trust.

Khan, H. (2010) *People powered health co-production catalogue*, London: National Endowment for Science, Technology and the Arts (NESTA).

Kymlicka, W. (1990) *Contemporary political philosophy: an introduction*, Oxford: Oxford University Press.

Lifelong Learning UK (2009) 'National occupational standards for community development'. Available at: www.lluk.org (accessed December 2009).

Little, A. (2002) *The politics of community: theory and practice*, Edinburgh: Edinburgh University Press.

Lukes, S. (2004) *Power: a radical view* (2nd edn), Basingstoke: Palgrave Macmillan.

Mayo, M. (1994) *Communities and caring: the mixed economy of welfare*, Basingstoke: Macmillan.

Mayo, M. (2000) *Cultures, communities, identities*, Basingstoke: Palgrave Macmillan.

Mayo, M. (2005) *Global citizens: social movements and the challenge of globalisation*, London: Zed.

Plant, R. (1974) *Community and ideology: an essay in applied social philosophy*, London: Routledge and Kegan Paul.

Popple, K. (1995) *Analysing community work: its theory and practice*, Buckingham: Open University Press.

Putnam, R. (2000) *Bowling alone: the collapse and revival of American community*, New York, NY: Simon & Schuster.

Pyles, L. (2009) *Progressive community organising: a critical approach for a globalising world*, New York, NY: Routledge.

Richardson, L. (2008) *DIY community action: neighbourhood problems and community self-help*, Bristol: The Policy Press.

Sandel, M. (1982) *Liberalism and the limits of justice*, Cambridge: Cambridge University Press.

Scottish Community Education Council (1998) *Guidelines for post qualifying community practice and development training*, Edinburgh: CeVe Unit, Scottish Community Education Council.

Somerville, P. (2011) *Understanding community: politics, policy and practice*, Bristol: The Policy Press.

Tam, H. (1998) *Communitarianism: a new agenda for politics and citizenship*, Basingstoke: Macmillan.

Taylor, M. (2011) *Public policy in the community* (2nd edn), Basingstoke: Palgrave Macmillan.

Williams, C., Burns, D. and Windebank, J. (2004) *Community self-help*, Basingstoke: Palgrave Macmillan.

Willmott, P. (1989) *Community initiatives, patterns and prospects*, London: Policy Studies Institute.

TWO

The historical and policy context: setting the scene for current debates

Marjorie Mayo and Jim Robertson

Introduction

This chapter sets the context for current debates on community practice. The aim is to provide a framework for the analysis of differing approaches to community practice in the 21st century. While the term 'community practice' is relatively recent, the social policies that managers of community practice set out to implement are not without their antecedents. There are echoes and continuities of earlier initiatives as well as important differences between programmes to tackle social disadvantage in the past on the one hand, and contemporary programmes to combat social exclusion on the other. This chapter aims to explore the similarities as well as the contrasts between differing approaches as these have shifted and developed over time. The intention is to focus upon unpacking the competing theoretical assumptions that have underpinned these debates, rather than to focus upon the historical detail of any particular social policy. For the reader who is interested in pursuing these histories in greater detail, because they are intrinsically fascinating in their own right, references to the relevant literature are included in the text.

After a brief overview of the rationale for community-based policies as these emerged in the 1960s and early 1970s, the chapter will move on to explore the very different approaches that emerged when neoliberal agendas predominated in the policy debates of the 1980s and early 1990s. This sets the context of the extent to which there may be similarities as well as differences between these earlier approaches and those of subsequent governments. These are contested questions; readers may reach differing conclusions about the balance between similarities and differences when they evaluate the evidence and consider the implications for community practice in the contemporary context. The intention of this chapter is that, armed with a critical understanding of the competing perspectives that underpin the current policy framework, those who manage community practice will be enabled to weigh up the varying implications for practice and develop their own strategies, as reflective practitioners, more effectively.

The rediscovery of 'community' and the development of community-based social policies in the 1960s and early 1970s

As a highly selective history of the past three decades or so, the focus here is upon those aspects of the 'rediscovery' of community and the development of community-based social policies that have contemporary resonances. These are as follows:

- the focus upon neighbourhoods, communities of location where problems of poverty and social deprivation were seen to be concentrated;
- the emphasis on coordination among service providers, to enable more effective ('joined-up' in more recent idiom) services to be provided to meet these concentrations of need; and
- the emphasis upon changing relationships between professionals, policymakers and service users, with greater user participation and enhanced community self-help, and with (and sometimes without) an associated commitment to empowering approaches to user and community participation and the pursuit of social justice agendas.

So, how and why did these agendas emerge in the 1960s and 1970s, not only in Britain, but elsewhere, including the US? In Britain, the Second World War period was followed by an era of economic recovery. There was considerable optimism about the potential for avoiding a recurrence of the Great Depression and the associated poverty and social deprivation that had followed the First World War now that governments had at their disposal the tools of Keynesian economics. In Britain, the social policies encapsulated in the 'welfare state', particularly the establishment of the national benefits system for sickness, unemployment and old age, would effectively eliminate poverty in the bud; or so it was widely believed.

For some, at least, of the Labour politicians involved, universal comprehensive state welfare provision was expected to render the traditional voluntary sector obsolete. In the words of Richard Crossman, a Labour politician who became Secretary of State for social services in the late 1960s, 'philanthropy was to us the odious expression of social oligarchy and churchy bourgeois attitudes. We detested voluntary hospitals maintained by flag days'. Illustrating this point of view about the negative associations of charity and everything connected with 'do-gooding', Crossman continues:

> Those of us who became socialists grew up with the conviction that we must in this point ally ourselves with the professionals and trades unions and discourage voluntary effort particularly since it was bound to reduce the number of jobs available. (Crossman, 1973, quoted in Brenton, 1985, p 265)

Crossman's comments typify the preferences for public-sector, rather than voluntary- or community-sector, provision and the trust in professionalism, rooted in economic and social planning, which have traditionally been associated with 'Old Labour'.

By the mid- to late 1960s, however, it was becoming only too clear that tackling the causes of poverty and social deprivation was more problematic than many of the architects of the welfare state had, perhaps, anticipated and the extent of voluntary activity was still 'staggering', as Crossman himself recognised (Brenton, 1985, p 274). Poverty was obstinately persistent, as the publication of Abel-Smith and Townsend's (1965) study of *The poor and the poorest* only too amply demonstrated. It was concentrated in, if not confined to, particular areas within cities (Townsend, 1979). Increasing public expenditure did not seem likely to provide the complete answer, and this was becoming less viable, in any case, as the post-war boom began to slow down.

There was also increased community action and new social movements, with the emergence of the Civil Rights Movement campaigning for African-American civil liberties in the US, followed by the development of student movements and the Women's Liberation Movement internationally. This was accompanied by expressions of tenant activism and trade union militancy. In this more critical climate of the 1960s and early 1970s, welfare state officials and welfare professionals were coming under fire. They were criticised for insensitivity, inflexibility, lack of effective coordination and, on occasion, downright arrogance towards their clients. Feminists were particularly critical of the patriarchal ways in which professional men took it upon themselves to control their female patients' and clients' lives, and anti-racists challenged institutional racism. This was also a period in which more overt forms of racism had emerged on the streets, as evidenced in the Notting Hill riots. Each of these attacks on the seemingly underwhelming reality of welfare state provision required some response from policymakers. Following the potentially inflammatory racism of Enoch Powell's infamous 'Rivers of Blood' speech in 1968, it was even clearer that something needed to be done – and be seen to be done – fast (Loney, 1983).

The existence of the welfare state per se was not generally being fundamentally challenged at this point, it should be emphasised, although there was, of course, a minority of critics from the political Right, notably the Institute of Economic Affairs, who argued against public provision, in principle, from the start. The majority of contemporary criticisms focused on the shortcomings of public welfare, particularly the inadequacies of services, which were all too often experienced as fragmented, inappropriately provided and overly controlling. This was the context, then, for the development of programmes targeted at particular neighbourhoods to promote better coordination between service providers, together with user involvement, community participation and self-help, to which we return in the next section of this chapter.

Meanwhile, there were differences as well as relevant similarities with the situation in the US. In summary, the social policy context was very different, with proportionately less public provision and greater emphasis on the role of the private as well as the voluntary and not-for-profit sectors of provision. Service coordination was, unsurprisingly, problematic here too, and there were concerns about the failure to address increasing social frustrations, especially in the cities where so many African-Americans had migrated from the deep South of the US, cities that were torn by riots in the 1960s. There were, in addition, political agendas to be addressed, as Democratic politicians sought to mobilise their potential constituencies of African-American voters. It was time for the federal government to be doing something – and to be seen to be doing something – about the problems of poverty and social deprivation in the ghettos. The 'War on Poverty' was launched in 1964 with federal government support for area-based programmes, including support for community action and the maximum feasible participation of the poor themselves – a phrase that turned out to be as problematic as it was ambiguous (Kramer, 1969).

As Marris and Rein (1972) pointed out:

> [the] fundamental flaws in the structure of government were exactly those with which community action was most concerned: over-centralisation, the lack of lateral communication between administrations, their indifference

to the effectiveness of their work, and their irresponsiveness
to the people they served.

But, as Marris and Rein went on to suggest, the faults were 'perceived
as lying within institutions rather than the structure as a whole' (Marris
and Rein, 1972, quoted in Mayo, 1975, p 6). The extent to which the
War on Poverty should address the underlying structural causes of
poverty and social deprivation was inherently problematic, then, from
the start.

British policy initiatives and US influences in the late 1960s and 1970s

Marris and Rein were invited to Britain in 1969 to advise the
government on the lessons of the US War on Poverty. This was to
inform the development of British area-based programmes, which
sought to tackle the problematic persistence of poverty and social
deprivation through administrative reform accompanied by community
development projects to stimulate self-help. Although there were
significant differences, the parallels with the US experience were
striking, and particularly so given the underlying differences in their
models of welfare. The US welfare system, with its emphasis upon
the roles of the private, voluntary and not-for-profit sectors, had been
experiencing similar problems to those experienced by the British
welfare state, with its emphasis upon the role of the public sector. As
will be suggested subsequently, this might have cast some doubt on the
supposed efficacy of private- and voluntary-sector solutions, 'rolling
back the state', which became the mantra of the Thatcher/Reagan
years in the 1980s and early 1990s.

Meanwhile, Marris and Rein's advice about the lessons of the
US experience – particularly the advice about the importance of
addressing structural issues such as the lack of employment and training
opportunities in the ghettos, and the importance of promoting social
justice as well as tackling the more technical administrative issues – was
somewhat sidelined. Effectively, the message from civil servants was
that it was fine to be critical, but not that critical. The government's
Community Development Programme (CDP), launched in 1969, was
to promote a new problem-solving machinery jointly operated by all the
normal services to enhance collaboration within and between central
and local government. At local level, neighbourhood offices were one
of the mechanisms for bringing officers and professionals together and
encouraging new ways of working with local communities. There were

steering committees at the local as well as central government level, which were the forerunners of more contemporary mechanisms, such as local strategic partnerships. There was also an emphasis upon the promotion of community participation and self-help.

The outcomes of the CDP were not quite as the government had intended (although they might perhaps have been anticipated on the basis of the advice from US). Although much of value was achieved at the local level (eg taking up issues of housing and welfare benefits), service coordination proved more difficult, especially at the central government level. In the light of these shortcomings, a number of local projects came together to develop alternative approaches. They produced a series of original and challenging reports analysing the structural causes of poverty and social deprivation, causes rooted in the impact of economic restructuring on Britain's older industrial areas and exacerbated by the inadequacies of public provision in key service areas, such as affordable housing (CDP, 1977a). In these project areas, far from being confined to the promotion of self-help, community participation had engaged a number of community activists and trade unionists around agendas for social reform and the promotion of social justice.

Although the CDP has been referred to as an example of this type of policy intervention, it was far from being unique. On the contrary, in fact, there was a range of policy initiatives from the late 1960s aimed to address area-based concentrations of poverty and social deprivation. Before the CDP, for example, there were Education Priority Areas, launched in 1967 to tackle educational disadvantage on an area basis, involving parents and communities in schooling and pre-schooling. Furthermore, 'Urban Aid', subsequently incorporated within the Urban Programme, was launched in 1968 to target resources to Britain's most deprived neighbourhoods.

By the mid- to late 1970s, meanwhile, the wider context for social reform was changing significantly, with the first major cuts in public expenditure from 1976. Although the importance of tackling the effects of industrial restructuring had clearly been recognised, the climate was less favourable to major public spending. There was less interest in opening the Pandora's box of community participation again in subsequent programmes. The partners who were to tackle inner-city economic decline, via the Inner Areas programmes in the late 1970s, were the government and local authorities (Lawless, 1981), with no specific mention of partnership with local communities. There were parallels here with developments in the US, where the more open-ended 'maximum feasible participation' of the War on Poverty was followed by far more tightly defined programmes, such as 'Model Cities'.

Market-led approaches in the 1980s and early 1990s

By 1979, a new government with a fundamentally different agenda had been elected. Both Thatcher and her counterpart in US in the 1980s, Reagan, were neoliberals, convinced that the health of the economy, both globally and locally, depended upon freeing up market mechanisms. Government intervention in the economy and public spending for social welfare both had to be reduced. Rolling back the state was key to the neoliberal strategy to promote economic growth via market mechanisms. Growth would then trickle down, it was argued, to benefit the population at large. According to this perspective, state spending programmes that interfered with the operations of the market were doing a disservice to the poor. Ultimately, the poor stood to gain more from a healthy economy than they would from state handouts, it was argued, and state handouts had the additional disadvantage of encouraging unhealthy relations of dependency.

There is an extensive literature on neoliberalism and its critics. Galbraith, one of the foremost critics, commented on the trickle-down approach as 'the less than elegant metaphor that if one feeds the horse enough oats, some will pass through to the road for the sparrow' (Galbraith, 1992, p 108). The point is not to develop the discussion in detail here, but simply to draw attention to the significance of the differences between the neoliberal agendas of the 1980s and early 1990s and the social-democratic agendas that had underpinned 'Old Labour' approaches to the welfare state in the preceding period.

'Old Labour' had supported state planning and public provision as the basis for a universal welfare system, based upon a national system of social insurance to guard against the risks of poverty and social deprivation. The rediscovery of poverty demonstrated that there were still gaps in the system, holes in the welfare net that needed to be plugged, rather than symptoms of more basic flaws. Similarly, professionals and officers of the welfare state were initially seen as key partners in this project, even if they were seen as needing to develop new, more sensitive and coordinated ways of working in response to the criticisms of the 1960s and 1970s. Some writers believe that during this period, community work, in its more traditional role, was frequently used by the state as a means of intervening at the local level to dampen social and political unrest (Popple, 1995).

Neoliberals, on the contrary, rejected the whole basis of the post-war welfare settlement. Public provision was the problem, rather than the potential solution. And bureaucrats and professionals were the self-serving villains of the piece, perpetuating an 'Old Labour provider culture', rather than a modern consumer culture of choice.

Accordingly, area-based programmes such as Enterprise Zones and Development Corporations were established to promote local economic development via market mechanisms. The private sector was to be the engine of growth. Poverty was off the official agenda (although welfare dependency was to be tackled by a range of measures). The powers of local government continued to be reduced (part of a longer trend in fact). Local government was to be bypassed by the Development Corporations, and the professions were to be reformed, brought to heel and made more directly accountable and cost-effective. Feminist and anti-racist critiques of patriarchy and institutional racism in public services were being taken up by professionals and pursued as part of very different agendas, while neoliberal strategies were attempting to restructure the welfare state through the promotion of the disciplines of market mechanisms and the new managerialism (Clarke et al, 2000).

By the late 1980s, however, it was becoming increasingly evident that neoliberal policies were not producing the expected results in the inner cities and outer estates where the problems of poverty and social deprivation were concentrated. On the contrary, in fact, area regeneration through Development Corporations such as the London Docklands Development Corporation had actually involved very considerable sums of public money, and questions of cost-effectiveness were being raised by the Audit Commission. Meanwhile, the problems of area-based concentrations of poverty had actually been increasing as social housing had become more and more residualised. Social polarisation had been taking place more generally as a result of neoliberal economic and social policies, and social inequality was growing faster than in any other Organisation for Economic Co-operation and Development (OECD) country except New Zealand (which was also experiencing neoliberal policy initiatives at this time). Globally, there was an increasing realisation that neoliberal development strategies – structural adjustment programmes – needed to be modified because of the negative impact on the poorest and most vulnerable – adjustment with a human face.

In summary, the next round of area-based programmes in Britain continued to be based upon neoliberal economic strategies, but the focus shifted. Local authorities were brought back as partners, to work alongside the private sector in public–private partnerships to deliver government regeneration programmes. There was renewed emphasis upon improving the social fabric as well as regenerating the economic base and/or promoting property development. There was also renewed emphasis upon community participation. City Challenge Programmes (launched in 1991) provided government resources to implement strategies for area regeneration to local partnerships that successfully bid for these. Subsequent programmes, such as the Single Regeneration Budget programmes (SRBs), similarly included provision for community participation within partnerships that emphasised the role of the private sector to coordinate regeneration strategies within localities. On the face of it, this sounds like a return to the area-based programmes of the late 1960s and early 1970s. But was it? Although there were some similarities, there were also significant differences.

In the 1960s and 1970s, programmes such as the CDP had targeted areas of deprivation, aiming to improve the appropriateness and effectiveness of services by better coordination between professionals and policymakers and through the promotion of user involvement, community participation and self-help. There were similar concerns in programmes such as City Challenge. But here the similarity ends. In the 1960s and early 1970s, there were pressures for cost-effectiveness as governments aimed to control the rise in public expenditure. But this was within the overall framework of the continuing commitment to public welfare (to a greater or lesser extent depending upon the politicians in question). However paternalistic and controlling, Old Labour was committed to a broadly social-democratic tradition that saw the welfare state in terms of agendas for social reform and redistributive approaches to social justice. Programmes such as City Challenge and the first SRBs, in contrast, were developed in the context of neoliberal strategies to promote private market mechanisms. And community participation was included as part of these wider strategies to replace the producer culture with a neoliberal alternative – a consumer culture.

This is in no way to suggest that the outcomes of these programmes were predetermined. Just as with the War on Poverty and CDP, promoting community participation could have the effect of opening a Pandora's box. Here, too, in City Challenge and SRBs, human actors developed their own strategies as individuals and within organisations. Community participation had varying effects, and these included outcomes that the participants themselves defined as empowering. For example, as a community representative commented on experiences of being involved from the first to the fourth round of SRB programmes: 'This has gotten better from SRB 1 through to SRB 4'. 'We gained respect and that has given us power', commented another (Anastacio et al, 2000, p 31). The point, then, is not that these programmes were entirely negative for local communities, but that the programmes were not intended to present challenges to the basic framework of neoliberal economic and social policies. Nor were they designed to promote social-democratic versions of social reform and redistributive justice.

The context for current policies

For some 30 years or so, local communities in some of Britain's inner cities and older industrial areas have experienced area-based programmes to promote service coordination, to improve relationships between professionals and service users, and to promote community participation and self-help, usually with associated commitments to empowerment and the pursuit of social justice agendas. Already by the 1970s, the CDP (1977b) report *Gilding the ghetto* referred to a 'decade of projects', pointing out that different government departments had been sponsoring different projects – but with little central coordination or preparedness to address the underlying problems. The report went on to quote a civil servant's comment that without serious political commitment, such initiatives were providing no more than the illusion of a response, 'gilding the ghetto or buying time' (CDP, 1977b, p 55).

This chapter has referred to a few examples only. Even in more recent years, over the past three decades, some neighbourhoods in England have experienced an urban development corporation, a Task Force, a City Challenge, a SRB programme, a Health Action Zone, an Education Action Zone, an Employment Zone, a 'New Deal for Communities' status, community cohesion policies and Local Strategic Partnerships designed to bring initiatives together under the previous New Labour government. Comments about regeneration fatigue were scarcely surprising, with understandable scepticism in some quarters about the novelty or, indeed, the likely impact of each latest initiative beyond the inevitable creation of a handful of jobs and promotions for the 'suits and dresses', the functionaries of the poverty industry. As the title of a chapter in a collection of essays on 'contested communities' puts this: 'You've fucked up the estate and now you're carrying a briefcase!' (McCulloch, 1997, p 51).

Reflecting upon the contradictions and tensions in the New Labour welfare project, Lister gave a limited welcome to the 'latest version in a long lineage of targeted area-based policies', rolled out 'largely under the auspices of the Social Exclusion Unit' (Lister, 2001, p 432), valuing the emphasis upon resident participation and the attempts to integrate local projects within a wider national strategy. In the face of growing concentrations of poverty and worklessness and the fact that, as the Social Exclusion Unit pointed out, 70% of all people from minority ethnic groups live in the 88 most deprived local authority districts compared with the rest of the population, there is a potentially important role for such area-based initiatives, Lister argued.

But, as she went on to point out, area-based programmes depend for their success upon wider action to address regional economic divisions, quoting Benington and Donnison's warning that: 'a small area focus can run the risk of diverting attention away from wider political economic forces which cause and maintain the concentrations of poverty and unemployment in these areas' (Benington and Donnison, 1999, p 65). Similar arguments have been applied to New Labour's approach towards community cohesion and the prevention of violent extremism in the wake of urban disturbances in 2001 and the London bombings in 2005 (Kundnani, 2007; Ratcliffe and Newman, 2011) – as illustrated by the Commission on Integration and Cohesion (COIC, 2007) report's recognition of the importance of addressing structural inequalities. So, was this effectively about re-gilding the ghetto, rather than confronting deep-seated economic and social divisions? Lister concluded by suggesting that 'New Labour has not shown sufficient courage in challenging many of the values associated with the Thatcherite legacy because of its fear of alienating a Middle England electorate perceived to be sympathetic to them' (Lister, 2001, p 441). For example, when it came to the role of the private sector, New Labour espoused neoliberal views on the value of involving the private sector in financing and running public services. These approaches were firmly included in the structures of area-based regeneration and neighbourhood renewal initiatives.

Reflecting on the limitations of New Labour policies towards deprived neighbourhoods, Syrett and North (2010, p 477) conclude that, despite deep-seated commitment:

> sustained policy activity over a 13 year period produced little impact upon the spatial patterns of disadvantage. In practice, successive NL [New Labour] governments struggled both to confront the economic basis of the problems of deprived neighbourhoods and to put in place the necessary governance arrangements to tackle the problem. The result was a plethora of initiatives and an ever-changing governance landscape which, although it produced some significant localised impacts, did not provide the basis for any

widespread reversal in the economic fortunes of deprived neighbourhoods.

Even before the impact of the banking crisis of 2008, in fact, inequalities were actually growing, the critics argued (Wilkinson and Pickett, 2010; Dorling, 2011).

So, that was the negative view, the 'glass half-empty' rather than the 'glass half-full' syndrome. Given limitations of space, the point is simply to note here the contested nature of such programme outcomes. In terms of New Labour's impact on civil society more generally, there were some more encouraging signs, however. Initiatives to promote active citizenship had enabled a significant number of people in deprived areas to make their voices heard more effectively, both as individuals and as members of communities (whether these were communities of locality or communities of identity or both) (Mayo and Annette, 2010). And there was increasing recognition of the importance of working in partnership with faith-based communities (Dinham, 2009).

Overall, however, critics pointed to the less positive effects of a decade or more of third-sector modernisation (Scott, 2010), pointing to increasing marketisation, enervation and inequality within the voluntary sector itself, as well as in society more generally. Critics questioned the extent to which these area-based programmes were actually succeeding in promoting community empowerment (however that contested term was defined). Conversely, they also questioned how far they were effectively geared towards building the voluntary and community sector's capacity to emulate the more business-oriented management styles of the new managerialism.

Given such criticisms, it would seem unsurprising that the Coalition government set out to promote a different approach following the UK general election of 2010. Like their predessor government in the 1960s, when the CDP was born, the new government looked to models from across the Atlantic. Drawing upon the experiences of mobilising for US President Barack Obama's election campaign, the Coalition government focused upon Alinsky-style organising (Alinsky, 1972; Gilchrist and Taylor, 2011) as the basis for training 5,000 community organisers, who were to facilitate the development of the so-called 'Big Society'. This was to add a hard edge – using more oppositional approaches to achieve immediate improvements and building broad alliances, including alliances with faith-based organisations in communities. This was contrasted with more community development-style approaches, inspired by the writings of Freire (1972), which had characterised citizenship learning and community participation programmes under New Labour (Gilchrist and Taylor, 2011).

Like previous programmes, however, the idea of the 'Big Society' was also concerned with mobilising voluntary effort, as public services were to be rolled back still further in an era of increasing financial stringency. In parallel with previous programmes too, the Coalition government has focused upon localities and partnership-working across sectors, with an emphasis upon area-based approaches to achieve these ends. Citizens were to become activated as volunteers and service users, exercising choice as informed consumers. The new localism was to apply more generally, however, in affluent areas too. And all this was to take place without addressing the market forces associated with the lack of job opportunities and affordable housing in the more deprived neighbourhoods.

Like previous governments too, the Coalition government has been concerned with issues of community cohesion and community safety in the context of continuing international migration, developing new initiatives to prevent violent extremism. As Gilchrist and Taylor (2011) have argued, anti-immigration panics illustrate the 'dark side' of community. But, in an increasingly globalised world, controlling immigration has proved to be easier said than done – and particularly so within the European Union's borders. The issues associated with social integration have continued to pose challenges for successive governments and for community practitioners alike, then, both in Britain and across the European Union, which has been developing its own initiatives in response.

Conclusions: implications for managers of community practice

This chapter started by suggesting that there were differing views about the extent to which the contemporary policy framework for community practice resembles the policy frameworks of preceding decades. Readers will come to their own conclusions on the basis of the evidence or their own experiences as managers involved in community practice. Whatever their conclusions, there are implications for community practice, however. This chapter has argued for the importance of human agency. The actions and, indeed, the inactions of individuals can and do make a difference to policy outcomes. The history of area-based programmes provides ample examples to illustrate the varying ways in which policies result in unintended consequences. Community participation initiatives, it has been suggested, have been cases in point. This has been demonstrated even in the more closely defined programmes of recent years – although the extent to which this room for manoeuvre can be expected to continue in the context of the challenges of the current economic, political and social climate remains to be seen.

This makes it all the more vital to reflect upon and learn from past experiences. There are positive lessons about opportunities grasped and initiatives developed from firm roots within local communities. There are also positive lessons to be learnt from past experiences of building bridges between different communities of interest and locality and the professionals working with them in the public and voluntary service sectors. But there are also negative lessons to be learnt, lessons about communities that have become increasingly fragmented and demoralised, caught up in competition for scarce resources, and grass-roots initiatives undermined and community energies diverted to fulfil the organisational requirements of programmes designed from the top down – struggling to cope with the loss of public services in contexts of increasing social needs. Reflecting upon the causes of past mistakes may be as valuable as reflecting on the ingredients of past achievements.

If managers of community practice and practitioners are seriously committed to making a difference, stretching the potential of the programmes that they work on to their limits, then they do need to develop a strategic approach based upon a clear understanding of their opportunities, rooted in a critical analysis of the structural and policy constraints. This involves unpacking the contested concepts and the competing agendas. Like a crew setting sail, community practitioners need to check the direction of the wind before setting their course. Like a crew, they also need to be constantly alert, adjusting for any changes of direction, if they are to use the wind effectively rather than allowing it to blow them off course. While navigational skills are essential, it is not only down to the captain, though. Teamwork is absolutely vital. A commitment to working in more empowering ways, as reflective practitioners, rooted in the values of equal opportunities and social justice, involves developing strategies in partnership with others. This will include professionals working alongside service users, community representatives and community activists. Through sharing the process of analysing the structural barriers and the policy constraints, together they may be enabled to develop a more effective jointly owned approach to maximising the opportunities for challenge and change.

References

Abel-Smith, B. and Townsend, P. (1965) *The poor and the poorest*, London: Bell.

Alinsky, S. (1972) *Rules for radicals: a political primer for practical radicals*, New York, NY: Random House.

Anastacio, J., Gidley, B., Hart, L., Keith, M., Mayo, M. and Kowarzik, U. (2000) *Reflecting realities: participants' perspectives on integrated communities and sustainable development*, Bristol: The Policy Press.

Benington, J. and Donnison, D. (1999) 'New Labour and social exclusion: the search for a Third Way, or just gilding the ghetto again?', in H. Dean and R. Woods (eds) *Social policy review 11*, Luton: Social Policy Association.

Brenton, M. (1985) *The voluntary sector in British social services*, London: Longman.

CDP (Community Development Programme) (1977a) *The costs of industrial change*, Newcastle upon Tyne: CDP Publications.

CDP (1977b) *Gilding the ghetto*, Newcastle upon Tyne: CDP Publications.

Clarke, J., Gewitz, S. and McLaughlin, E. (2000) *New managerialism: new welfare?*, London: Sage.

COIC (Commission on Integration and Cohesion) (2007) *Our shared future*, Wetherby: Communities and Local Government Publications.

Dinham, A. (2009) *Faith, public policy and civil society: problems, policies, controversies*, Basingstoke: Palgrave Macmillan.

Dorling, D. (2011) *Injustice: why social inequality persists*, Bristol: The Policy Press.

Freire, P. (1972) *Pedadogy of the oppressed*, Harmondsworth: Penguin.

Galbraith, J. (1992) *The culture of contentment*, London: Sinclair-Stevenson.

Gilchrist, A. and Taylor, M. (2011) *The short guide to community development*, Bristol: The Policy Press.

Kramer, R. (1969) *Participation of the poor*, Englewood Cliffs, NJ: Prentice-Hall.

Kundnani, A. (2007) *The end of tolerance? Racism in 21st century Britain*, London: Pluto.

Lawless, P. (1981) *Britain's inner cities*, London: Harper and Row.

Lister, R. (2001) 'New Labour: a study in ambiguity from a position of ambivalence', *Critical Social Policy*, vol 21, no 69, pp 425–48.

Loney, M. (1983) *Community against government: the British Community Development Project 1968–78*, London: Heinemann.

Marris, P. and Rein, M. (1972) *Dilemmas of social reform: poverty and community action in the United States*, London: Routledge and Kegan Paul.

Mayo, M. (1975) 'The history and early development of CDP', in R. Lees and G. Smith (eds) *Action-research in community development*, London: Routledge and Kegan Paul.

Mayo, M. and Annette, J. (eds) (2010) *Taking part? Active learning for active citizenship and beyond*, Leicester: NIACE.

McCulloch, A. (1997) '"You've fucked up the estate and now you're carrying a briefcase!"', in P. Hoggett (ed) *Contested communities*, Bristol: The Policy Press, pp 51–67.

Popple, K. (1995) *Analysing community work*, Buckingham: Open University Press.

Ratcliffe, P. and Newman, I. (eds) (2011) *Promoting social cohesion: implications for policy and evaluation*, Bristol: The Policy Press.

Scott, M. (2010) 'Critical reflections on a decade of third sector modernisation: another sector is possible', *Local Economy*, vol 25, nos 5–6, pp 367–72.

Syrett, S. and North, D. (2010) 'Between economic competitiveness and social inclusion: New Labour and the economic revival of deprived neighbourhoods', *Local Economy*, vol 25, nos 5–6, pp 476–93.

Townsend, P. (1979) *Poverty in the United Kingdom*, Harmondsworth: Penguin.

Wilkinson, R. and Pickett, K. (2010) *The spirit level: why equality is better for everyone*, London: Penguin.

THREE

Organisational management for community practice: a framework

Hugh Butcher

Introduction

The central challenge of this chapter is simply stated: what management systems and what organisational structures will best enhance the work of community practitioners, enabling them to maximise their effectiveness in supporting communities to take action? Too often, there is an assumption that there is 'one best way' to manage work organisations. This chapter represents a plea for 'organisational alignment', so that work practices of community practitioners are supported by appropriate, customised organisational and managerial contexts.

This chapter is in four parts. It begins with a brief overview and critique of 'one best way' thinking about organisation and management. Building on the discussion of the nature of community practice in Chapter One – on how the power and goals of a wide variety of institutions and practitioners interact to create the complex field of community practice – the chapter goes on to identify a number of key features of community practice as a work process that should influence its organisation and management. This leads to the presentation of a simplified operational model – comprising organisational structure, culture, systems and procedures – required to support such work. Finally, the chapter considers aspects of managerial roles and management styles that, pursued within the context of this organisational model, will best promote effective, high-quality practice.

This chapter, in short, offers frameworks for thinking about and modelling organisation and management for community practice. Such frameworks and models need to be carefully selected and adapted, taking into account the goals and constitution of particular employing organisations, the kind of community practice implemented, and the nature of the geographical and cultural context in which the work is undertaken. It would, indeed, be ironic if the frameworks and models discussed here were to be construed as prescriptions for 'the one best way'.

'One best way'?

It is now over a century since Frederick Taylor (1911), prototype management guru and early advocate of 'scientific management', first proclaimed that it was possible to discover the fundamental and immutable principles of organisational management. 'Mechanistic' models of management should, according to Taylor, mirror the forms of mechanised (motor car assembly line) mass production being pioneered by his friend Henry Ford. Standardised working practices, top-down job design, strict coordination and control through hierarchical layers of management and supervision, and disciplined compliance to rules and regulation increasingly became accepted dictums of much 20th-century industrial and commercial management.

The idea that there is 'one best way' to design and manage work organisations continues to cast its long and baleful shadow over much organisational theory and practice. As Morgan (2006, p 31, emphasis in original) notes:

> Classical management theory and scientific management were each pioneered and sold to managers as the one best way to organise. The early theorists believed they had discovered *the* principle of organisation which, if followed, would more or less solve managerial problems forever. Now we only have to look at the contemporary organisation scene to find that they were completely wrong on this score. Indeed, we find that their management principles often lie at the root of many modern organisational problems.

In seeking models for the organisational management of community practice, we certainly need to look beyond Taylorist thinking. Post-Taylorist thought has emphasised that organisational design and management practice needs to recognise that 'one best way' thinking is inadequate because:

1. The nature of most organisational work is no longer (if it ever was) akin to assembly-line car production. As Morgan (2006, p 27) notes: 'Mechanistic approaches to organisation work well under conditions when machines work well, but in more and more work situations machine-like management and organisation is massively dysfunctional'. The work process of the community practitioner is about as far away as you can get from that of the worker on the assembly line.

2. Managers are now acutely aware that they need to be able to adapt their organisations to the particular (and changing) contexts and environments in which they operate. Social, economic and cultural change is ubiquitous and, as we argue in Chapter Four, organisations need to maximise their capacity for adaptability and change and to become 'learning organisations'. Community practice has, historically, been deployed to support a wide variety of evolving social and political goals and programmes (Butcher, 1993; Somerville, 2011) and there is no reason to believe that this will not continue to be the case.

3. Following from the previous points, organisations – including those responsible for supporting community practitioners – need to be seen as more akin to 'organisms' than machines. The organic image prompts us to think in terms of open systems (rather than in closed structural terms), of interaction with (and reciprocal adaptation to) changing environmental contexts, and of growth and evolution.

Community practice as work process: the '5P + C' model

So, what are the key features of community practice as a work process and what implications – for organising and managing such work processes – follow from this? It may be useful to approach these questions through use of a particular model of community practice. This involves us asking, first of all, how can we best characterise the Purposes, Policies, Programmes, Practices and Processes of community practice (the '5Ps'), and the operating contexts of that practice ('C')? I will call this the '5P + C' model. We can then go on to ask: what do such characteristics imply for the organisation and management of the practitioners responsible for undertaking such work?

Briefly, the elements in the model may be described as follows:

- *Purposes*: these are the broad overall intentions of the work, incorporating the aims, the underlying principles and values, and the macro-objectives of the work. For example, the intention of working towards a more socially inclusive society, based on values of equality and community, may be seen as a guiding *purpose* behind much community practice.

- *Policies*: the specific, mandated frameworks for action that community practitioners are employed to pursue in particular organisations at particular times. For example, a government may promote a strategy for neighbourhood renewal, thus providing a policy framework and context for a particular form of community practice.

- *Programmes*: the specific plans of action through which community practitioners seek to implement policy. For example, a local authority may pursue a policy of area decentralisation and local democracy – with community practitioners employed to support a *programme* designed to establish and support a system of area forums.
- *Practices*: the general working methods and operations, underpinned by associated skills, that are used by community practitioners, for example: networking, group work, action research and so on. Many such practices are characteristic of a variety of other human service occupations of course, and are not specific to community practice.
- *Processes*: the routine series of practices and operations that coalesce in ways that *do* characterise community practice as an occupation; for example, community capacity-building is seen as a characteristic work process of some community practitioners.
- *Contexts*: the operating and socio-political environment in which the community practitioner is employed, for example: inner-city or rural community; locality community or interest community.

With these distinctions in mind, we can begin to look in a little more depth at the realities of the community practitioner's occupational role and remit under each of these headings.

Purposes

Active community

The contemporary purposes of community practice are presented schematically in Figure 3.1. At the very centre of the diagram – the 'bullseye' – we identify 'generating and supporting active community' as a key purpose of community practitioners. This was stressed in Chapter One (p 11). Whether working with locality, interest or identity communities, the community practitioner's aim is to support members of communities in developing the motivations and dispositions, skills and knowledge, to work to achieve their common goals. Alan Barr has conducted research among community practitioners and community activists into the characteristics that help define, for community members, 'quality of life' in the community (see Chapter Eight, this volume, p 176). Figure 3.2 draws on the research of Barr to link 'quality of life measures' to the idea of 'active community'.

Figure 3.1: Community practice: purposes

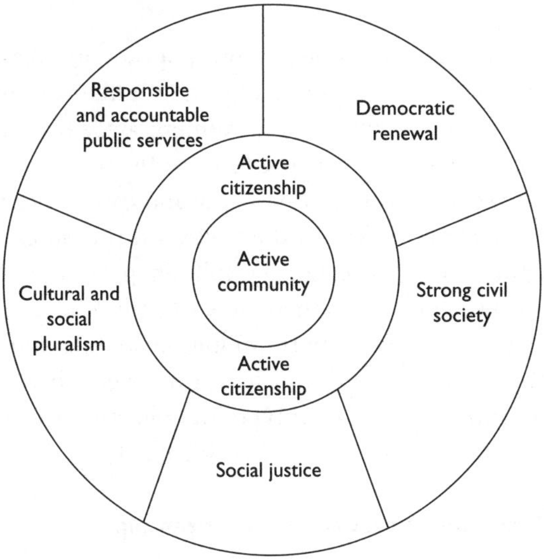

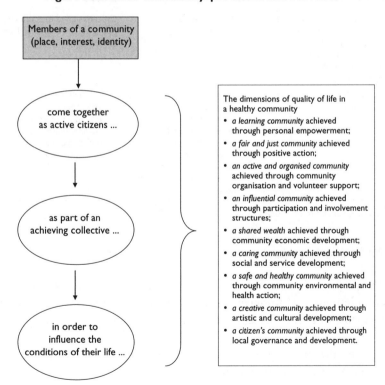

Figure 3.2: Active community: processes and outcome

Sources: See Alan Barr et al (1996) and Chapter Eight, this volume.

Active citizenship

The concept of active community presupposes an enlarged role for the citizen in society – represented by the middle ring in Figure 3.1. Community practice embraces a movement away from narrow ideas of citizenship – as concerned predominantly with rights to use or consume state services on the one hand, and cast a vote for someone to represent their views within the polity on the other. Goss (2001) and Benington and Moore (2011), following Moore (1996, 1999), usefully conceptualise an enlarged view of active citizenship – one in which the citizen embraces both a range of public deliberation and decision-taking roles (in addition to voting every four or five years) as well as engaging in a range of types of collective action to produce (as well as consume) public value (see Table 3.1).

Table 3.1: Community practice: active citizenship

	Role of active citizens	
Consumers	**Governors**	**Doers**
Citizens active in pursuing rights and entitlements to public services/access to public programmes and to services provided by activists/producers:	Citizens active as owners/authorisers:	Citizens active in producing public value for themselves and other citizens:
– beneficiaries – clients – service users	– voters – taxpayers – participators/ decision-takers (in social enterprises, neighbourhood and community councils, community associations, etc)	– self-helpers and volunteers – providers of services – co-producers – meeting obligations and responsibilities

Source: Adapted from Moore (1999) and Goss (2001)

Public 'end-state' purposes

The previous two purposes of active community and active citizenship complement and underpin a third set of purposes (the five outer segments of Figure 3.1 are contemporary examples):

- to ensure public provision and services are more responsive, open and accountable to all citizens;

- to extend, and render more participatory, democratic institutions in society;
- to promote social inclusion and equal opportunities and to work for greater socio-economic equality and social justice;
- to strengthen the range of voluntary, charitable and community organisations that comprise a vibrant civil society; and
- to deepen social and cultural pluralism, promoting positive interactions and public deliberation between diverse groups and cultures.

The challenge of public, contested, purposes

These are ambitious purposes, and they share a number of distinctive features that have an important bearing on the organisation and management of workers who are employed to bring them about. In the first place, their exact meanings are highly contestable. They generate debate, and sometimes conflict, and this becomes part of the occupational context and climate of those who are working to achieve them. Moreover, they are 'public' purposes and belong to the 'public domain' (Ramsden and Stewart, 1994; Benington and Moore, 2011), and are, thus, subject to the political debates, prioritisation and decision-making that characterise that domain. Working for equality or democracy, or open and accountable public administration, for example, are 'end-state' public purposes, and determining how they are to be shaped and achieved is generally seen as the responsibility of legislators or senior decision-makers. It is they, conventionally, who shape how such purposes are to be pursued; others are responsible for implementing the programmes and procedures put in place in order to secure their achievement. Community practitioners, unusually for front-line workers, find themselves engaging with those citizens (and their 'active communities') who are directly seeking to influence the shape as well as the detailed implementation of these large, end-state purposes.

This is challenging work in a number of respects. If community practitioners are to support citizen action effectively and responsibly, then it requires that they have a sympathetic and well-developed understanding of the nature and complexity of the underlying values themselves, as well as the difficulties inherent in securing their practical realisation. It can be irresponsible and harmful to the goal of active citizenship for community practitioners to work with people to achieve influence and power in the public arena in an ineffective or tokenistic way. On the other hand, if community practitioners *are* effective, they may well become publicly identified with the aims and actions of the community groups and organisations with which they are working, and so be accused of trespassing on political territory that legislators and appointed decision-makers regard as their own.

The practitioner's situation can also become fraught if the goals of the community groups and organisations they are working with are significantly at odds with those of powerful interest groups. In the hurly-burly of everyday politics, it can become difficult for those involved to respect the distinction between support for the general idea of 'active citizenship' (a value to which most can sign up) and supporting the particular concrete purposes that comprise the bone of contention in a particular place and at a particular time.

Policies and programmes

Trends in policies; diversity in programmes

As noted, the purposes of community practice find expression in a wide range of community *policies*, pursued by government at the local, central and international levels, as well as by voluntary, mutual-aid, social enterprise and community organisations. Such policies are implemented through action *programmes* that identify the specific goals and strategies to be pursued, establish the resources made available, and specify the implementation plans to be followed. In terms of the key *purposes* of community practice identified earlier, over recent decades, community *policies* have been developed in many countries claiming to help secure:

- *Responsive public services*: decentralisation of services, along with local multi-agency working, has been introduced with the aim of increasing the responsiveness of public services to citizens.
- *Democratic renewal*: as part of plans to 'modernise' government, devolution of decision-making in public, social enterprise and charitable agencies to locality levels has been pursued, for example, to advance the cause of democratic participation.
- *Civil society*: elements already identified in the two points above (eg recognition of the importance of social enterprises and charitable bodies in multi-agency working) rest on a recognition of how community development, community capacity-building and community organisations, along with other strategies to enhance local social capital, have sought to strengthen civil society.
- *Social justice*: more often than not, community policies are designed to help promote values of equity and fairness; sometimes their *primary*

goal is about supporting the poor or disadvantaged, as, for example, in some community and neighbourhood renewal initiatives, health action projects and child/family support programmes.

- *Cultural and social pluralism*: 'localism' (sometimes an implicit, sometimes an explicit, ingredient in all the previous policy purposes) embraces a belief in the values of pluralism; but social and cultural pluralism is generally regarded as much more than a beneficial spin-off of pursuing community policies – community projects and programmes often put enhancement of diversity and pluralism as a primary purpose of their programme.

A weakness inherent in Figure 3.1, and the brief overview of purposes outlined in the preceding five bullet points, is a failure to acknowledge the degree of ideological and political contestability that arises whenever attempts are made to unpack the precise meanings of the terms employed. Just as the term 'active community' is highly contested, so, of course, are terms like 'justice' and 'democracy'. An example of this idea of ideological and political contestability is illustrated with respect to the politics of localism and 'place community' in Box 3.1.

Box 3.1: Policies and programmes: localism and the 'place' community – ideological and political contestability

Community policies claiming to promote localism in various forms have often been pursued by governmental and non-governmental agencies of various stripes in different countries over the last 50 years. Decade by decade, political and organisational agendas, influenced by broad social, economic and cultural changes, have shaped the nature of community policies concerned with decentralisation and devolution.

To illustrate, in the UK during the 1970s, some local authorities sought to achieve decentralisation (of some of their mainstream local government services) and experimented with devolution of aspects of service decision-making, buttressed by consultative procedures and neighbourhood forums (Blunkett and Jackson, 1987; Butcher, 1993).

Two decades on, the localism of the first New Labour administration under Prime Minister Blair (1997–2001) was underpinned by a belief that central government needed, on the one hand, to *drive* local change and, on the other, to ensure that the *scope* of local change initiatives should be broadened out beyond traditional local government services to embrace health, economic development, policing, education and so on (Stoker, 2007; Somerville, 2011). At the same time, policies were advanced that were committed to developing communities of place per se (promoting a 'New Deal for Communities', 'Neighbourhood Renewal' etc).

During the first years of the 21st century, the weaknesses of New Labour's centralist, top-down approaches were increasingly acknowledged; it was seen that the benefits of localism could only be properly realised if standardised, centrally driven policy implementation was replaced by an awareness that local problems needed to be addressed through local problem-analysis along with locally driven, innovative problem-solving. A plurality of more direct forms of neighbourhood government needed to be established in the belief that more locally responsive and joined-up approaches to local problems would result from significantly more local democratic engagement. The idea of 'double devolution' entered the vocabulary of localism (Department for Communities and Local Government, 2006).

With the return to power of a Conservative–Liberal Democrat Coalition in 2010, the new government was faced with a 'perfect storm' of financial and economic crises. Such difficulties were attributed in part to the secular growth of 'big government', along with the associated escalation of sovereign debt, over the Labour years (Bowles, 2010; Boardman, 2011). In addition to reforms of the market and state, the way forward was seen to lie in the revitalisation of civil society. An active citizenry, freed from disabling statism and red tape, could be liberated to run community businesses and associations, and be commissioned to provide local social care, education and health services through locally owned and managed social enterprises. A new form of 'sub-localism' was envisaged, which, at least partly, echoed the previous administration's notion of 'double devolution'.

Change and evolution

An important implication of such policies and programmes for their management and organisation derives from the increasingly rapid rate at which they are developing and evolving. Organisational analysts suggest that under such conditions, management systems that encourage non-rigid and adaptable structures, organisational learning, and 'adhocratic' forms of organisation need to be brought to the fore. We will return to this important point later in the chapter.

Development through partnership

Another significant feature of community policies and programmes is that they often have a 'process' and developmental focus. Such work processes can rarely be standardised and pre-programmed in much detail. Community practitioners are employed to create and sustain social environments in which members of communities can:

• realise their 'voice' (see Chapter One);
• contribute to partnership-working, joint planning initiatives and network organisations (see Chapter Six); and
• develop 'community capacity' capable of creating and then utilising, through active community, what is increasingly referred to as 'social capital' (Field, 2008).

Once again, the work process entails flexibility in the exercise of expert judgement within evolving situations.

This leads to another significant feature of community policies and programmes that also deserves mention. Programme goals are determined and driven, in theory at least, through the aspirations and efforts of a range of interested parties, including 'active communities'. Front-line community practitioners will, therefore, be operating in conditions of evolving coalition-building. As we shall see, the successful management of professionals engaged in such work will rest on rigorous recruitment and selection procedures, along with professional training and mentoring that encourages critical-reflexive practice, supported by sustained and skilled managerial supervision.

Processes and practices

Processes and practices comprise those routine activities undertaken by community practitioners on a day-to-day basis. *Practices* are those general working methods (entailing the exercise of associated skills) used in a wide range of human service occupations. Examples include task-based group work, networking, administering, informal education, counselling, planning, brokering, profiling and researching, consulting, and so forth. *Processes*, on the other hand, are those configurations or clusters of practices that characterise the work of a specific occupation. For the community practitioner, these include inter-agency and partnership-working, community research and evaluation, community organising, support for experiential community learning, and so forth.

Boundary work

Once again, a number of features of such practices and processes have implications for the management and organisation of the community practitioner's work. They involve, for example, working at the interface between formal agencies responsible for delivering public policies and services to communities, between individual community members and their own community organisations, and between the coalitions of groups and agencies that come together in alliances to create public value. Henderson, Jones and Thomas (1980) called this 'boundary work', drawing attention to the way that community workers occupy a position and perform a role *between* people, communities and organisations. Theirs is an 'interjacent' role:

> lying between other components in society, and in relation to which it has some function ... this 'space' between community groups and organisations, local and central organisations, is not a static one – it is fluid and changes as the worker is pushed and pulled by various forces that emanate from community groups and bureaucracies. (Henderson et al, 1980, p 2)

Practitioner attributes

Following Henderson, we can also note that the process of community practice is 'worker-centred'. The success of community practitioners' work, and the efficiency of their transactions with individuals, groups and organisations, depends greatly on their 'personality, energy, stamina and skills', and their capacity to be effective is significantly mediated through the power of their personality. Such personal power is contingent, in turn, on the development of trust, confidence and affinity between community practitioners and the networks of people and agencies with whom they are working. All this has two further implications.

'Messy' problems and 'emergent' solutions

As noted, it is clear that community practitioners work in and with dynamic situations – situations that evolve through the ongoing interaction and negotiations between different stakeholders and their respective interests. Under such circumstances, it is difficult to plan or 'script' the community practitioners' work schedule in advance in any detail. Typically, they work with 'messy' (unbounded) problems, and such problems are likely to confound the application of neat, pre-planned solutions. Such problems are likely to be subject to redefinition, and action responses may be 'reframed' as they are addressed. Community problem-solving thus has an emergent quality about it. The process of community practice also has an important mutual learning dimension to it; as work evolves through joint activity by key stakeholders, so new 'lessons' and new solutions are developed and refined. The result is that as community and agency capacity for action is developed jointly, so the sustainability of initiatives is thereby enhanced.

Inner compass

Second, and as a result, the community practitioner's 'inner compass' of values, principles and professional identity become a vital contributory ingredient to the success of their work. In circumstances where 'recipe' solutions are unlikely to be successful, workers require the confidence to innovate flexibly, with others, through processes of reflection and review, underpinned by a well-grounded professional ethic.

Democratic professionalism

This leads us to highlight another key feature of the community practitioner's professionalism – what has been called its 'democratic professionalism'. The development of approaches to co-production of public- and third-sector services has prompted the development of new models of professional practice, changing what it *means* to be a professional. Co-production of services regards people as partners in the design and delivery of services, not just as passive recipients of policies and programmes determined and provided by experts. Co-production relies on the mutuality, reciprocity and engagement of citizens in reconfiguring services as equal partners *with and alongside* professionals. The conventional distinction between service provider and service recipient becomes blurred; the professional becomes 'other-directed', a facilitator of change rather than a provider of services – an approach clearly akin to community practice. Jenkins and Brotherton (1995, p 280) were early advocates of what they called 'democratic' forms of professionalism. Drawing attention to the way in which modern forms of occupational therapy distance themselves from conventional professional norms (which tend to emphasise practitioner expertise and client dependency), they recognised and advocated a model of professionalism that rests on partnership, negotiation and power-sharing between worker and stakeholders. A NESTA report (Boyle et al, 2010) argues that such a partnership model is developing strongly on the periphery of public services, especially in social care and supported housing, and advocates that 'co-production' should become the default model for a range of other services, including health care and criminal justice. The model of professional practice developed within co-production thinking clearly enjoys a good fit with the goals and methods of community practice, along with its notions of active community, responsive services and a strengthened civil society. Dzur's (2008) research takes the argument one stage further by locating the idea of democratic professionalism within the current discourse on deliberative democracy: for him, professionals (read 'community practitioners') can play a key role in opening up opportunities for citizen participation in democratic reform.

Context

The operating context within which community practice is undertaken consists of its social, geographical, organisational and policy environment. Our discussion in this and previous chapters has already touched on a range of such factors. We have noted in Chapter One, for example, how Acts of Parliament have placed a statutory duty on local authorities in England to prepare community strategies and to develop and implement these through a system of local strategic partnerships. Chapter Two has charted some of the wider socio-political changes that have helped to shape the development of community practice over the past three or four decades.

Organisational context

We will not rehearse such factors again here, but focus on a feature that deserves systematic attention in this book – the *organisational* context for such work. Community practitioners work within a highly diverse range of agencies and organisations:

- Government agencies at the central, regional and local levels support initiatives concerned with area and neighbourhood democracy, delivery of housing, and youth and educational services, and are involved in, for example, local community capacity-building and community consultation.
- Voluntary-sector organisations and social enterprises while often funded to implement aspects of government policy, also pursue their own independent work with communities, encouraging mutual aid, local campaigning and project work.
- Community groups constitute a further, informal, focus for active citizenship and community service.

• Finally, and as Chapter Six points out, community practice is increasingly pursued through cross-sector partnerships and development programmes concerned with economic, social and neighbourhood regeneration and renewal.

The structure, culture, operating procedures and management styles within these organisations vary and this significantly influences how effective their workers will be in delivering programmes and policies.

Community practice: key organisational variables

This organisational context is, then, an extremely variegated one and it is important to take account of some of the key dimensions of such variability:

• In the first place, such organisations differ in how far community practice constitutes their 'core business' or is a subsidiary activity supportive of one or more aspect of their central mission. As noted in Chapter One, more and more human service agencies are incorporating a community engagement focus in their work. This can give rise to incompatibilities in management styles and lead to difficulties in coordinating diverse activities within particular roles.
• Such organisations can also differ in the extent to which their approach to community practice is 'agency-focused' or 'community-focused'. Is their community practice approach primarily 'top-down', where the 5Ps are shaped by agency mission, or is it primarily concerned with 'bottom-up' work, where the configuration of the organisation's 5Ps are led by community priorities?
• Third, organisations differ in the emphasis they give to 'process' or 'task' goals in their work. For example, a goal may be to fulfil a statutory duty or policy requirement; or the goal may be to support a step change in the mindset (and associated skills) of community members.
• Fourth, and interrelated to the previous factors, community practice organisations differ in the primary target of their change efforts: is it community, organisation, inter-agency network or institutional-level change that is the primary goal? Thus, community development is likely to focus on direct work at the neighbourhood level in order to enhance the effectiveness of community groups. Alternatively, the focus may be on strengthening the agency's capacity for responsive service delivery via community consultation, or achieving an

effective community voice within an inter-agency partnership pursuing joined-up policy implementation.

We have summarised four ways in which organisations responsible for supporting community practice and community practitioners differ. In reality, there is a significant overlap and clustering among the variables, which gives rise to recognisable types of organisational form. The underlying analytical distinctions nevertheless remain helpful because they enable us to pinpoint a range of key organisational and management issues that are central to the concerns of this chapter:

- How to achieve and retain organisational control over such practice when it is implemented as a bottom-up, community-driven process.
- How to best monitor and appraise performance when the community practice is primarily of a process-oriented nature.
- How to encourage an organisational climate and provide managerial leadership in multi-agency partnership organisations.
- How to best support the continuing professional development of community practitioners who work in exposed and isolated circumstances and who may be subject to cross-cutting demands and conflicting allegiances.

Before taking our discussion of management and organisation further, it may be helpful to pull together the strands of the discussions so far. In Box 3.2, we provide a summary list of the key characteristics of community practice that are likely to impact on its organisation and management, pointing out similarities and differences.

Box 3.2: Characteristics of community practice as work process

- Such work is carried out in dynamic and evolving situations:
  - work is rarely 'routine', it entails creative problem-solving and action-learning; and
  - project work often develops its own momentum over time, there is often an 'emergent' quality about it.
- It is a 'young' occupation and its mission is itself developing.
- In a time of ubiquitous socio-economic change, the roles given to community practice are broadening.
- Community practitioners' working environments are often the site for clashes of interest over contested, public values.

- All of which requires on-the-spot decision-making and puts a premium on adaptability and resilience.
- The worker's 'inner compass' of values and principles and reflexive mode of operation becomes key.
- Such work is founded on relationships of trust, confidence and affinity between practitioner and community members and other workers.
- It often involves working at the cutting edge of change.
- It is inter-professional work. Characteristically, it involves working in partnership with other professionals.
- While it embraces certain strategic goals and principles, its operational goals are likely to be those of 'others'. There is a commitment to work to enhance the agency of community members.
- It is often as much process-driven as task-driven.
- It is carried out in naturalistic contexts; it deals with 'messy' (unbounded) problems.
- Its work with people involves a mutual, experiential, learning experience.
- It is a democratic, other-directed, professional activity.
- It involves work at the 'boundary' between community groups and formal organisations, and at the point of connectivity between various occupations and professions.
- It involves 'partnership'-working – building on inter-organisational relationships and boundary-spanning roles.
- It is concerned with people and problems 'in the round' and embraces holistic thinking.
- The work of the community practitioner relies on their personality, energy, stamina and skills and their use of self and resources in a purposeful and disciplined way.
- The methodological approach to change is 'we-centred' – it is democratic and egalitarian in its emphasises on community.
- The 'collective' has primacy, it is the public/social aspects of problems that are paramount, and the beneficiaries of community action constitute a larger collective than the membership of the group or organisation taking action.

Organisation and management: a systems model

So far, we have concentrated on identifying important key features of community practice that inform the distinctive demands placed upon its organisation and management. In this section, we present a simplified model of organisational and management processes that helps us to make sense of such demands in a more systematic and holistic way. Writers on organisation have provided a number of helpful syntheses of relevant organisational and management theory, and our model draws on the work, in particular, of Mintzberg (2007, 2011), Sadler (2001), Handy (1985), Hales (2001) and Salaman (1995). The model is presented here as a kind of conceptual map, a way of thinking about and addressing the requirements of organising and managing community practice (see Figure 3.3). It consists of four interlinked components: organisational culture, organisational systems, management roles and standard operating procedures. The arrows in the diagram indicate that they form a dynamic, working system.

Taken together, they enable us to address the key question preoccupying us in this chapter, namely, the form each element should take in order to best serve the goal of producing effective, high-quality community practice. Or, looking at matters from the practitioner's point of view, the question becomes: 'How should organisational and management systems be constituted in order to enable me to do my work as effectively as possible?'

Figure 3.3: Systems model: organisational management for community practice

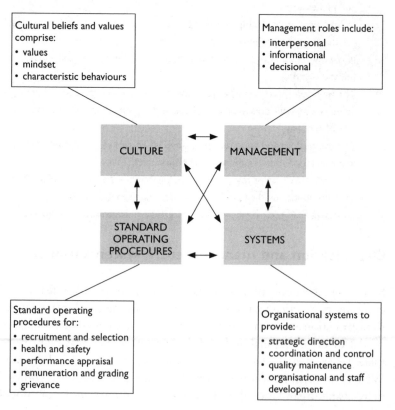

In the following, we outline the four major components of our model in turn.

Organisational culture

We draw upon Sadler (2001) here, who suggests that organisational culture may be regarded as comprising three elements:

- *Shared values* – the things 'organisational members collectively see as important and which consequently tend to guide their behaviour' (Sadler, 2001, pp 22–3).
- *Mindset* – comprising the sets of beliefs held by organisational members.
- *Characteristic behaviours* – in any organisation, it is possible to identify 'how we do things around here' in terms of codes of dress, how people relate to each other, how decisions are made and so forth.

Organisational systems

Mintzberg (2007), Hales (2001) and other writers on organisations have pointed out that managers have responsibilities for providing their organisations with direction and momentum, for ensuring that diverse activities are coordinated, and for ensuring that quality standards are met. These are usually achieved through a variety of organisational systems set up for such purposes. Organisational management is in many respects about putting such systems in place, and then ensuring their smooth running. Systems concerned with individual and organisational development, it may be noted, are dealt with in Chapter Four.

Management roles

Many attempts have been made to identify the core roles and tasks of organisational managers. Mintzberg's (1973, 2007) model of managerial work, the result of detailed empirical research, suggests that managerial work, whether carried out by the chief executive or workshop supervisor in a private company, or the senior health service administrator or a ward manager in a publicly funded hospital, involves carrying out very similar roles. He identified 10 specific roles within three overall categories, as follows:

1. Interpersonal category
    - Figurehead role: managers perform symbolic duties as head of their organisational unit.
    - Leader role: managers establish organisational goals and motivate organisational members to achieve them.
    - Liaison role: managers develop and use webs of contacts outside their organisational unit.
2. Informational category
    - Monitor role: managers collect and analyse many kinds of information useful to the organisation.
    - Disseminator role: managers transmit information from the outside to members in the organisation.
    - Spokesperson role: managers transmit information from inside the organisation to outsiders.
3. Decisional category
    - Entrepreneur role: managers initiate controlled change in order that the organisation adapts to the changing environment.
    - Disturbance handler role: managers are called upon to deal with the unexpected.
    - Resource allocator role: managers make decisions about the use of organisational resources.
    - Negotiator role: managers deal with other organisations and individuals.

Standard operating procedures

These are the established, formally prescribed and standardised 'how to' routines of an organisation – its procedures for grading jobs, for conducting performance review and appraisal, for handling complaints and disciplinary matters, its health and safety systems, and so forth. Each 'system' will have any number of such standard operating procedures, but we will not elaborate further on these in this chapter.

Organisational management for community practice

We are now in a position to suggest a number of conclusions from our discussion. In this final section of the chapter, we *illustrate* the kind of alignment that can be sought between the key features of the community practice work process and the basic requirements for the effective organisational management of such a process. Within the scope of this chapter, it will not be possible to provide a complete analysis, but hopefully a sufficient flavour of the usefulness of the general approach offered here will come across for the reader to apply the model to the specifics of their own circumstances.

Organisational culture

We make no excuse for examining 'cultural' alignment first. This book demonstrates the critical importance to community practice of its value base, mindset and behavioural norms. We have seen, for example, that a key characteristic of community practice is its heavily value-driven nature – that practitioners tend to see themselves as making a contribution to realising robust end-state values such as active community, strong democracy, social inclusion and social justice.

We have also noted that practitioners' 'inner compass' of values and principles is key to their effective practice, given the kind of contexts and processes with which they work. Theirs is a culture of collective problem-solving and an 'other-directedness' that acknowledges the need to allow community strategies to 'emerge' through dialogical processes of action-learning. In Chapter One, the value-driven 'principles of action in community practice' were thus summarised as:

- Equality and diversity: recognising and valuing diversity in individuals, groups and communities, and counteracting discriminatory and oppressive behaviours and attitudes.
- Empowerment: facilitating individuals and groups to take more control over their lives.
- Participation: promoting and respecting the rights of individuals to take an active part in action and decision-making relating to aspects of their lives.
- Partnership and collaboration: working together and sharing responsibility and power, and recognising the contribution of skills and expertise offered by different people.
- Learning: creating the climate through which mutual learning can occur.
- Social justice: identifying and challenging the underlying causes and effects of imbalances of power, wealth, status and opportunities.

Such values underpin the '5Ps' of community practitioners' work process discussed earlier in this chapter.

Turning to 'mindset', Chapter One again makes it clear that distinctive beliefs characterise how community practitioners see the world:

- that people are constituted and define themselves and their needs and aspirations by their membership of collectivities such as communities;
- that such communities exhibit diversity, which when underpinned by differences in access to power and resources, results in negative and damaging experiences of exclusion and discrimination; and
- that a community's collective expression of its needs and aspirations, particularly when expressed through organised action, can bring about beneficial change.

In terms of characteristic behaviours, community practitioners tend to put a premium on open communication, participative and inclusive approaches to decision-making, and what Hofstede (1991) calls low levels of 'power difference' (low emphasis on status differentials, deferring to formalities of rank, etc), and demonstrate what he calls the 'feminine' attributes of nurturance, care and support. There will be scepticism about undue respect for procedural norms if these are perceived to be based on little more than tradition or ingrained habit. The work of community practitioners often involves challenging established ways of doing things, and this attitude transfers to their approach to organisational life too!

Charles Handy's (1985) well-known categorisation of different types of organisational cultures helps us draw out the implications for the kind of organisational context most likely to support effective community practice. He suggests that organisational cultures typically derive from a combination of the following ideal-typical models:

- *The club model* – This model of organisation rests on the power, authority and influence of a particular individual (or executive group). It is a highly centralised form of organisation and its strategic direction and modus operandi derives from its leader. The metaphor of a spider's web can be invoked – power emanates outwards, from the leader at the centre of the web, and is exercised through the appointment of loyal lieutenants together with direct interventions from the centre. Handy likens this model to a club – where the organisation is an extension of the head or founder.
- *The bureaucratic organisation* – This model of organisation is based on a careful delineation of organisational roles, defined by procedural rules within carefully defined parameters. The metaphor here is of a number of Greek columns topped off by a capstone; work is divided between departments (the columns) and coordinated by the corporate management team at the top (the capstone).

- *The team-based task organisation* – This form of organisation operates through project teams and networks set up to tackle particular problems and projects. Teams are composed according to the requirements of the project, and are given considerable devolved authority to get on and complete the task(s) that they have been set. Handy's metaphor here is of a net, with the work teams being cells at its interstices; power and influence are distributed to the nodes that comprise the net.
- *The loose coupled independent professional structure* – In this model, the organisational structure exists only to serve the needs of the expert individuals who comprise it. The professionals in such an organisation basically work on their own, but capitalise on the advantage of shared accommodation, office services and other back-up. Handy says that this kind of organisation has a person–oriented culture. The organisational idea is that individual talent is of the greatest importance but can be usefully serviced by some sort of minimal organisation.

These are clearly 'models', and Handy is the first to recognise that real-world organisations will comprise a mixture of such types. His conceptualisation does, however, enable us to sharpen our analysis. Many community practitioners are likely to find the team-based task organisation the most supportive environment in which to work. The 'club' model will be too 'top-down'; the independent professional model too individualistic. The 'bureaucratic' model is, of course, characteristic of many of the public organisations that employ community practitioners. The features of this model – departmentalism, power and status following office, rigid structures, and slow responsiveness to change – can prove uncomfortable to those with the mindset of the community practitioner. Organisations that support a team-based work culture, on the other hand, are likely to be more appropriate. They are more likely to be effective in circumstances that demand innovative, multidisciplinary problem-solving skills, applied by workers brought together from different backgrounds and disciplines with the flexibility and decentralised authority to confront 'messy', unbounded problems.

Mintzberg (2007, p 199) identifies the key features of this organisational form (he labels it the 'innovative' organisation) as follows:

> highly organic structures, with little formalisation of behaviour; specialised jobs based on expert training; a tendency to group the specialists in functional teams for housekeeping purposes but to deploy them in small project

teams to do their work; a reliance on teams, or task forces ... and considerable decentralisation to and within teams.

Organisational systems: strategic direction

So, what forms of organisational systems are consistent with, and supportive of, such a culture? Community practitioners are likely to find person-centred, open, democratically run systems for determining *strategic direction* of their own organisational unit the most valuable and also the most functional. Why this should be is fairly obvious. As we have seen, community practitioners value collective, participative and inclusive decision-making. They value holistic thinking and their approach to managing change is naturally 'we-centred'. They are used to partnership-working and encourage inter-organisational approaches to problem-solving. It would be strange indeed if support for such values was not deemed to apply to them as employees within their own organisation. But it is not just a question of values; there is a strong case for finding ways of fully involving community practitioners in their employing organisation's strategic planning system on instrumental grounds too. We have noted that community practice is itself developing, and the momentum for this comes from many different quarters. A very important driver comprises the needs, demands and aspirations of the communities they engage with, and the learning and insights of those who work with such communities on a day-to-day basis. The community practitioner's own organisation would, instead, be trying to plan and move forward in a strategic way with one arm tied behind its back if it did *not* involve both the communities who are its prime beneficiaries, its raison d'être, as well as its front-line workers. Wide involvement in the process of strategic thinking and decision-making is clearly necessary if it is to be consistent with the core values and aims of community practice as outlined earlier.

Engagement with key stakeholders does not stop there, however. As we have seen (refer back to Figure 3.2), supporting community empowerment and enhancing the quality of community life requires an active engagement by many people and agencies whose work impacts on communities. An important message of this book is that all those whose decision-making has an effect on employment and jobs, care and welfare, safety and environment, learning and education, and so forth, have a key 'community practice' dimension to their work. *Their* strategic intentions need to be worked out in concert with, and to compliment, each other, *as well as* being responsive to community members themselves. The discussions in Chapters Four and Six are very relevant here. Chapter Four makes use of the idea of the 'learning organisation' to tease out how the aspirations for joined-up thinking and action can be realised through concerted attention to the disciplines of organisational learning. Chapter Six discusses the pitfalls and benefits of pursuing good practice through networks and inter-organisational partnerships.

Organisational systems: coordination and control

Turning to how strategic goals can be realised, and intentions realised, brings us to questions of organisational coordination and control. 'Joined-up' thinking and planning demands 'joined-up' action. Organisational writers (see Hales, 2001; Mintzberg, 2007) suggest that a number of approaches can be delineated. Mintzberg (2007, p 101) identifies the following coordinating mechanisms:

- Mutual adjustment – where coordination is achieved through the simple process of informal communication between people working together.
- Direct supervision – managers direct, and workers carry out the instructions given.
- Standardisation of work processes – managers devise standard operating procedures for the accomplishment of tasks and ensure that the worker has the minimum competences necessary to follow the procedures.
- Standardisation of outputs – the emphasis here is on the achievement of specified end results. Coordination and control is achieved through target-setting, benchmarking, the implementation of appropriate quality assurance processes and so forth.
- Standardisation of skills – coordination of work is secured through careful selection of skilled staff. 'Skills' may seem to be a rather narrow way of describing what we mean here. Earlier on, we invoked the idea of the worker's 'inner compass', and this perhaps better expresses the idea behind this approach to organisational coordination and control. The worker approaches their role and task not only with the requisite skills, but also with the values, mindset and motivation to work towards satisfactorily reaching, in cooperation with others as necessary, the goals specified in the strategic plan.

In terms of community practice, the first and last in this list of coordination and control mechanism are probably the most effective and common ones in use. The community practitioner's work processes and context renders direct supervision and standardisation of work processes virtually impossible, and standardisation of outputs is only possible at the most general level.

It is 'mutual adjustment' and 'inner compass' that characterise work coordination in (Handy's) team-based task-oriented organisation and, as we saw earlier, this is a highly functional organisational framework for much community practice (see Box 3.1).

Organisational systems: quality maintenance

Like coordination and control, the maintenance and assurance of 'quality' poses particular organisational problems for community practice. Arguably, the definition of quality is itself more problematic than in many educational, social care and other human service fields, but finding the most appropriate method to assess quality, and then promote its enhancement, is also fraught with difficulties. These difficulties stem from the following characteristics of community practice as a work process, as listed in Box 3.1:

- initiatives evolve over time, often as a result of the experiential community learning that has itself been enabled and encouraged by the community practitioner – goals, processes and outcomes can all become 'moving targets', thus making the establishment of such things as quality 'benchmarks' and measurements of linear 'quality improvements' of dubious utility;
- it is concerned with addressing 'unbounded' and 'messy' problems in which variables interact in highly complex, systemic ways; identifying the influence of particular features, and then being confident about the kinds of effect that may result from bringing to bear some influence on that feature, is often extremely costly and time-consuming; and
- it is often inter-professional work and involves working in partnership with other organisations and professionals; establishing the contribution of community practice is not only complex, but also ill-serves the holistic approach to which it aspires.

None of these features imply that quality measurement, and the nature and extent of its improvement, must remain totally elusive and unknowable – only that it is often very difficult. Chapters in this book show what can be done by management to help. Chapter Eight, for example, outlines the considerable work that has been done by Alan Barr and his colleagues towards developing robust approaches to participative evaluation skills. Chapter Four discusses the importance of disciplined reflection for improving individual practice, and the contribution that collective learning can make to organisational improvement. Organisational systems can help to institutionalise and legitimate these quality improvement approaches.

Organisation systems: managerial roles

We have noted that management has been researched and analysed in terms of clusters of operational roles that tend to shape the typical manager's working day. Again, our efforts to identify some of the defining features of community practice can help us to understand the distinctive features of the management role for this particular kind of work and occupational group. Some examples will suffice.

- *Interpersonal role cluster* – We can see that *leadership* of a community practice team will take a particular form. As an 'other-directed' occupation, and one that seeks to develop the independence and agency of community groups and organisations, the team management role will err on enabling and facilitating, supporting and advising, and revert to prescribing and authoritatively directing only when absolutely necessary. The *liaison* role is a vital one; the 'boundary' role of community practice will be greatly helped by a team leader who *is* proactive in seeking out and developing new contacts and potential supports. This relates to aspects of the informational role cluster (see following point).
- *Informational role cluster* – Community practice management has an extremely important role to play in ensuring the dissemination of information as a two-way process, both *within* the team, and between the team and organisations and people in its operating environment. Information is a critical resource for 'active community', and community practice managers have the authority to access and disseminate information and intelligence of value to their front-line workers and the communities with which they work. The manager's spokesman role is also an important one within this cluster. As a 'young' occupation, awareness and understanding of the purposes and working processes of community practitioners may be sketchy at best or misconceived at worse. Managers have a valuable role to play in both raising general levels of awareness about the role and remit of community practice, as well as disseminating information about the specific work currently undertaken by their front-line workers.

- *Decisional role cluster* – Dissemination of information can become a key ingredient in the manager's role as 'disturbance handler'. We have noted how some kinds of community practice can take workers into challenging and contentious political and value debates and struggles. In addition to ensuring that robust mentoring and supervisory systems are in place to support workers through what can sometimes become quite difficult and stressful times, the skill and energy with which managers promote and explain the nature of the work undertaken within their organisation can be invaluable. The manager's entrepreneurial role ('initiating controlled change in order that organisations adapt to a changing environment', as Mintzberg (2007, p 19) put it) is especially important in times of rapid change, and this theme is taken up in Chapter Four, where we argue that developing a 'learning organisation' approach to organisational structure, process and management is one of the most effective ways of fulfilling this role.

Conclusion

This discussion of the organisational management of community practice has used the concept of 'alignment' as an organising concept. This concept incorporates the idea of ensuring that management and organisation achieves the best 'fit' with the work that it exists to support. And it also embraces a concern with the 'fit' between the organisation and its macro-social and operating environment.

The '5P + C' framework has enabled us to focus in a systematic way on the characteristics of the community practice work process *as well as* the relevance of broader contextual factors and changes. In utilising this model, we hope that we have demonstrated some of the advantages of seeing organisations as 'organic' systems, interrelating in complex and adaptive ways with their environment. Only a partial sketch can be provided in one chapter, and we are conscious that the 'broad-brush approach' adopted here fails to do justice to the range and variety of work that can properly be characterised as community practice. Equally, we have done little to qualify our arguments in terms of the range of different environments (organisational, political, social, policy) that community practitioners and their managers will find themselves working in.

This chapter will, however, have served its purpose if it has provided some useful working concepts and frameworks with which community practice managers can reflect on, analyse and then use to improve their work within their own organisational units.

References

Barr, A., Hashagen, S. and Purcell, R. (1996) *Monitoring and evaluating community development in Northern Ireland*, Belfast: Department of Health and Social Services.

Benington, J. and Moore, M. (2011) *Public value: theory and practice*, Houndmills: Palgrave-Macmillan.

Blunkett, D. and Jackson, K. (1987) *Democracy in crisis: the town halls respond*, London: The Hogarth Press.

Boardman, F. (ed) (2011) *Making policy in an age of austerity*, London: Public Management and Policy Association.

Bowles, M. (2010) *Time for change: new models of support for community action*, London: Community Development Foundation.

Boyle, D., Coote, A., Sherwood, C. and Slay, J. (2010) *Right here right now – taking co-production into the mainstream*, London: NESTA.

Butcher, H. (1993) 'Why community policy? Some explanations for recent trends', in H. Butcher, A. Glen, P. Henderson and J. Smith (eds) (1993) *Community and public policy*, London: Pluto Press, pp 55–71.

Department for Communities and Local Government (2006) *Strong and prosperous communities*, Cm 6939-I, London, CLG.

Dzur, A.W. (2008) *Democratic professionalism: citizen participation and the reconstruction of professional ethics, identity and practice*, Pennsylvania, PA: Pennsylvania State University.

Field, J. (2008) *Social capital*, London: Routledge.

Goss, S. (2001) *Making local governance work; networks, relationships and the management of change*, Basingstoke: Palgrave.

Hales, C. (2001) *Managing through organisation; the management process, forms of organisation and the work of managers*, London: Business Press.

Handy, C. (1985) *Understanding organisations* (3rd edn), Harmondsworth: Penguin Books.

Henderson, P., Jones, D. and Thomas, D. (eds) (1980) *The boundaries of change in community work*, London: George Allen and Unwin.

Hofstede, G. (1991) *Cultures and organisations*, London: McGraw Hill.

Mintzberg, H (1973) *The nature of managerial work*, London: Harper and Row.

Mintzberg, H. (2007) *Mintzberg on management; inside our strange world of organisations*, New York, NY: The Free Press.

Mintzberg, H. (2011) *Managing*, London: Financial Times/Prentice Hall.

Moore, M. (1996) *Creating public value*, Harvard, MA: Harvard University Press.

Moore, M. (1999) 'The job ahead', in Moore, M. (ed) *Community, opportunity, responsibility. Accountability: Report of symposium on the future of public service*, London: Office of Public Management.

Morgan, G. (2006) *Images of organisation*, Thousand Oaks, CA: Sage.

Ramsden, S. and Stewart, J. (1994) *Management for the public domain; enabling the learning society*, Basingstoke: Macmillan.

Sadler, P. (2001) *The seamless organisation*, London: Kogan Page.

Salaman, G. (1995) *Managing*, Buckingham: Open University Press.

Somerville, P. (2011) *Understanding community: policy, politics and practice*, Bristol: The Policy Press.

Stoker, G. (2007) *New localism, participation and networked government*, Manchester: University of Manchester, Institute of Political and Economic Governance.

Taylor, F.W. (1911) *Principles of scientific management*, New York, NY: Harper and Row.

FOUR

Individual and organisational development for community practice – an experiential learning approach

Hugh Butcher

Introduction

This chapter poses two related questions. First, what kind of individual *development* can best support the work of community practitioners and enable them continually to improve the quality of their work with communities? Second, what kind of *organisational development*, of those agencies and departments that have a responsibility for resourcing and implementing community programmes, can best enable community practice to flourish?

These two questions draw on the general discussion of the management and organisation of community practice presented in Chapter Three. Here, however, the focus narrows to a consideration of the more specific question of how continuous quality improvement at the individual practitioner and organisational levels can be assured. We argue the case for utilising a particular model of reflective practice based on Kolb's (2007) theory of experiential learning. His original 'learning cycle' model, updated by subsequent refinements and additions, provides a compelling framework for enhancing continuous improvement of community practice at both the individual and organisational levels.

The learning challenge

Before exploring the specifics of the learning cycle concept itself, it may be helpful to make explicit some of the reasons for promoting 'learning' as a fruitful idea for thinking about how best to support individual and organisational development for community practice.

It is now something of a cliché to suggest that in almost all aspects of life, people are dealing with ever more rapid, discontinuous and far-reaching patterns of change. Vaill (1996) uses the apt metaphor of 'permanent white water' to capture how change is now experienced by more and more people, in more and more areas of their lives. The majority of professional workers – including those working for community change – feel continuously buffeted and thrown off balance by never-ending torrents of change, each of which requires ever greater reserves of flexibility, adaptation and resilience to survive, and yet more to move forward. Since the appearance of the first edition of this book, both the level and all-pervasiveness of 'white-water' change have become ever more insistent.

'Permanent white-water' change requires that community practitioners continually update their knowledge, develop their skills and expand their mindset to enable them to effectively embrace new and ever-expanding ways in which their core competencies are called upon to contribute to more innovative policy and practice agendas. They are obliged, then, to become more competent at learning new ways of thinking and doing – in short, to become resourceful and resilient lifelong learners.

Thus, whether considering the established or newer-emerging models of community practice, its practitioners are required to offer improved core competencies in:

- processual ways of working with community systems that strengthen their capacity for civic and community action;
- developmental methods of working with democratic institutions to render them more inclusive and participatory; and
- creative ways of engaging with social policy programmes to make them more relevant, holistic and sustainable.

Learning – personal and organisational

Learning may be defined as the process through which changes in the state of knowledge ('know-what'), skills ('know-how') and values and dispositions ('know-why') of an individual or of an organisation occurs. Learning processes will on the whole, though not inevitably, result in changes in action and performance (by individuals or organisations). Needless to say, the kinds of learning that are the focus of this chapter are those that *do* result in new actions or improved performance as a result of changes in knowledge, skills and values and dispositions. There are, of course, differences between individual and organisational learning (which is addressed in the later part of this chapter). However, in short, organisational learning is a systems-level phenomenon. Such learning stays within organisations even though individual members come and go over time (see Nevis et al, 1995; Sanchez and Heene, 2000).

Experiential learning

This chapter is concerned primarily with learning that goes on in the context of workplace, community and organisational settings. It is this 'experiential' learning that is of most interest to community practitioners – learning that occurs in and through engagement with lived day-to-day problems and issues. It is, in other words, learning that takes place: while planning to do something; while actually doing it; while reflecting on how it was done; in drawing out generalisations ('lessons') from the experience of doing it; and on deciding how things might be tackled differently in the future.

Theories of experiential learning have much to offer precisely because they have been developed to provide a framework for thinking about the day-to-day learning that takes place in these everyday contexts. These 'sites' of learning very often provide as many, and arguably more, opportunities for powerful learning than do the more formal, structured ones of the lecture hall and training centre. Further, experiential learning theory suggests ways in which such learning can be consciously accelerated and deepened. From this perspective, the work activity of the community practitioner is, thus, not only about planning and implementing programmes and processes that empower and benefit the 'community'; it is also about continuous, active, experiential learning by practitioners themselves. I will use the term 'practitioner-learner' in the following paragraphs whenever the context makes it appropriate to emphasise this dual, reflexive approach implied by experiential learning.

Kolb's model of experiential learning and its development

Kolb (2007) draws on earlier thinking by Dewey, Lewin, Piaget and others to construct a model of experiential learning that can be represented diagrammatically, as in Figure 4.1.

Figure 4.1: Kolb's learning cycle

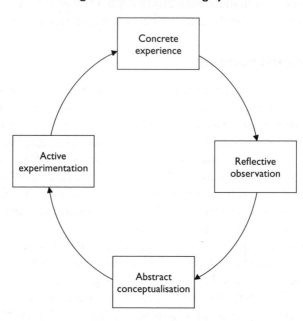

Source: Adapted from Kolb (2007)

Dixon (1999, pp 40–1) summarises this learning cycle succinctly:

> The cycle begins when we each experience the world through our senses. Kolb calls this step 'concrete experience', to indicate that he does not mean the vicarious experience we have through books or plays, but a real world experience. Examples of concrete experience could be as varied as sitting through a boring meeting or suffering the distress of losing a job. Kolb suggests that to learn from our experience we must engage in a second step of consciously reflecting on what occurred. This step he calls 'reflective observation'. We are able to reflect on much less than occurred in the actual experience. Reflection is selective, and … is influenced by our expectations and our existing meaning structures. The third step in the learning cycle is making sense of what we have experienced … [which] involves relating new information to existing meaning structures and out of that relationship creating new meaning. Kolb calls this 'abstract conceptualisation'. The final step in Kolb's model is active experimentation. At this step we test out the meaning that we have constructed by taking action in the world.

In this summary, Dixon introduces a further, very useful, concept: that of an individual's 'personal meaning structures'. Our personal meaning structures comprise: our beliefs about ourselves and other people; our understandings of the communities, organisations and policy systems within which we work; our attitudes and values; our ways of feeling and thinking; and so forth. They are, in a sense, the 'sedimented' results of our past attempts to organise and make sense of our experiences and interactions in our everyday world. They comprise our own individual frameworks of beliefs and understandings about our world, our selves and the relations between the two. Such understandings may be more or less tacit, more or less coherent, and more or less unique to us. And, importantly, they shape the perceptual 'lens' through which we filter current experiences and seek to make sense of them – thus confirming and/or revising and/or replacing aspects of our personal meaning structures. This may, in turn, lead us to adopt new ways of interacting with the world.

Figure 4.2: The experiential learning cycle

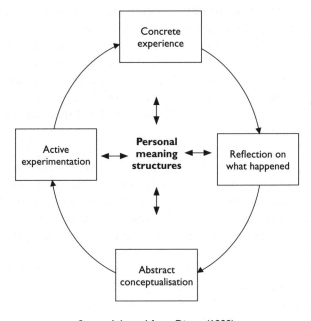

Source: Adapted from Dixon (1999)

The task of being a truly effective experiential learner, following Kolb (2007), is not an easy one; it requires the practitioner-learner to exercise four distinct kinds of learning abilities:

- concrete experience abilities – our ability to involve ourselves fully, openly and without bias in new experiences;
- reflective observation abilities – our ability to observe and reflect upon our experiences from a variety of different perspectives;
- abstract conceptualisation abilities – our ability to use or create concepts that integrate our observations into coherent frameworks of understanding and 'theories'; and
- active experimentation abilities – our ability to deploy our theories to aid decision-making and solve problems.

Four features of the experiential learning approach deserve particular note:

1. In this model, learning is seen as an *active interpretive process*, rather than an outcome. The diagrams depict one 'cycle', but in reality there are many, indeed, a never-ending series of 'cycles', as understandings grow out of reflections on experience, which in turn lead to new, modified actions and then to new insights and so on. This model is best regarded as a process model of *continuous lifelong learning*. We see again, from the 'practitioner-learner' perspective, that all practice is both a context and an opportunity for new learning, offering us the chance for new learning to feed back into improvements to the quality of practice. The 'trick' is to find the way of ensuring that this potential for 'learning through action' (and, as we shall see in a moment, 'learning in action') is optimised and then translated into improved practice.

2. Second, in calling this learning process an 'active interpretive process', we are drawing attention to another key feature: it draws upon *constructivist* and *critical realist* thinking about learning and knowledge. These perspectives (Kelly, 1955; Sayers, 2000; see also Illeris, 2009) assert that our knowledge of reality (our personal meaning structures) will always be an interpretation, a mental construction; they result from our attempts to make sense of the world and they always remains provisional, contestable and subject to revision. This is in direct contrast to a particular version of the 'objectivist' tradition, which, as Norton (1987, p 2) explains, 'assumes that knowledge exists independently of the learner and understanding is a process of coming to know that which already exists'. Norton (1987, p 2, emphasis added) notes that:

If we take a constructivist view of knowledge, then we must accept that *the world of the learner* becomes crucial. Everything a learner receives is filtered through her or his own personal construct system and made sense of in terms of what is important to him or her. A constructivist perspective takes a model of learning that puts the student at the centre of creating meaning which carries with it the assumption that the teacher becomes a facilitator of learning rather than a transmitter of knowledge.

Kolb's great contribution (along with those who have built on his insights) has been to help us to gain a more detailed understanding of the processes involved when we construct meaning out of our engagement with the world. A similar process is involved, of course, when the community practitioner helps those engaged in community action to collectively construct new meanings for themselves about their own communities. It also helps them critically investigate the way the dynamics of the wider world impact, often negatively, on their communities, and the way such new understandings can provide the foundation for collective action (Freire, 1996). A further advantage of this model of learning is, thus, its alignment with existing ways in which community practitioners think about their work.

3. Another consequence of the 'cyclic' nature of the experiential learning process is worth spelling out: learning has not been fully internalised until the cycle is complete. Research by Mumford (1993) has built on an insight of Kolb's that individual learners differ in their proficiency in using each of the steps in the cycle. This may lead some of us to prefer particular steps over others, and, as Dixon (1994) puts it, to the extent that we 'slight' any of the steps in the cyclical process, our learning is that much less effective. The concept of different learning styles is important and theorists have categorised these in many different ways. One example is that of Lank and Mayo (1994, pp 136–7), who provide a graphic illustration of each style, summarising them as follows:

Activists:

• tend to thrive on the challenge of new experiences;
• try anything once;
• tend to revel in short-term fire-fighting;

- constantly involve themselves with other people; and
- are relatively bored with implementation and longer-term consolidation.

Reflectors:

- like to stand back and review experience from different perspectives;
- collect data and analyse it before coming to conclusions;
- tend to be cautious; and
- like to consider all possible angles before making a move.

Theorists:

- prize rationality and logic;
- are keen on basic assumptions, theories, models and systems thinking;
- tend to be detached and analytical;
- are unhappy with subjective or ambiguous experiences; and
- like to make things tidy and fit into rational schemes.

Pragmatists:

- take the first opportunity to experiment with applications;
- positively search out new ideas or techniques that might apply to their situation;
- respond to problems and opportunities as 'a challenge';
- are keen to try out ideas from training and management courses; and
- like to get on with things that have a clear purpose.

The idea of preferred learning styles has a variety of implications, one being that practitioner-learners may be wise to keep under review their own learning styles, to seek to extend them, to bear them in mind when working with others and so on. Managers can help people do this, and later on we summarise three techniques (journaling, mentoring, action-learning) that can aid the community practitioner in doing this.

4. Finally, Kolb's learning cycle model has been developed to help us understand different 'levels' or 'depths' of learning. These have sometimes been referred to as 'single-loop', 'double-loop' and 'triple-loop' learning (Schön and Argyris, 1974; Swieringa and Weirdsma, 1992). Single-loop learning occurs when new insights into a problem help us to adapt and cope better within the parameters of

a predefined situation. This has also been called 'corrective learning', because the parameters themselves (which may well be part of the problem as experienced) are taken as a 'given' and are not themselves addressed within the learning cycle. Much problem-solving occurs by applying a formula or recipe – 'do it this way if you want such and such a result'. This can often be an appropriate response; it can lead to useful incremental improvements in work routines, overcome shortcomings and result in an improvement in performance.

However, in many instances, the practitioner-learner will find such an approach deficient or even counterproductive. Double-loop learning occurs when we *do* question how the issue or problem has been defined or 'framed'. We realise that if we redefine it or 'see it' in another way, then new solutions can present themselves, and altogether different problem-solving strategies can be pursued. In double-loop learning, for example, a practitioner or their organisation may set about questioning and then *changing* its routines ('the way we do things around here') in order to bring about improvements. It does not just rely on trying to improve, or 'tighten up', the operation of the routine itself. So, we might see the 'solution' to low levels of engagement with public consultation exercises as requiring quite different approaches to consultation, rather than seeking ways of improving existing methods.

Triple-loop learning, somewhat confusingly, has been used with a number of different meanings. For some, it refers to the way an individual or organisation goes beyond questioning the operational assumptions behind the 'routines' and asks still more searching questions – about the basic principles or the fundamental purposes laying behind them. It does not just lead to doing things better (an outcome of single-loop learning) or differently (an outcome of double-loop learning), it leads to doing *different things*. The kinds of innovative approaches to policy and practice described in reports from 'think tanks' like Demos, the Institute for Public Policy Research, the New Economics Foundation and ResPublica provide useful illustrations of attempts to think afresh the basic assumptions that underpin traditional models of welfare and community practice.

Turning to another meaning of triple-loop learning (sometimes called 'deutero-learning'), this happens when we reflect on our learning processes themselves. We reflect on 'how' we are experiencing, reflecting on and trying to make sense of a 'problem'. We may, for example, begin to see that our negative feelings about particular situations curtail our reflecting upon them in a full or 'open' manner. Or, it may be that we come to see that our 'preferred learning style' leads us to a general tendency to 'slight' the reflective step in the learning cycle. In such cases, we are involved in deutero-learning, in 'learning how we learn', and this further refinement of the experiential learning cycle model provides us with a way of thinking about how we can become more proficient, more creative and more insightful 'practitioner-learners' and problem-solvers.

Referring back to our definition of learning, it is through these processes, applied in real-life situations, that changes in practitioners' knowledge, skills and values and dispositions occur, which can result, in turn, in important changes in action and performance.

Applications: supporting the experiential learner

So, what tools and organisational supports are available to practitioners to assist them in becoming more effective, lifelong, experiential learners? In Dixon's (1999) language, how can practitioner-learners be supported in improving the functional effectiveness of their personal meaning structures? A growing literature on the theory and practice of supporting the development of the 'reflective practitioner' points to some very practical things that community practice managers can do to support their professional workers in this regard.

As noted, 'reflective observation' is the fundamental first step in turning experience into learning. It is what we do when we take a mental step 'back' from our active involvement in concrete experience and become a more detached reviewer and cogitator on the events and processes that we have been involved in at first hand. Kolb followed philosopher John Dewey (1997 [1938]) in seeing reflection as akin to 'turning something over in the mind', treating it to focused, sustained and serious mental attention; this is much more than a kind of daydreaming, it is a purposeful activity directed at quarrying insights from experience.

Boud et al (1985; see also Moon, 2004; Ghaye, 2010) have done much to develop our understanding of the reflective process, agreeing that it has to be seen as a deliberate process. These authors give it a prominent place in their work on experiential learning, noting that it involves 're-evaluating' experience through the use of a number of elements (which may or may not occur in sequence):

- 'association', that is, relating new data and ideas to that which is already known;
- integration, which is seeking relationships among the data and ideas;

- validation to determine the authenticity of the ideas and feelings which have resulted; and
- making knowledge one's own (Boud et al, 1985).

One of Boud's most important contributions to our understanding of the reflective process is his insistence that the key to improving the quality and depth of our reflection lies in how we deal with the feelings and emotions that are brought to the surface as we review past experiences in our minds. Unless this emotional content is dealt with properly, our learning will be that much less effective.

Thus, for Boud, the process of reflection is comprised of three interlinked aspects, or components:

- We return, in our minds, to our experience; we 'relive' it, 'observe' it and 'turn it over in our minds' in some detail, as accurately and fully as we can. This may involve us in reviewing events as they unfolded over time; or we may seek to place them into a wider context, or try to trace the causes of the way they developed as they did; or we may look at how our perceptions and understandings evolved as events developed, or the way we reacted (or did not react), thereby affecting the course of events.
- In doing this, it is crucial that we attend to the personal reactions and feelings that the experience evokes in us; these may be positive (helpful) or negative (obstructive). To recognise them, and then focus on them, enables us to interpret and, thus, deepen our understanding of the roots of those feelings. We ignore or bypass this aspect of the

Figure 4.3: Boud's reflection process in context

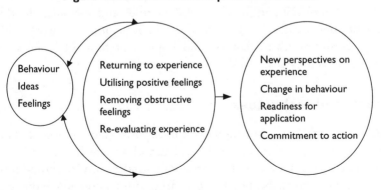

Source: Adapted from Boud et al (1985)

reflective process at our peril. Burying or denying our feelings can prevent us from effectively learning from our experience.

• Thus, we become better able to re-evaluate our experience in the light of new insights and learning gained during the first two aspects of the process. Such new learning may lead us to modify (or confirm) our personal meaning structures and, thereby, our subsequent actions. Boud represents this process diagrammatically, as shown in Figure 4.3.

It is worth taking this analysis one stage further. Implicit in the conceptualisation of the reflective process presented so far is the idea that we reflect on *past* action. We 'return' to prior experience and 'relive' it in our minds in order to construct new meaning and modify our practice. Schön (2009) has drawn the useful distinction between this type of reflection (what he called 'reflection on action') and what he calls 'reflection *in* action'. This latter type of reflection – a defining characteristic of the expert professional – enables us to observe 'concurrently' an unfolding situation in which we are implicated, and to 'turn it over in our minds', while at the same time acknowledging its emotional impact on us, all in 'real time'. This kind of reflection is of particular value under two sets of circumstances (circumstances that often characterise the work of community practitioners): when the problem or issue at hand is ill-defined, 'messy', ambiguous and marked by uncertainty; and when the action to be pursued is to be undertaken through dialogue and mutual adjustment between a number of actors. Under such circumstances, deciding what to do, and then doing it, is necessarily pursued through a process of incremental change within an evolving understanding of a fluid situation. The artistry of the professional resides in the ability to handle such indeterminacy, and differs markedly from a model of practice predicated on pre-planned implementation of established rules and formulas. To the practitioner-learner whose goal is to empower others to work with their communities to develop and implement *their* preferences, to 'reflect in action' is a vital skill.

Tools and techniques

Reflection, then, is a key ingredient in all three (single-, double- and triple-loop) types of experiential learning. So, how may it be developed? A number of approaches are worthy of consideration by community practitioners (preferably, but not necessarily, with support and resourcing by community practice managers); they can be employed singly or in combination, and differ only in the extent to which they require the active cooperation of one or more other people. Three will be outlined here:

Journals – Keeping a journal is now well recognised as a disciplined aid to reflective practice. The process of recording a critical incident or noting an evolving piece of work aids focus and concentration; feelings can be noted and explored and understandings of how to account for events can be reviewed. Such recordings can take a narrative form or, depending on the writer's 'learning style', use can be made of mind-maps and other forms of diagrammatic representation. Metaphors can be created that aid the framing process. Reflective writing enables us to return and review initial thoughts sometime later, and so add further to an evolving understanding. On occasions, a subsequent insight can lead to quite radical rethinking and reinterpretation – a move from single- to double-, or even triple-loop, learning (Walker, 1985; Buzan, 2000; Ghaye, 2010).

Peer support and mentoring – Engaging in dialogue with peers who have a shared commitment to learning through experience will almost certainly prompt examination and discussion of different perspectives. Probing questions can be posed that stimulate new thinking. The dialogue that flows from a consideration of different perspectives on the experiences at hand can open up new ways of 'seeing' and understanding. There is much to be said for encouraging and making time for such dialogue between peers. Interpretations and thoughts can be shared, unmediated by considerations of seniority or authority relationships. Well-run training events can involve participants sharing 'similar' experiences in different contexts, which can further accelerate the learning process. Exploration of 'difference' in such circumstances can generate energy and motivation for learning, as well as pose alternative perspectives that stimulate further reflection and review (Garvey et al, 2009; Brockbank and McGill, 2011).

Action-learning – Participation in action-learning sets can also aid deep reflection and learning. An action-learning set comprises a group of people (say, six or seven) who contract to meet together mutually to encourage and support each other's reflective learning, through a systematic question and answer process. The set may arrange, for example, to meet for a full day, once a month for eight months, to explore work-related issues that each member brings to the set. Each set member describes and then 'thinks aloud' about their issue as it unfolds over the eight months. At each meeting, each member has their own time-slot (of, say, 45 minutes), during which the set's total focus is on that person's issue. The role of other members of the group is to pose questions that will stimulate thinking, but *not* to enter into discussion or, still less, offer suggestions about actions that could or should be taken. The question-posing process becomes a powerful tool for prompting reflective thought, and encouraging new insights, analysis and learning (Weinstein, 1995; McGill and Beaty, 2001; Beard and Wilson, 2002; Pedler et al, 2008).

Community practice and the learning organisation

So far, the focus of this chapter has been on individual learning and individual professional development. An organisation that supports and rewards its members for undertaking continual professional development can certainly claim, in an important sense, to be a 'learning organisation'. Peter Senge (2006), for example, in his mould-breaking discussion of the learning organisation, identifies 'personal mastery' and a commitment to continual improvement as key components of an organisation worthy of such a description. However, he also argues that a learning organisation is more than an organisation whose individual members are committed to (and receive support to achieve) continuous individual learning. Rather, it is one in which learning takes place and is resourced to happen at the *collective* level, when such opportunities for learning are woven into the very fabric of the organisation – an outcome of organisational culture, structure and operational processes. It is to this type of learning, which happens collectively in and through the agency employing the practitioner-learner, to which we now turn. We look first at the meaning of organisational learning, and then explore how organisational action can be taken by managers to encourage and accelerate such learning.

Including personal mastery, the five key 'disciplines' of this kind of organisation are, according to Senge (2006, pp 6–12):

- *Systems thinking* – the discipline of analysing and managing organisational dynamics in holistic, systemic terms; this involves 'seeing interrelationships rather than linear cause–effect changes, for seeing patterns of change rather than snapshots' (Senge, 2006, p 68).
- *Building shared vision* – powerful, generative learning occurs when people are highly committed to accomplishing things that matter deeply to them, in concert with their peers.

- *Team learning* – this encourages collaboration and energy flow between people and ideas; teams can be synergistic – ideas spark off ideas, and the outcomes can be much more than the sum of the parts.
- *Building personal mastery* – as noted, individual learning does not guarantee organisational learning, but without it, no organisational learning can occur. Learning organisations provide their members with continuing opportunities for personal and professional development.
- *Mental models* – the powerful influence of 'taken-for-granted' ways of seeing things and patterns of thought are recognised and exposed to critical examination in a non-defensive manner. The learning organisation builds in processes to ensure that double- and triple-loop learning occurs routinely.

But *how* does collective (organisational) learning occur, and how does an organisation structure and manage itself to support such whole-system learning?

Nancy Dixon's (1999) illuminating account of the organisational learning cycle takes Kolb's model of experiential learning further and, utilising her conceptualisation of 'personal meaning structures', she provides us with a way of understanding, and then supporting, the process of learning at an organisational level. An adapted version of her organisation learning cycle is presented in Figure 4.4.

To understand how organisational learning occurs, Dixon suggests that it is helpful to differentiate between three types of meaning structure: the 'private', the 'accessible' and the 'collective'. In Figure 4.4, the inner circle represents the personal meaning structures of the organisation's members: these are individuals' (sometimes shared, sometimes not) interpretations of how their organisation works, their own place and role within it, and so on.

Members of an organisation may well choose to keep much of their personal meaning structure private and to themselves. The reasons for this can be many and varied: they may have received certain information in confidence; they may fear the consequences of disclosing certain opinions or perspectives; or they may believe that keeping certain information to themselves strengthens their hand in the game of 'organisational politics'. 'Collective meaning structures', on the other hand, represented by the outer ring, are those parts of the organisation members' cognitive map that *are* held jointly with other members. Dixon points out that these will comprise taken-for-granted:

Figure 4.4: The organisational learning cycle

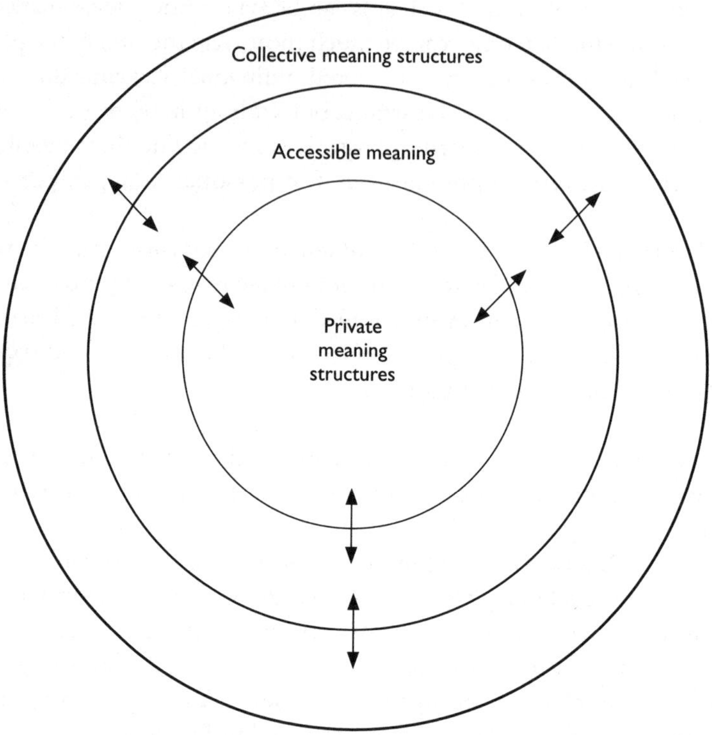

Source: Adapted from Dixon (1999)

norms, strategies and assumptions which specify how work gets divided up and how work gets performed. Collective meaning structures may be codified in policies and procedures, but to be collective they must also reside in the minds of organisational members. (Dixon, 1999, p 48)

There will clearly never be total agreement among those that make up an organisation; nevertheless, there will be sufficient agreement for members to work together 'as if' there was agreement. The organisation can then get along and do things – schedule and run meetings, allocate work, and so on – without the need for repeated and protracted discussions about, or explanations for, the ground rules. Collective meaning structures are what allow an organisation to act 'autonomously, swiftly and in concert'. In many organisations, a good deal of time and resources – on induction of new staff, devising and then training them in standard operating procedures, and so on – is taken up with ensuring that collective meaning structures are understood and complied with.

The most interesting part of Dixon's (1999) model is the intermediate ring, what she refers to as members' 'accessible meaning structures'. These are the parts of members' cognitive maps (of their organisation) that they are willing to share with others, but over which there may well be considerable variation in interpretation or, indeed, significant disagreement; where meanings, in other words, are contested.

Organisational learning occurs when the content of the intermediate ring – members' accessible meaning structures – are openly shared, and via a process of constructive dialogue are then used to explore and develop new, shared sets of collective meanings capable of guiding organisational action. Existing collective meaning structures come to be criticised and evaluated in the light of such new thinking and, subject to organisational inertia being overcome, necessary changes in organisational practices, processes and, ultimately, strategy and culture may be introduced. This gives rise to a number of important questions:

- What can an organisation do to enhance the motivation and confidence of its members to engage in such collective, dialogical learning?
- How can such dialogical action-learning be built into the routine operations of the organisation?
- What can be done to improve the quality of the inputs, and therefore the outputs, of such dialogue?

In short, what we are asking here is: how can organisations 'learn to learn' more effectively, improving their deutero–learning capability? Nevis et al (1995) offer a useful framework here, suggesting that the answers to these questions lie in improving the following processes, which can be seen to mirror at the collective level the stages in Kolb's cycle:

- processes through which people at all levels in the organisation can acquire and develop new knowledge and perspectives;
- processes through which such knowledge and perspectives can confidently be disclosed, disseminated, shared and discussed with others in the organisation;
- processes through which the validity and usefulness of new knowledge and processes can be sifted and evaluated in the light of their potential contributions to organisational improvement; and
- processes through which proposed improvements can be checked, trialled and – if effective – rolled out for wider adoption within the organisation.

Applications: supporting organisational learning

Features of organisational design and management practice that maximise the realisation of such processes can be grouped under the following headings (see Marquardt and Reynolds, 1994; Argyris, 1999; Pedler et al, 2008):

1. Organisational culture
2. Organisational processes
3. Organisational structure

We now look at each of these features in turn, with a particular focus on aspects that have immediate relevance to organisations involved in supporting community practice and community practitioners.

Organisational culture

Learning organisations tend to be 'outwardly oriented', systematically clarifying, agreeing and working towards achieving the maximum desired impact on the people, communities and other organisations in their operating environment. Both organisational vision (where the organisation aspires to be in the long term – thus providing it with 'direction') and mission (the organisation's major purpose – its reason for existence) are important here, providing the organisation and its members with a sense of what is important, a yardstick against which to 'realise the future' in creative and innovative ways. It is better still if the vision and mission of the learning organisation stresses the importance of whole-organisation learning to the achievement of its primary organisational goals. In such organisations, learning goes beyond education and training for job-specific skills and knowledge development. Learning (and related terms like innovation, creativity and problem-solving) is part of such an organisation's mindset. These organisations embrace a concern that everyone shall have opportunities for continuing development. The goal is to equip organisational members with the necessary problem-solving and other transferable skills (of team-working, networking, etc) that provide the foundation stones for accelerating new ways of thinking and working and embracing new responsibilities.

Again, learning organisations tend to see change not as an exceptional event, but as a normal, continuous process. Linked to this, the members of such organisations place a high value on enquiry and experimentation; old methods are to be continuously questioned for their contemporary relevance, and new ideas are to be tested out. The learning organisation is not 'risk-averse'; some risk-taking – and thus failure – is acceptable, so long as positive learning for the future is the outcome.

Finally, learning organisations value participative policymaking; all members are believed to have a potentially valuable contribution to policy development, particularly those closest to the operational 'front line' (who in most other organisations are expected to be conformist, compliant and passive).

Organisational processes

Aligned to such values, a number of key processes assume prominence in the learning organisation. All organisational members are seen to take responsibility for continually monitoring external environments and internal operations. Everyone has a role in 'environmental scanning' – searching for and recording innovations adopted elsewhere, and then reflecting on how they can be incorporated or adapted as part of their own organisation's practice. Looking 'internally', all have responsibility for identifying how things can be done better, and specific 'improvement programmes' (such as Total Quality Management and Quality Circles) are used as a way of encouraging review and generating ideas for new ways of doing things.

Such techniques also underpin and support what is probably the most important learning process of all: encouragement of open, transparent communications both vertically and horizontally through team dialogue. Ideas emerging from both outside the organisation and from inside need to be discussed and evaluated. Dialogue, within a team minimally encumbered by status differences and motivated by a desire to establish valid and useful ideas or innovations, has the best chance of reaching quality conclusions. Team learning through dialogue must replace 'debate' if the latter implies a 'battle' between ideas and 'positions' that is likely to prove counterproductive.

Many advocates of the learning organisation, including Dixon (1999), point to the important role that new technology can play. Marquardt and Reynolds (1994, p 36) note that in the learning organisation, the collection and interpretation of valid and reliable information is vital; knowledge creation and transfer 'includes the continual creation of knowledge and the ongoing circulation process'. Learning technology, which includes information technology, assists this process. Knowledge can be gathered, sorted and disseminated seamlessly across functions, levels, borders and cultures.

New technology can enable information (collected from internal and external sources) to be rapidly and widely distributed among most, if not all, members of the organisation. Such 'networked intelligence' can powerfully improve learning through maximising openness, communication and team dialogue.

Organisational structure

A highly useful organisational precept is that 'structure' should follow 'function' (see Chapter Three, this volume). When applied to the structural arrangements of the learning organisation, this leads to the design of 'flat, non hierarchical and holistic structures ... [which maximise] contact, information flow, local responsibility, and collaboration within and outside the organisation' (Marquardt and Reynolds, 1994, p 36). A flat structure supports two other structural features that are said to be key to the learning organisation, namely, team-working and networking: 'organisational members are brought together to work collectively with other people in the organisation and to network whenever possible with the resources outside the organisation through ... alliances, informal relationships, and so forth' (Marquardt and Reynolds, 1994, p 109). This, in turn, facilitates empowerment, where the authorisation and power to act is delegated as near as possible to the point of interaction with the community, thus enabling learning to happen through the exercise of responsibility.

The learning organisation thus seeks to devolve decision-making and control of operations to relatively small, decentralised units; coordination is likely to take place through mutual adjustment, communication and shared information rather than through top-down instruction or bureaucratic rule-following. Rules in the learning organisation – and they do, of course, exist in all organisations – set limits on what is permissible rather than prescribe how things should be done in fine detail, identifying the parameters to team or organisational behaviour. Organisational control is exercised, then, less through rules than through generating, encouraging and resourcing members' commitment to the achievement of task goals; the 'how' is delegated downwards.

Conclusions

This chapter has argued that managers of community practice should consider adopting an 'experiential learning' approach to improving the quality and effectiveness of their groups' or agencies' practice. In drawing on the work of organisational theorists, we have followed the dictum that 'few things are as practical as a good theory'. The theory we have summarised provides the basis for implementing programmes of personal and professional development, as well as 'whole-organisational' development programmes designed to implement continuous learning and improvement at the systems level. More than this, however, the chapter argues that the models described are consistent with the general approach to organisation and management presented in Chapter Three. Because this chapter, like Chapter Three, shares so many of their assumptions and prescriptions with community practice itself, its recommendation will be readily acceptable to practitioners.

References

Argyris, C. (1999) *On organisational learning*, London: Wiley-Blackwell.

Beard, C. and Wilson, K. (2002) *The power of experiential learning*, London: Kogan Page.

Boud, D., Keogh, R. and Walker, D. (1985) *Reflection; turning experience into learning*, London: Kogan Page.

Brockbank, A. and McGill, I. (2011) *Facilitating reflective learning: coaching, mentoring and supervison*, London: Kogan Page.

Buzan, T. (2000) *Make the most of your mind*, London: Pan Books.

Dewey, J. (1997 [1938]) *Experience and education*, New York, NY: Touchstone.

Dixon, N. (1999) *The organizational learning cycle*, London: Gower.

Freire, P. (1996) *Pedagogy of the oppressed*, Harmondsworth: Penguin.

Garvey, B., Stokes, P. and Megginson, D. (2009) *Coaching and mentoring: theory and practice*, London: Sage.

Ghaye, T. (2010) *Teaching and learning through reflective practice*, Abingdon: Routledge.

Illeris, K. (2009) *Contemporary theories of learning*, Abingdon: Routledge.

Jenkins, M. and Brotherton, C. (1995) 'In search of a theoretical framework, part 2', *British Journal of Occupational Therapy*, vol 58, no 8, pp 332-6.

Kelly, G.A. (1955) *A theory of personality; the psychology of personal construct theory*, New York, NY: W.W. Norton.

Kolb, D. (2007) *Experiential learning: experiences as the source of learning and development*, London: Prentice-Hall.

Lank, A. and Mayo, E. (1994) *The power of learning*, London: Institute of Personnel and Development.

Marquardt, M. and Reynolds, A. (1994) *The global learning organisation*, New York, NY: Irwin Professional Publishers.

McGill, I.A. and Beaty, L. (2001) *Action learning: a guide for professional, management and educational development*, London: Kogan Page.

Moon, J. (2004) *Reflection in learning and professional development*, Abingdon: Routledge.

Mumford, A. (1993) *How managers develop managers*, Aldershot: Gower.

Nevis, E.C., DiBell, A.J. and Gould, J.M. (1995) 'Understanding organisations as learning systems', *Sloan Management Review*, Winter, pp 73–85.

Norton, L. (1987) 'Taking a deep approach to learning', unpublished paper presented to GNU Workshop 'Development and dissemination of good practice in seminar teaching', Liverpool Hope College.

Pedler, M., Burgoyne, J. and Boydell, T. (2008) *The learning company*, London: McGraw Hill.

Sanchez, R. and Heene, A. (2000) 'A competence perspective on strategic learning and knowledge management', in R. Cross and S. Israelit (eds) *Strategic learning in a knowledge economy*, Woburn, MA: Butterworth Heineman.

Sayers, A. (2000) *Realism and social science*, London: Sage.

Schön, D.A. (2009) *Educating the reflective practitioner*, San Francisco, CA: Jossey-Bass.

Schön, D.A. and Argyris, C. (1974) *Theory in practice: increasing professional effectiveness*, San Francisco, CA: Jossey-Bass.

Senge, P.M. (2006) *The fifth discipline*, New York, NY: Random House.

Swieringer, J. and Wierdsma, A. (1992) *Becoming a learning organisation*, Wokingham: Addison-Wesley.

Vaill, P.B. (1996) *Learning as a way of being; strategies to survive in a world of white water*, San Francisco, CA: Josey-Bass.

Walker, D. (1985) 'Writing and reflection', in D. Boud, R. Keogh and D. Walker (eds) *Reflection: Turning experience into learning*, London: Kogan Page.

Weinstein, K. (1995) *Action learning, a journey of discovery and development*, London: Harper Collins.

FIVE

Negotiating values, power and responsibility: ethical challenges for managers

Sarah Banks

Introduction

By its very nature, community practice is fraught with ethical challenges – especially in relation to the extent to which community participants are given, take or create power and control. On a daily basis, grassroots practitioners work with these issues, and seek, or are given, support from managers to tackle them. In addition to supporting and supervising practitioners, those managing community practice face their own ethical difficulties, relating, for example, to: conflicts of interest between various stakeholders; political imperatives; resource allocation; and staff management decisions. This chapter will highlight some of the specific ethical dilemmas and problems that arise in the context of managing community practice. It will: discuss the nature of ethical dilemmas and problems in general; outline some of the key features of community practice that generate ethical difficulties for managers; and introduce the concept of 'dilemmatic space'. The chapter draws on semi-structured interviews and case materials from managers working in the fields of neighbourhood regeneration, community education, community social work, youth offending, community safety, community support and community development. Two case studies are explored, based on the work of a UK neighbourhood regeneration programme and a non-governmental organisation (NGO) working in conflict-ridden areas of Pakistan.

Ethical dilemmas and problems: the role of 'ethics work'

What makes a dilemma an ethical dilemma, as opposed to a practical, technical or political dilemma? Usually, a dilemma is defined as a choice between two equally unwelcome alternatives – when it seems that 'whatever I do will be wrong'. A dilemma belongs to someone and is about making a choice. A situation, event, case or story itself is not a dilemma, but may raise dilemmas for certain people. Any event or situation has practical, technical, political and ethical dimensions. But these are not inherent in the nature of the event itself; they are constructed by the actors involved in the situation or commentators reflecting on it. Pulling out the 'ethical' dimensions of a situation is inevitably artificial, as they are deeply embedded and intertwined with the practical, technical and political. The following simple case example is designed to illustrate this point.

Box 5.1: Case example – framing an ethical dilemma

A volunteer is putting up a shelf in a community resource centre. She is anxious to complete the job as she has promised the youth group that it will be fixed before their next session, which is in 30 minutes' time. The volunteer only has two sizes of screws: small and large. Neither is the right size for fixing the shelf. She may initially see her choice as merely a technical dilemma – choosing between the small screws that might not support the shelf, and the big screws that would be extremely difficult, perhaps impossible, to fit. But this situation could also be construed as having ethical dimensions. The centre manager comes along and asks how safe the shelf will be, expressing concerns about the risks of it falling and hurting someone; she suggests that the installation is delayed until the right-sized screws are obtained. The manager has reframed the choice as not just between two technically imperfect jobs, but also between risking human safety versus breaking a promise. Adding the dimensions of human safety and promise-keeping brings the situation into the sphere of the 'ethical'.

The subject matter of ethics is often said to be the welfare of living beings, although it should arguably be extended to cover the flourishing of the whole ecosystem. This is a broad area to cover: most situations and events have dimensions relating to the welfare of humans, animals or other elements of the ecosystem. But we tend to focus on this more when there is a difficult choice to be made – when a problem or dilemma is perceived. It may be useful to distinguish between ethical dilemmas and problems (see Banks, 2012, p 20):

- *Ethical dilemmas* occur when someone faces a choice between what appear to be two equally unwelcome alternatives and it is not clear which choice is the right one. So, for the volunteer in Box 5.1, the choice may be between risking the safety of the centre users and breaking a promise to the youth group.

- *Ethical problems* arise when someone sees a situation as involving a difficult ethical choice, but is clear what course of action is the right one. For example, the manager in Box 5.1 may be very clear that the shelf must be fixed as safely as possible, as the welfare of the users of the centre is of paramount concern. She is prepared to wait to get the right-sized screws. She knows this will entail breaking the promise to the youth group and she may risk upsetting them, but is willing to do this.

The role of the manager in the hypothetical case set out in Box 5.1 has several features:

1. *Encouraging the volunteer to reframe the situation in broader context* – the manager encourages the volunteer to reframe her dilemma in ethical as well as technical terms – to see wider implications than first imagined. This is part of the role of a manager in giving professional supervision – to support volunteers and workers to see the bigger picture and to explore options.
2. *Sharing or taking over the dilemma* – the manager could be regarded as sharing the ethical dilemma with the volunteer by discussing and advising on the situation, or she may, indeed, be taking responsibility for decision-making herself (she 'suggested' that the installation of the shelf was delayed).
3. *Framing the situation from a manager's perspective* – the manager herself frames the situation as giving rise to an ethical problem rather than a dilemma. Some of the reasons why the manager sees it in this way are perhaps due to: her greater experience; the responsibilities attached to her role as manager (particularly, the overall welfare of service users); the fact that she personally did not make a promise to the youth group and therefore has less personal engagement with the young people; the fact that she does not have to work regularly with them on a face-to-face basis and so it may not affect her relationship with them greatly; and the specific rights and duties attached to the role of the manager that make it easier for her to take difficult decisions and also make it imperative that she regards safety as paramount.

An indication is given in this short example of the cognitive and emotional *work* that goes into seeing an everyday situation in ethical terms and working out how to proceed. I call this process 'ethics work' – which includes not only framing and reframing situations, but also work at an emotional level, choices of roles, performance of professional identities and ethical reasoning (Banks, 2012, pp 204–5; 2013).

Ethics in managing community practice

In reviewing the literature, and through discussions with managers working in the field of community practice, it is possible to identify certain features of community practice that generate ethical problems and dilemmas both for community practitioners and for those who manage them. These are now summarised.

Community practice as a value-based activity

As outlined in Chapter One, community practice has at its heart a set of values and ethical principles. It is not unique in this respect. Many occupations and practices would make the same claim, especially those in the welfare or caring field. For example, in social work, youth and community work, and health and social care work, principles relating to the kind of society we want to achieve (healthy, just, caring, egalitarian) and the ways we achieve this (with respect for individual rights and freedoms, through processes that are participative, fair, sensitive and accountable) underpin the work. But community practice is, perhaps, more focused on values as its defining feature than some other occupations or professions. Unlike social work, community work or medicine, community practice is not an occupation as such. It is a set of practices that may be carried out by people belonging to a variety of different occupational and professional groups – ranging from planning officers to nurses. What makes it community practice is not that it is about planning or nursing, but that it is about acknowledging and developing 'the active community', based on principles of empowerment, participation, collective welfare and social justice. There are several features of community practice as a value–based activity that give rise to problems and dilemmas:

- *The principles of community practice are essentially contested.* Managers of community practice are likely to get caught up in these value disputes, which may often be implicit. For example, local authority planners and engineers may assume that 'participation' is a process of consultation, whereas community development officers see it as power-sharing with local people (Banks and Orton, 2007). The manager of a community development team has to hold and manage this tension. Some community practitioners and politicians may adopt a critical or radical approach to community practice, with the aim of mobilising the active community to challenge the current balance of power and highlight structural inequalities (Banks, 2007a). This may lead to misunderstanding, or even conflict, when managers of community practice need to translate, mediate and decide when to take a stand.

• *The principles themselves may often conflict.* This may give rise to dilemmas about how to prioritise. For example, the promotion of the collective welfare of the residents of a neighbourhood may conflict with the empowerment of a subsection of residents. Promotion of equality for project participants may conflict with the promotion of their safety and welfare (as in Case study 5.2, when a Pakistani NGO withdrew from an unsafe area). Managers face such dilemmas themselves and also have to support the workers they manage in handling dilemmas and conflicts.

• *Community practice may take place in contexts where these values are not recognised or understood.* For example, community practice may be seen as simply locality-based or decentralised service delivery, or as a means of finding community representatives required to sit on a board in order to gain funding for a neighbourhood-based project. This ignores the key values that stress the importance of encouraging the participation and empowerment of community members. Managers of community practice may have to offer explanations, justifications and education to colleagues in the same agency or other organisations. Furthermore, some managers may themselves be unfamiliar with the values and approach of community practice, yet find themselves managing workers undertaking community practice.

Community practice works through complex relationships with service users, residents and interest groups

The essence of community practice is its relationship with 'active citizens' and 'active communities'. But the nature of this relationship and how it is achieved is far from straightforward. Some of the issues include:

• *Defining 'the community' with which to work.* It may be assumed that 'community' includes all residents in a neighbourhood, or all members of an interest or identity group. However, a 'community' may in fact comprise many smaller 'communities', families and individuals, with different interests and agendas, often in conflict. Dilemmas and problems may arise when sections of a 'community' or individual service users or residents become dominant or are excluded. Managers may find that they need to mediate between different sections of a community, or between communities. Case study 5.2 shows how, in order to work with girls and young women, the managers and board of an NGO in Pakistan had to acknowledge the power of, and work with, tribal leaders.

• *Difficulties in achieving 'community participation'*. Often a distinction is made between consultation and participation, with participation seen as a higher point on a ladder (Arnstein, 1969). Yet only a few representatives can sit on a board or committee and be involved in decision-making. Issues arise about the process by which individuals become 'community representatives', how accountable they are to their 'constituencies' and how competent they are to take part. Ethical dilemmas and problems emerge on occasions when: residents, participants or service users have no desire to become active; they are prepared to take power, but not responsibility; they are given responsibility but little real power; they lack the skills but do not wish to undertake training; members of boards or committees have their own personal and political agendas; or the real power lies outside the board or committee and is used to control or manipulate participants. Managers have to support workers to handle some of these challenging issues.

• *Knowing when parentalism ('paternalism') of professionals is justified*. The stated aim of much community practice is to be 'community-led', so issues arise about the role of managers and professionals in supporting community members to plan and make decisions. Banks and Shenton (2001) report how members of a local partnership felt 'community capacity-building' to be insulting. The manager of the project in Case study 5.1 gives several examples of situations where she felt that she had to exercise her professional judgement to persuade local activists to scale down ambitious projects and plans. This raises questions about when parentalism (deciding for people in their best interests) is justified and what the limits to autonomy (freedom of choice) are.

Community practice often involves inter-agency, inter-professional and other forms of collaborative working

Community practice developed initially within specific areas of work, often involving professionals in particular fields becoming more 'community-oriented', such as community police, community care managers or community arts officers (Butcher et al, 1993). A large part of the recent growth of community practice, however, tends to be associated with initiatives relating to inter-agency and inter-professional teams and partnership-working. Community practice may also involve coalitions of organisations and interest groups working together on a common cause or campaign, as in the traditional model of community organising (Alinsky, 1989; Pyles, 2009). The bringing together of a range of organisations, interest groups and individuals also entails a meeting of different organisational systems, cultures and values. The managers of the partner agencies, or of the projects, teams or alliances spawned by the partnerships, then have to handle the organisational inflexibilities, misunderstandings, competition and cultural conflicts that inevitably arise (Banks, 2004, pp 125–48). This may raise dilemmas in relation to:

- *Differences in organisational systems and ways of working.* Different agencies and groups may have different systems for allocating and prioritising work or for recording and sharing confidential information. Some community groups may be run entirely by volunteers and have few formal systems. If different organisations operate differently, this may raise questions of fairness in the distribution of resources, respect for individuals' rights to privacy and whether larger, professional organisations should impose/demand common systems or work creatively with the differences.
- *Differences in professional cultures and values.* The core purpose of the work of each professional group is different, which affects their cultures and values. For example, in working with young people, youth workers may have a focus on informal education and welfare; nurses on health; and police officers on law enforcement and crime prevention. This means that the role of these professionals in a youth offending team is complementary, but their approaches to the work and their values may sometimes be in conflict. Some community-based projects are explicitly organised as inter-faith partnerships – working across different faith groups and organisations (Weller, 2009). In such projects, it is often the role of the manager to ensure that the practitioners work to their strengths, develop a team identity and are able to recognise and respect each other's professional cultures and secular and spiritual values.
- *Differences in professional competences and identities.* These may create problems in inter-professional teams where there has been a move towards sharing work traditionally done by each professional group. For example, in some youth offending teams, a youth worker, police officer or nurse may complete pre-sentence reports on young people – a job previously done by social workers and probation officers.

The manager may be faced with a youth worker saying that she does not have the competence to do this task, she believes it is contrary to youth work values and unfair on the young people, and that the generic work is undermining her professional identity.

Community practice entails multiple accountabilities

This is a feature of many work practices. For example, Clark (2000) talks about 'complex accountability' in relation to social work and Harrison and Dowswell (2002) refer to 'bureaucratic accountability' in medicine. Arguably, in the field of community practice, the situation can be as complex, if not more so. This is especially the case when there is clear accountability owed to service users, participants or residents, as well as employing agencies and outside funders. Accountability means being liable to be called upon to give an account of what one has done or not done (Holdsworth, 1994; Banks, 2004). This usually entails giving descriptions, justifications or excuses and gives rise to a number of issues:

- *Deciding where accountability lies.* In community practice, there is the potential for a complex layering of accountability, as managers may be employed by one agency (such as a local authority) to manage work funded by several other bodies (such as central government, a charitable foundation and European Social Fund), working for a multi-agency board with an explicit commitment to the democratic participation of local residents. Voluntary organisations (NGOs) may have contracts to provide services for local government, yet managers are also accountable to their boards and community members. Managers may be drawn in different directions, having to balance competing and contradictory demands from several legitimate sources.
- *Deciding which/whose outputs are prioritised.* Balancing the demands of the funders for predefined targets and outputs with the needs and desires of residents/participants is another dilemma that may arise for the manager of community practice.
- *Finding space for flexibility and creativity.* Faced with conditions of financial austerity, the increasing demands of managerialism and the imposition of rules, regulations and targets on community practice, managers are often limited in the degree to which they can respond to local needs. They may also manage staff and volunteers who are reluctant to subscribe to detailed and standardised requirements for monitoring and recording their work.

Community practice occupies a 'dilemmatic space'

All these features of community practice could be regarded as part of what it means to occupy what Honig (1996) calls 'dilemmatic space'. Hoggett et al (2008, p 30) use this concept in their study of UK regeneration workers to describe 'a space in which there is no longer any obvious right thing to do'. While Honig's concept of 'dilemmatic space' is rather complex, one of the points she makes is that we tend to think of dilemmas as discrete events, as specific situations that arise and demand that choices are made. But it might be helpful to locate these events in dilemmatic space or spaces that form us as human agents and that are the terrain in which we negotiate our lives: 'Rather than springing up *ab initio*, dilemmas are actually the eventful eruptions of a turbulence that is always there. They are the periodic crystallisations of incoherences and conflicts in social orders and their subjects' (Honig, 1996, p 259).

This idea of operating within an inherently turbulent space is very familiar in the field of community practice, and, indeed, all social welfare work, where the rationale for the work is built on contradictions (between state support and self-help; care and control; individual choice and the common good) (Banks, 2012). The role of the community practitioner is to negotiate these contradictions and undertake skilful and sensitive 'ethics work' in holding the tensions and navigating this everyday dilemmatic space (Banks, 2013). The role of the manager is to chart and navigate the dilemmatic terrain, to support and guide workers and volunteers in their practice, and to handle strategic issues relating to mission, resources, politics and policy.

Issues of democracy, power and responsibility in practice

I will now explore the nature of the dilemmatic space and some of the ethical dilemmas and problems faced by managers in two case studies. The aim is not to give specific guidelines on how to resolve ethical difficulties, as each practice situation is different, and in coming to a decision about what is the right action to take, each manager, management team or board will take account of unique relationships and commitments to the people involved and their own styles of working, competence and confidence. Rather, I will give an account of these situations, including what the managers actually did, which may help readers identify what issues are at stake in such situations and what factors are taken into account in negotiating the bumpy terrain and making difficult ethical decisions. The case studies clearly illustrate the importance and value of an experiential and reflective learning approach to managing community practice, as discussed in Chapter Four.

Case study 5.1: Managing a regeneration programme in the UK[1]

Introduction

This case study relates to a large regeneration programme. As outlined in Chapter Two, during the 1990s and early 2000s, there was a growth of multi-agency programmes to tackle social exclusion in both urban and rural areas in Britain. There was also an increasing recognition that residents of an area should be actively involved in the regeneration process, both as a democratic right and because they have useful insights into the needs of an area. Furthermore, they will continue living there after any short-term scheme ends, and hence need to feel ownership of any developments that have happened and have the skills and confidence to pursue further development work (Taylor, 1995; Purdue et al, 2000). This led to a requirement for community participation in both the planning and implementation of large-scale neighbourhood regeneration schemes, such as those funded through the Single Regeneration Budget or New Deal for Communities programmes in England, and the integration of 'community capacity-building' into these programmes (Banks and Shenton, 2001).

While this process may have worked well in some areas, in many others it did not. According to Gardner (2007), much community engagement in regeneration schemes was 'shallow and ephemeral'. This may reflect the fact that community engagement was manufactured for an external purpose rather than arising from a spontaneous or organic development from within a community itself (see also Hodgson, 2004; Banks and Vickers, 2006). Not surprisingly, many residents resented the invitation to be co-opted as community representatives onto boards to manage schemes that they had neither desired nor initiated. While this simply led to disinterest and non-participation in some cases, in other cases residents engaged in more openly hostile and confrontational participation, as described by Dargan (2009) in her study of one of the New Deal for Communities areas. There has been a growing critique of 'managed participation', with Cooke and Kothari (2001) coining the phrase 'the tyranny of participation' to characterise the potential of participatory approaches to contribute to the further oppression of the poor and marginalised people whom such schemes seek to empower. Cornwall (2002) makes the telling distinction between 'invited' spaces for community control and those 'demanded' by people themselves.

This suggests that it is important to take a critical approach to community engagement and participation, to assess what it entails and what it means in a particular context. Variations on Arnstein's eight-stage 'ladder of participation' are often used in the literature on community participation – suggesting that there are degrees of power-sharing, ranging from the bottom rungs of non-participation (manipulation and therapy), through informing, consulting and partnership, to citizen control (Arnstein, 1969). This image of a ladder is not always helpful, in that it implies a hierarchy of achievement, moving from the bottom of the ladder to the top. First, it does not take account of the complexities of participation that may have elements of 'partnership' while also being managed or 'manipulated'. Second, in some circumstances, informing or consulting may be entirely appropriate and should not be regarded as 'inferior' or evidence of a shortcoming. Abrioux (1998, p 26) prefers the visual image of a sphere, which suggests a circular, non-hierarchical continuum. In the following discussion of the case, it may be useful to bear in mind the basic distinction between consultation (listening to people's views and giving them feedback) and participation (people taking an active part in a project or process, often having some power to shape the project).

The programme and its challenges

> "There's been not many occasions ... when I came to a different view to the residents.... I think part of my dilemma ... is [that] I think it's naive and unprofessional to say residents are always right, you know. So occasionally I've made a judgement and come to a decision, which has been against the wishes of the residents." (Director of a regeneration programme)

This comment was made in an interview by Theresa, the director of a seven-year regeneration programme covering a housing estate with a population of roughly 2,000 on the edge of a British city. The programme had a budget of £13 million from public-, private- and charitable-sector sources and was managed by a partnership comprising various local authority departments, police, health, voluntary-sector agencies and community representatives. According to Theresa, the area is divided by a long history of conflict between different parts of the estate and between families and factions, including violence and criminal activity committed against each other. Traditionally, there has been a low level of community-organised activities and involvement. Theresa raised a number of issues relating to resident involvement in the partnership and in decision-making during the course of the interview, of which several are summarised below.

Reluctant residents: from participation to consultation

When Theresa first arrived, she found the partnership working well. However, she said it seemed "very top-down" – dominated by the main agencies, with minimal resident involvement: "Some community work had been done, but ... it was about dragging residents along to come to meetings they didn't want to go to and they didn't understand."

The first thing Theresa did was to persuade the Partnership Board to accept that the residents did not want to come to their meetings, and instead to run activities in parallel. This meant engaging the residents in what they wanted to do through 'blitzing' the area with opportunities and community development support. Eventually, a community forum was established, supported by a development worker and training opportunities. Yet, after several years, resident involvement in the partnership was still problematic:

> "It's become a bit more difficult more recently to continue to engage residents in those bigger-picture conceptions really, in a meeting which takes place once a quarter. I mean, they do ... but we've lost off some people.... We've had to have other things taking place, to make sure that residents have a say, and so ... for example, they had a mid-programme review. We just had loads of stuff, you know. We did a door-to-door survey, a sample survey, we plonked a marquee in the middle of the estate, celebrating achievement plus interviews for people – lots of people came into that ... some younger kids were involved in painting, model-making, writing on tiles, what they thought."

What Theresa seemed to have managed was a move away from token resident representation on the partnership, through the setting up and supporting of a parallel community forum, to consultation via review days and other activities with as many residents as possible. On the surface this could seem like a move from residents participating in decision-making to mere consultation and opinion surveys to inform decisions taken by professionals and outside agencies. Yet it was a realistic acknowledgement of the 'token' nature of the participation in the partnership, and of the levels of ability and willingness of local residents to engage in decision-making in these formal settings. The process seems to represent an enlightened move backwards through the stages usually regarded as progress on the 'ladder of participation' – resulting in the engagement of a much wider range of people.

Complex accountability: residents' wishes versus long-term sustainability

Residents were very keen to build a large community resource centre. Theresa thought this a risky venture, given the small population and the proposed location of the building in the middle of the estate (not on a main road), which would be unlikely to attract other users to generate additional income. Theresa was concerned that when the regeneration programme finished, a building would be left that was unsustainable – both financially and in terms of support for the residents to manage it: "I would have felt much happier with a converted house with an extension", she commented. Theresa felt that the residents should think through the project carefully. The partnership made the decision not to be the majority funder of the project, although this would have been possible if this building project had been prioritised. This meant that the message to the residents was:

> "'Here's a challenge to you. If you want this, you're going to have to raise most of the money. We'll give you a big chunk ... but ... as well as persuading us, you've got to persuade a whole lot of other people. You've got to persuade the European secretariat ... you've got to persuade the National Lottery Charities Board ... you've got to have a really robust business plan'... So because we knew it was risky, it was very important if you wanted it ... we had everybody concerned, including ourselves, to be as thorough as we could with it. Even now it's risky, I can't guarantee it'll be up in five years' time, you know, I think there's a good chance it will be, but ..."

Theresa mentioned the terms 'sustainable' and 'self-sustaining' several times. For her, this was an important feature of the regeneration programme. It would be too easy to please residents and funders in the short term with a series of 'quick fixes' but leave nothing behind.

She was also conscious of her accountability not just to this group of residents now, but to the wider community in the future, as well as to the funders of the project. As she commented, "in terms of risks and value for money, I mean, I had a responsibility to the funders".

Professionals and residents as 'co-producers': an example of an ethical problem

Another of the situations Theresa described as raising ethical problems also relates to the use of her professional judgement and experience – taking a long-term view:

> "An issue that's quite important to me is childcare. But we [the partnership] haven't put a huge amount of money into it. We've got a children's project, which in terms of some of the regeneration projects is not a huge project … it doesn't provide day care or anything. But it does run some crèches and it does some development work and has a breakfast club, that kind of thing. Basically, it comes from my experience of working in the east end of [nearby city], you know … setting up day nurseries … and loads of after-school clubs, you know, which were wonderful, really well funded, really well run, really professional, you know, but incredibly expensive. So I think to give that to people for five years and then take it away, I think is awful, you know. So … people rely upon it, you know, so … I was really hard on that really. Really hard. So I just said: 'OK, it's important but in terms of what we put into it, we're not going to fund all the project from the start. You need to find some of the funding, and then if it grows, you've got to grow from other sources of funding.'"

For Theresa, one of the main dilemmas in this situation was the question of whether her approach was excessively parentalist:

> "Occasionally, you see, I do something which I sometimes feel uncomfortable with, in a sense, really, in that I suppose I'm using my professional judgement and experience almost to say 'I know what's best for you', you know, which is sometimes not easy to do."

Yet she obviously decided that it was right to be 'hard'. Although she did not express it in this way, it was as if she felt that she had a duty to draw on her experience and professional expertise to promote the general welfare of the community in the longer term. It would have been irresponsible not to do so. She could not stand by as a neutral facilitator of residents' wishes and desires. Her role was also as an educator (to help develop the community as a learning community), a director (with responsibility for public money) and a professional (with experience, expertise and professional duties). A little later in the interview, she commented:

> "I don't go along with this cliché stuff about this 'resident-led' stuff ... I think it's nonsense really ... expecting people on a voluntary basis to manage services and serve on committees and things ... I don't think sustainability is about independence for local communities.... The term I'm comfortable with is 'interdependence'. We need each other. We bring different things. The residents are professionals in one way, because they obviously know what it's like to live here; they know what they want, but we're not doing them any service by coming along and agreeing with them all the time."

From the comments Theresa made during the interview, it was clear that she was concerned to ensure that residents' views were listened to and respected. But her view of respect was that it entailed treating residents as people whose rights to make choices carried with them some responsibilities for implementing the choices, and for considering the consequences of their choices for others, now and in the future. This is a theme taken up in an account of this project several years later, when the paid manager of the new community centre struggled to encourage volunteer management committee members to undertake training and take responsibility for managing the centre (Banks, 2007b).

Case study 5.2: Managing a women's NGO in Pakistan[2]

Introduction

This case study is set in a very different context from Case study 5.1. It is about an NGO working with women and children in an area of armed conflict, terrorist activity, extreme poverty and very conservative attitudes – the Federally Administered Tribal Areas (FATA) of Pakistan. The organisation has a commitment to empowering women and children, but works with the whole community, including the local men, to pursue its goals. Working in such conditions brings very specific challenges, often relating to dilemmas about how much risk to take, when to withdraw and how far to compromise organisational values in order to achieve basic improvements in people's health, education and well-being. Managing such NGOs is a challenging task, requiring great commitment and courage and a tenacity to keep going in spite of setbacks (Slim, 1997; Desai, 2002; Lavalette and Ioakimidis, 2011). One of the prerequisites for such work is good knowledge and understanding of the local area – its politics, terrain, culture, religion – and the building of trust with key power-holders. Although many NGOs working in areas of conflict are international aid agencies, some of the most effective work is done by locally based indigenous NGOs, which develop their own careful and creative ways of operating.

The FATA of North West Pakistan are poorly developed, and women are severely restricted in what they can do. They are not, for example, allowed by their male relatives to see male medical staff or meet women outside their family other than for approved activities such as collecting water. An estimated 3% of women can read, the rates for child and mother mortality are among the highest in the world, and almost 70% of people live below the poverty line. In addition to these problems, the area is very unsafe, as the Taliban dominate much of the region and exert their authority by force.

The project and its challenges

Khwendo Kor is a women's and children's NGO that undertakes health, education and advocacy work with women and children in the FATA and Khyber Pakhtunkhwa of Pakistan (see: www.khwendokor.org.pk). The NGO is locally run and was established in 1993 by Maryam Bibi, a woman who is herself from the FATA and remains the Chief Executive. Starting with a staff of four, Khwendo Kor now employs more than 300 staff, runs over 200 schools for girls, has trained over 1,000 traditional birth attendants, runs micro-credit schemes and female adult literacy classes, and helps women obtain identity cards and vote in elections. It receives funding primarily from overseas donors. It has a clearly stated purpose relating to promoting women's and children's education, based on principles of: rights for all; empowered communities, especially women and children; and a just and equitable society.

Traditionally the Taliban do not approve of female education, and staff from the NGO are at risk of being shot or kidnapped and their offices have been bombed. Their ability to work in the area at all depends on negotiations with whoever has power in the particular villages they target. The ability to conciliate those in power is thus crucial to their ability to work in the area at all and often to the safety of their staff. If this initial negotiation is successful, Khwendo Kor then has to approach the men in the village and only through them can they eventually work with the women. The NGO involves *maliks* (headmen) in its activities at all stages of its interventions. However, this is not easy. The *maliks* usually ask for personal favours such as jobs, monetary incentives and the upper hand in decision-making. As the Chief Executive and founder of the NGO commented in an interview (Ali, 2011):

> We are also very sensitive to local conservative and patriarchal culture so are very careful in not to offend the local communities in any way....
>
> The security situation is precarious. Working for a women's NGO is extremely difficult. People take us as US spies; elders think we are bad women; women think we're doing things against tribal culture; Taliban attack us for doing things against Islam. Therefore we invest a lot of time and energy in building trust with the people to achieve their support, and once this is accomplished, it's only then with their support that we try to actively engage the women and girls.

The commitment to the mission of Khwendo Kor and the strong value base of the organisation come across very clearly when listening to the Chief Executive. A key part of her role is to provide moral leadership and serve as a role model for the staff, as well as promoting the work and explaining the dangerous, sensitive and painstakingly slow nature of the task to international funders, as she explained:

> "If you are trying to achieve improvements for women and children then you meet opposition from men and, in my case, from groups such as the radicalised Taliban. It is important not to react defensively and not to attack them as that will achieve nothing. You need to take such people with you, to help them to see what they can gain

for themselves and their families through allowing their women and daughters to come more forward.

... it is important for me as the head of my organisation to talk regularly with my staff at all levels and take notice of what they tell me – and that I keep visiting people in the villages as well as talking to high level international people."

The following two examples illustrate some of the issues facing the Chief Executive and Programme Managers who work for Khwendo Kor.

How far to go in compromising principles

In a village in Khyber Agency, the acting *malik* agreed to support a girls' school, and one of his female relatives was appointed as a teacher. However, he later insisted that his brother be employed as Khwendo Kor's field supervisor and asked for a rise in the salary of the female teacher beyond the NGO rules. He avoided the collective community meetings and insisted on his demands. Although the other members agreed to have a second teacher from outside the village, the *malik* said he would not be able to take responsibility for her security.

At this point, the Programme Director faced an ethical dilemma. Khwendo Kor had put a lot of effort into developing the school, with the support of the acting *malik*, and it was of great benefit to the young women of the village. However, the acting *malik* was now showing himself to be too powerful to allow the village community itself to make collective decisions with regard to education. In such situations, the withdrawal of support from one person (the *malik*) could jeopardise the whole enterprise and female education could collapse. Taking all these factors into account, the Programme Director insisted that Khwendo Kor could not go beyond certain limits in compromising its principles, and eventually the school had to be shifted to a nearby village. Although fewer students were enrolled in the new school (at least initially) and only a handful of girls from the original school were allowed by their families to attend, the involvement from the 'new' village through the establishment of a men's education committee and a women's education committee was far greater, thus putting it onto a much firmer footing. Although Khwendo Kor itself decided to withdraw from the school in the first village, it took the decision to leave the teachers behind and negotiate for the government to provide some input into its continuation.

Reflecting afterwards, the Chief Executive felt that she and the senior staff of Khwendo Kor had learnt from this experience that they should not move ahead with their education plans without a broad base of effective support from the wider community, even if an individual in a highly influential position is supportive and the early soundings look positive. This incident also heightened the importance of Khwendo Kor senior staff being aware of interactions between influential villagers and more junior staff. For example, it was the *malik*'s attitude to the latter that first started the alarm bells ringing about the insecurity of the situation; this had not been apparent in the dealings of senior staff with him.

Prioritising safety

Similarly, in FR Bannu a *malik* allowed the traditional training for birth attendants to take place on condition that it was only for his wife and a few close female relatives. This *malik* was influential outside his village and the NGO needed his blessing to work in the area. Khwendo Kor staff do not usually provide the training for fewer than 10–12 women. At this point, the managers and board had to decide whether to proceed or not. They decided to go ahead because the area was a stronghold of the Taliban and any invitation to make inroads was to be welcomed. Therefore, the NGO agreed to provide the traditional birth attendants' training to only three women. This then resulted in the wife of the *malik* getting paid employment in a government Basic Health Unit in his village. However, after achieving his personal objective, this *malik* became disinterested in the NGO and did not support them against the Taliban. Soon after the training was delivered, the security situation in the area deteriorated.

Again a decision had to be made about what to do. It was agreed to close the local office and withdraw the staff. However, Khwendo Kor continues to believe that their approach was sound. The fact that the wife went on to become employed by the government as a result of receiving the training will, they believe, have some benefits. She will act as a role model for other local women insofar as she received training from an 'outside' women's NGO and is now employed outside the home – and this was with the support of the wider village community. The *malik*'s increased income (the wife's salary will go directly to him) is likely to provide him with an incentive to support women's development in the future, perhaps when the security situation eases and Khwendo Kor is able to reopen their office.

Working on being acceptably pragmatic

The dilemmas faced by the managers and board of Khwendo Kor are often to do with knowing when their approach is acceptably pragmatic and when it has tipped over into risking the compromise of their values. There are times when the delivery of a service can appear to be effective (or hold the potential to be) but can jeopardise the safety of staff, collude with activities that might be regarded as corrupt, undermine its sustainability or otherwise compromise the values that the organisation purports to uphold. As the Chief Executive commented:

> "You need to be clear about your values, you need to always act with integrity even if you feel tempted to take shortcuts and you need to understand the importance of building relationships. In that way, you will keep going no matter what the obstacles and hurdles are. Slowly, slowly things change."

This case study about managing a women's NGO in an area of traditional religious and cultural values and armed conflict highlights what it means to negotiate dilemmatic space. It graphically illustrates Honig's (1996) idea that the actual events and noticeable decision points that constitute dilemmas (eg whether to work in an area and whether to withdraw) are, indeed, a bubbling to the surface of the issues that underlie the very nature of the work and the terrain – physical, cognitive, emotional and ethical – on and in which the work takes place.

Conclusions

The details from the two case studies give some impression of a range of issues managers of community practice have to face, the kinds of approaches they use and the language in which they describe their ethical problems and dilemmas. What is clear from talking to these and other managers is that a strong value base usually informs their work. Although each manager tackles the issues faced in their work differently, the kinds of principles and values to which they subscribe relate to:

- promoting the empowerment of residents/service users/participants;
- promoting the well-being of the 'community'/residents/service users/participants;
- promoting social justice and equality; and
- acting with professional integrity, competence and honesty.

However, none of these principles is straightforward in its interpretation and implementation, and many of the ethical dilemmas and problems involve conflicts between them. How we interpret 'empowering participants' depends on our view of who the participants are. If they are construed as lacking adequate information, knowledge or competence, this entails a commitment to increasing people's awareness of possibilities, their confidence and abilities to make choices and act on them. If they are oppressed and marginalised within their own families and communities, this may involve working to change the underlying conditions very slowly.

Regarding 'promoting well-being', we need to ask what is meant by 'well-being' (it could be health, wealth, satisfaction, etc) and whose well-being should be promoted. For the managers in both case studies, it was a question not just of considering 'these residents living here now', but also about thinking of future generations and sustainability. Promoting well-being needs to be implemented in conjunction with promoting social justice – the idea that whatever 'well-being' or goods are being produced should be distributed fairly. What counts as fair is itself contestable – is it according to need, desert or pre-existing rights (to property through inheritance, or to health care through insurance)?

The final value, 'professional integrity', seemed to be important to both Theresa and the Chief Executive of Khwendo Kor. It involves an awareness of a person's power and expertise as a manager and a duty to use these wisely, to reflect, to take responsibility and be prepared to take considered risks as well as dissuade people from ill-considered risks. 'Professional integrity' may, in some cases, be related to the profession of origin – for example, community work or social work – but, equally, it may also be related to the generic 'professionalism' of the manager. Having a clear set of values, the ability and commitment to reflect on their implications in practice and to weigh up conflicting priorities, and the courage and confidence to implement them are all very important in occupying the contested and uncomfortable dilemmatic space of community practice and in tackling the inevitable ethical dilemmas and problems that emerge in the management of community practice.

Acknowledgements

I am grateful to the managers upon whose interviews this chapter draws, particularly those who provided material for Case study 5.1; to Khwendo Kor for permission to use materials relating to Case study 5.2; and to the Leverhulme Trust for a research fellowship, during which some of the interviews were conducted.

Notes

[1] This case was drawn from interviews with a manager of a regeneration scheme and other participants, to whom I am grateful for their contributions, and from documentary sources. The area and people have been anonymised; the name 'Theresa' is not the manager's real name and aspects of her identity have been changed.

[2] I am grateful to Khwendo Kor for giving permission to use this case study, to Friends of Khwendo Kor, especially Marilyn Crawshaw and Ian Sinclair, for providing much of the material, and to Maryam Bibi for an inspiring conversation about her approach to her work. The organisation was happy for its real name to be used. A shorter version of this case study is also published in Banks and Nøhr (2012, pp 204–6) and I am grateful to Routledge for giving permission for it to be reused. Additional material has been taken from the websites of Khwendo Kor and Friends of Khwendo Kor (see: www. khwendokor.org.pk and http://frok.btck.co.uk), from a speech given by Maryam Bibi on receiving an honorary doctorate at the University of York, UK, July 2011, and from an interview with Maryam Bibi available at: http://thewomenseye.com.

References

Abrioux, E. (1998) 'Degrees of participation: a spherical model – the possibilities for girls in Kabul, Afghanistan', in V. Johnson, E. Ivan-Smith, G. Gordon, P. Pridmore and P. Scott (eds) *Stepping forward: children and young people's participation in the development process*, London: Intermediate Technology Publications, pp 25–7.

Ali, F. (2011) 'Interview: Maryam Bibi fights to empower women in dangerous Northwest Pakistan'. Available at: http://thewomenseye. com/2011/07/04/interview-maraym-bibi-on-empowering-pakistani-woman/ (accessed 1 January 2012).

Alinsky, S. (1989) *Rules for radicals*, New York, NY: Vintage Books Edition (1st published in 1971 by Random House).

Arnstein, S. (1969) 'A ladder of community participation', *American Institute of Planners Journal*, vol 35, no 4, pp 216–24.

Banks, S. (2004) *Ethics, accountability and the social professions*, Basingstoke: Palgrave Macmillan.

Banks, S. (2007a) 'Becoming critical: developing the community practitioner', in H. Butcher, S. Banks and P. Henderson, with J. Robertson (eds) *Critical community practice*, Bristol: The Policy Press, pp 133–52.

Banks, S. (2007b) 'Working in and with community groups and organisations: processes and practices', in H. Butcher, S. Banks and P. Henderson, with J. Robertson (eds) *Critical community practice*, Bristol: The Policy Press, pp 77–96.

Banks, S. (2012) *Ethics and values in social work* (4th edn), Basingstoke: Palgrave Macmillan.

Banks, S. (2013) 'Negotiating personal engagement and professional accountability: professional wisdom and ethics work', *European Journal of Social Work*, doi: 10.1080/13691457.2012.732931

Banks, S. and Nøhr, K. (eds) (2012) *Practising social work ethics around the world: cases and commentaries*, Abingdon: Routledge.

Banks, S. and Orton, A. (2007) '"The grit in the oyster": community development in a modernising local authority', *Community Development Journal*, vol 42, no 1, pp 97–113.

Banks, S. and Shenton, F. (2001) 'Regenerating neighbourhoods: a critical look at the role of community capacity building', *Local Economy*, vol 16, no 4, pp 286–98.

Banks, S. and Vickers, T. (2006) 'Empowering communities through active learning: challenges and contradictions', *Journal of Community Work and Development*, vol 8, pp 83–104.

Butcher, H., Glen, A., Henderson, P. and Smith, J. (eds) (1993) *Community and public policy*, London: Pluto Press.

Clark, C. (2000) *Social work ethics: politics, principles and practice*, Basingstoke: Macmillan.

Cooke, B. and Kothari, U. (eds) (2001) *Participation: the new tyranny?*, London: Zed.

Cornwall, A. (2002) 'Locating citizen participation', *IDS Bulletin*, vol 33, no 2, pp 49–58.

Dargan, L. (2009) 'Participation and local urban regeneration: the case of the New Deal for Communities (NDC) in the UK', *Regional Studies*, vol 43, no 2, pp 305–17.

Desai, V. (2002) 'Informal politics, grassroots NGOs and women's empowerment in the slums of Bombay', in J. Parpart, S. Rai and K. Staudt (eds) *Rethinking empowerment: gender and development in a global/local world*, London: Routledge, pp 218–36.

Gardner, G. (2007) 'Recognising the limits to community-based regeneration', paper presented at 'What is the added value of the community-based partnership approach', School of Oriental and African Studies, 16 July. Available at: http://extra.shu.ac.uk/ndc/ndc_presentations.htm (accessed 1 December 2009).

Harrison, S. and Dowswell, G. (2002) 'Autonomy and bureaucratic accountability in primary care: what English General Practitioners say', *Sociology of Health and Illness*, vol 24, no 2, pp 208–26.

Hodgson, L. (2004) 'Manufactured civil society: counting the cost', *Critical Social Policy*, vol 24, no 2, pp 139–64.

Hoggett, P., Mayo, M. and Miller, C. (2008) *The dilemmas of regeneration work: ethical challenges in regeneration*, Bristol: The Policy Press.

Holdsworth, D. (1994) 'Accountability: the obligation to lay oneself open to criticism', in R. Chadwick (ed) *Ethics and the professions*, Aldershot: Avebury, pp 42–57.

Honig, B. (1996) 'Difference, dilemmas and the politics of home', in S. Benhabib (ed) *Democracy and difference: contesting the boundaries of the political*, Princeton, NJ: Princeton University Press, pp 257–77.

Lavalette, M. and Ioakimidis, V. (eds) (2011) *Social work in extremis: lessons for social work internationally*, Bristol: The Policy Press.

Purdue, D., Razzaque, K., Hambleton, R. and Stewart, M. (2000) *Community leadership in area regeneration*, Bristol: The Policy Press.

Pyles, L. (2009) *Progressive community organising: a critical approach for a globalising world*, New York, NY: Routledge.

Slim, H. (1997) 'Doing the right thing: relief agencies, moral dilemmas and moral responsibility in political emergencies and war', *Disasters*, vol 21, no 3, pp 244–57.

Taylor, M. (1995) *Unleashing the potential: bringing residents to the centre of estate regeneration*, York: Joseph Rowntree Foundation.

Weller, P. (2009) 'How participation changes things: "inter-faith", "multi-faith" and a new public imaginary', in A. Dinham, R. Furbey and V. Lowndes (eds) *Faith in the public realm*, Bristol: The Policy Press, pp 63–81.

SIX

Linking partnerships and networks

Alison Gilchrist

Introduction

This chapter looks at how networking can be used in community practice to support inter-agency, community-level collaboration, particularly through the involvement of residents, service users and community representatives. There are good and bad sides to networks, reflecting different influences and identities. On the one hand, they can favour certain individuals, organisations and sections of the community who are 'in the loop', giving them an unfair advantage over those who are not so 'well-connected'. On the other hand, networks constitute excellent systems for communication, shared learning, support and organising. I will argue that the informal conversations and cooperation characteristic of networks often complement formal structures by allowing trust and mutual understanding to emerge, and that this web of personal relationships forms the basis of most successful partnerships. It is important that managers of community practice understand how community networks operate and how they can be supported to contribute positively to service outcomes, such as improved health, community safety, neighbourliness and so on.

After a brief look at how the policy context has promoted partnerships and community participation, the chapter reveals how networks can contribute to the implementation of these themes. It sets out evidence on the social value of networks and explores issues relating to power, inequalities and inclusion. The second half of the chapter examines networking as an aspect of community practice. It identifies some dilemmas and implications for managers arising from boundary-spanning work, especially regarding accountability, uncertainty and demonstrating impact.

The overview of policy developments in Chapter Two indicates how the idea of 'community' has been a continuous thread in the approach of UK and other governments to partnership-based decision-making and service delivery. It draws on important concepts of collective action, co-production and social capital and, most recently, under the guise of the 'Big Society', has emphasised self-help and devolved forms of empowerment (Taylor, 2011). Increasingly, informal interpersonal networks are recognised as a vital, but ever-changing, aspect of people's experience of community and civil society, shaping their sense of identity and belonging (Ipsos-Mori, 2010).

Communities of all descriptions are difficult to work with from the outside. It is not easy to find reliable 'entry points' and there are often schisms within even the most apparently uniform populations, arising from earlier feuds or differences that are invisible (or seemingly irrelevant) to the outsider. Understanding community networks requires a sophisticated, but active, engagement with the web of connections within communities, and between these and the 'outside' world.

Networking is an essential component of community practice. It involves establishing, maintaining and then using links between individuals and organisations based on personal relationships, respect and reciprocity. It introduces a degree of coordination that allows the diversity of experience and opinions to be articulated, compared and constructively managed. The shifting pattern of connections poses a considerable challenge to anyone trying to develop channels of communication and consistent cooperation across the community–institution boundary. It is not possible (or desirable) to impose any kind of structure over what happens in such situations, though much *can* be achieved by keeping open and flexible relations with a broad range of key actors.

Partnership in policy

Due to the changes in UK government policy and the global economic downturn already referred to in Chapter Two, it appears that formal partnerships are losing significance in terms of strategic planning and resource allocation. The Localism Act 2012 downplays their role, scarcely mentioning the word 'partnership', and in many areas local strategic partnerships (LSPs) are being dismantled or becoming platforms for sharing data and airing views between different local government departments, other statutory services and the private sector. In the future, they are likely to have an increasing focus on enterprise and commissioning. For communities, networking remains as important as ever but may need to take place outside of official structures – for example, through attendance at voluntary-sector assemblies, coordinated by infrastructure organisations, which are themselves experiencing dwindling resources (eg Livingstone and

Cotton, 2011). Notwithstanding the effect of public spending cuts, intermediaries and infrastructure bodies (such as councils for voluntary service or community forums) are important vehicles for boundary-spanning work, ensuring that diverse views are expressed and debated. There has been a belated acknowledgement that the attitudes and corporate practices of the other partners (usually local authorities and business interests) may need to change in order to accommodate the less formal styles and needs of community representatives.

The collaborative advantage offered by partnership-working should not be underestimated. It allows agencies to develop a more holistic and strategic approach to their work by sharing resources and responsibility, and setting up at least a shell of common ownership and purpose. Cross-sectoral partnerships bring together key decision-makers in the relevant agencies in order to reach a consensual overview of a particular problem (eg training provision for people leaving prisons or care), but leaves the separate agencies to manage the actual delivery of services in a coordinated way. Sometimes, it is possible to provide access to services through a single 'one-stop-shop' arrangement, which eases referrals and generally makes more sense to the user. The focus of this might be a particular client group, such as homeless people, who can come for advice or care on a range of issues, such as drug use, housing, health care, benefits information and so on. A more advanced version of this model could be the establishment of a new agency, with representation from the various stakeholders, but with its own identity, legal powers and status.

Encouraging individuals who are working together in partnership to see each other as 'rounded' people, and to be aware of other aspects of their lives beyond the business of the partnership, can lead to a greater willingness to see things from different perspectives, compromise and deal constructively with disagreements. Opportunities for people to get to know each other outside the formal meetings are helpful, as are shared training events where participants learn from each other and tackle common problems (Maguire and Truscott, 2006). This enhances partners' negotiating and problem-solving skills, and can subtly shape patterns of influence within the group. A good example is to be found in Eastburgh (a pseudonym), on the north-east coast of England, described in Box 6.1.

> **Box 6.1: Case example of networking by a local council**
>
> The elected members of the local council in Eastburgh decided to organise an 'awayday' to discuss strategic challenges facing their town. They invited key stakeholders along, including resident leaders, service managers, planners and 'front-line' community practitioners. In addition to the more formal sessions focusing on specific problems, there was also plenty of time for semi-structured social networking. As a result, the various players all felt that they knew each other better as individuals and also understood their different roles and perspectives on a range of issues. Over the next few years, this meant that communities received more 'joined-up' services, departments worked together to tackle long-standing concerns rather than 'passing the buck' between tiers in different authorities, and councillors felt more engaged with the people they represented. Participation in local elections increased, as did attendance at assorted community forums, because residents believed that their involvement really did make a difference and they wanted to maintain their connections with other community members.

The most effective community representatives are usually key members of extensive informal networks and have high levels of self-efficacy. Over-reliance on personal connections can, however, distort the representative's judgement in favour of the views of like-minded people, meaning that minority or unpopular experiences are overlooked or suppressed. Therefore, more formal democratic structures, which are open and accountable to all members of the relevant community, are also needed. These might already exist in the form of tenants' and residents' associations, a youth council, or neighbourhood committee. However, they may need cajoling to become genuinely representative. Building cooperative relationships and trust takes time and can sometimes benefit from an outsider who can play the role of 'broker' and mediator.

Participation in practice

Over the past few decades, there has been a growing trend to involve residents and service users in decision-making and service delivery; hence the emergence of community practice as offering a model for institutions to work with communities in ways that are empowering and inclusive. As Chapter Two indicates, public participation through active citizenship and community engagement have been strong themes of British public policy for many years, with numerous reports advocating and examining how users of services can be actively involved in decision-making (Henderson and Vercseg, 2010; Mayo and

Annette, 2010; Brodie et al, 2011). The idea of government programmes being delivered through consortia of public, private and voluntary organisations has been pursued under successive governments since the 1980s, especially in the field of urban regeneration and economic development. Under the New Labour government (1997–2010), various programmes specified that local residents would have some input into the design and delivery of regeneration schemes through community representation on the relevant decision-making bodies. Evaluations of these initiatives revealed that local community members were often marginalised at meetings and genuine participation was distorted through the prism of voluntary-sector liaison, with paid professionals assuming the role of local leaders.

It is recognised that in many instances, 'community participation' was superficial or non-existent and that effective and long-lasting impact could not be achieved without the expertise and commitment of local residents or service users. Accordingly, capacity-building programmes were instigated, which produced a cohort of volunteer activists, but they have had only limited impact in the long run (eg Batty et al, 2010). It has not proved sustainable and research shows that effort is needed to tap into local networks, align organisational cultures and improve communication processes; otherwise, the poor quality of relationships can obstruct the delivery of desired outcomes as well as being inefficient for all concerned.

In theory, community or 'user' representatives sit as equal partners on a partnership board and are expected to express considered opinions across a range of issues. Ideally, this will be based on deliberation with other members of the community to reach a united view on what should be done. The reality rarely conforms to this standard for a number of different reasons, which will be examined later in the chapter. For now, the important point to remember is that effective networking encourages, enables and empowers community members to participate using skills and strategies that:

* honour differences;
* acknowledge competing interests; and
* address inequalities.

The limitations of partnerships

Partnerships sometimes provide a facade for the same old practices and 'usual suspects', whereby delivery agencies decide 'what is best' for residents and users, and continue to work separately (and occasionally in competition with each other) to provide services according to the conventional wisdom and budget limitations. Over several decades of research, evidence has accumulated that community engagement on partnerships is complex, fragile and problematic to sustain (see Case study 5.1 in Chapter Five of this volume; see also Mayo and Taylor, 2001; Foot, 2009; Taylor, 2011, ch 9). Often, the partnership seems to exist on paper only, with community representation merely tokenistic or non-existent. This happens when there is a lack of clarity and respect as to what communities can contribute, or when the unequal power dynamics within the partnership are not sufficiently analysed, acknowledged and addressed (Gilchrist, 2006). In both instances, the more powerful partners will need to examine their own attitudes and procedures with a view to making them more accessible and relevant to people used to working in communities, rather than institutions. It may also be necessary to consider how informal networking (notably, behind-the-scenes wheeling and dealing) excludes some partners from decision-making.

One of the most frequent complaints made by community representatives is that they do not understand the material provided and therefore cannot make an informed contribution to decision-making. Experience tells us that good communication is a vital component of community practice, ensuring that information is provided in accessible formats and languages, and that papers are circulated in good time for people properly to consider their response. Community representatives who are unused to technical reports or formal policy documents may need help in interpreting these, either from independent advisors or from officers of public authorities. This can be difficult for those professionals who are not accustomed to being accountable to lay people or who rely on jargon for their explanations (eg Ray et al, 2008). Citizen-centred governance requires that community practice managers support colleagues throughout the organisation to understand the implications for their own area of work and persuade them that the benefits of adapting to this new approach outweigh initial disruptions and uncertainties (Barnes et al, 2008).

When undertaking joint-working across organisational or sectoral boundaries, it is helpful to have a set of protocols or a compact that sets out how the partnership operates and to undertake early 'visioning' exercises to develop shared goals. This phase often takes longer than expected, as people usually bring very different aspirations and needs to the partnership. For agencies, it may be about meeting targets within a given time frame. For communities, this could be a chance to get their voices heard at a strategic level, and they want to make sure that their ideas are listened to and given credence. Unless decision-making is seen as transparent and inclusive, this swiftly results in scepticism and withdrawal.

The value of networks

Networking complements and underpins formal partnership procedures. It creates spaces and opportunities for dialogue, reflection and building informal relationships. Networks consist of overlapping sets of 'nodes' and links, directly and indirectly connecting individuals, organisations and groups. They form a vital substrate of community life, often operating 'under the radar', and comprise a distinct, if largely invisible, layer of independent voluntary activity (Phillimore and McCabe, 2010). Their membership is often fluid and indeterminate, depending on recent encounters and exchanges. Organisation theory identifies networks as effective forms of organisation in what are sometimes known as turbulent environments and complex systems, where many different elements interact and influence each other's behaviour (Thompson et al, 1991; Brafman and Beckstrom, 2006). Network models of working are effective in circumstances where resources are dispersed over several agencies, and where there is a high degree of uncertainty over possible outcomes. In these situations, an organisation will find it useful to have connections that allow information to be collated and compared from a range of sources, as illustrated in Box 6.2.

> ### Box 6.2: Case example of community participation in a rural area
>
> A Development Trust was set up to support the 20 or so village halls operating in a fairly isolated rural area. All were facing similar problems around funding, community participation in activities and recruiting volunteers to manage the buildings. In addition to a useful website, the Trust undertook a survey of needs and aspirations, followed by a series of networking events to disseminate the findings, explore options and develop a shared strategy for combining resources and sharing information better. Those who attended the meetings found them both useful and enjoyable, making connections with like-minded people and renewing their sense of the vitality of community activities in sustaining village life.

Networking sets up these kinds of links but can also blur lines of accountability and role demarcation. The 'fuzziness' of networks and their lack of defined decision-making structures make them effective vehicles for mobilising community participation but often unsuitable for the formal management of resources. They can facilitate representation, but not replace it. This is mainly because networks are inherently undemocratic and riddled with inequalities that can be difficult to challenge (Small, 2009). Conflicts and power imbalances are often hidden and networks can sometimes be exclusive, dominated by a tight circle of powerful friends or family members. This can mean that erroneous assumptions and oppressive attitudes towards 'others' go unchallenged, as informal networks usually lack the mechanisms for resolving differences or addressing inequalities. Nevertheless, social networks are themselves valuable assets for individuals, communities and partnerships. They provide support, motivation and a collective resilience that can help people through difficult times or to face multiple challenges.

In recent years, information technology (IT) has been developed to provide an array of platforms for online networking that support community activities and exchanges. It is said that 'virtual communities', especially those based around shared identities or interests, have created inclusive spaces for networking, assuming of course that everyone has equal access to the Internet and IT facilities. Many neighbourhoods have developed their own websites, which act as a source of information about local events, enable people to connect with community members sharing similar concerns and interests, and create forums for debate about shared issues (Hampton and Wellman, 2003; Hampton, 2007; Harris and Flouch, 2010).

Many also offer an interface between public authorities and communities, which is potentially a means for direct communication that overcomes stigma and suspicion, thus enabling communities, authorities and public service agencies to work together on local issues. Community practitioners and managers could make more use of social networking tools to ensure that communities are able to influence decisions and have the capacity to communicate and organise themselves. They can be used to debate issues and arrive at a position that can be communicated to decision-makers, including members of local partnership bodies.

Social benefits

There has been a growing interest in the idea of social capital as a significant dimension of community life, defined in terms of trust, networks and social norms (Putnam, 2000). Populations and individuals with strong social capital are found to enjoy higher levels of health, happiness, educational attainment and economic growth (Halpern, 2005; Foxton and Jones, 2011). In addition to the benefit of close personal bonds, weaker connections that link different sections of society contribute to cohesion and stability, perhaps by joining clusters of people in a community to open up opportunities, enhance mutual understanding and establish norms of behaviour (Granovetter, 1973; Csermely, 2009). These bridging and linking forms of social capital (Woolcock, 2001) create a sense of collective efficacy associated with both 'voice' and 'agency' (Wellman and Frank, 2001; Dale and Newman, 2010).

As indicated earlier, there is substantial evidence that people's reported well-being is correlated with the quality of their social networks (Helliwell and Putnam, 2005; Cacioppo and Patrick, 2008; Hothi et al, 2008; Searle, 2008; Umberson and Montez, 2010) and general life satisfaction (Gow et al, 2007). Robust and diverse networks seem to make people more resistant to disease, more resilient to emotional and other forms of trauma (Cornwell and Waite, 2009; Christakis and Fowler, 2010; MBF, 2010), less prone to experiencing long-term unemployment, and less likely either to perpetrate or suffer from criminal activity (Halpern, 2005). It comes as no surprise to find that a recent government report on mental capital recommended five 'steps to happiness', two of which emphasise the importance of positive interaction through connecting and giving (Foresight, 2008). An important aspect of sustainable neighbourhoods is to be found in the design of the built environment and provision of community activities because these foster social networks that, in turn, enhance stability and community cohesion (Bevan and Croucher, 2011).

Everyday encounters in local public spaces generate familiarity and a sense of 'community'. However, this is not always a positive experience. Divisions and prejudices within communities breed hostility, misunderstanding and resentment, as witnessed in periodic disturbances and inter-ethnic conflict in British cities. Helping people with different backgrounds and interests to communicate and cooperate is therefore crucial in encouraging integration and managing diversity. Community practice needs to recognise that networking should be both skilled and strategic – nurturing the more difficult links between sections of the community in order to foster a degree of civic cohesion and meaningful interaction (CoIC, 2007). This might involve working across different communities to set up, for example, an inter-cultural sports activity or a campaign around a shared problem, such as clearing up a local eyesore or tackling drug abuse. The community practice manager would need to create or develop links into all the relevant communities to ensure that key individuals and organisations are kept informed and, wherever possible, involved in the initiative and that their concerns are taken on board.

At a local level, strengthening informal networks will achieve many of the objectives desired by various partnerships, for example, around cohesion, poverty reduction, resilience and neighbourliness (Rowson et al, 2010; Bashir et al, 2011; Wilding, 2011). This might be irrespective of changes in service delivery and may be due to local circumstances such as opportunities for social interaction, demographic factors (such as population mobility), prevailing customs and the quality of 'place' – the accessibility and pleasantness of public spaces. However, in terms of benefits to individuals, it should be noted that it is meaningful social interaction and the development of close relationships that generate positive outcomes, rather than simply contact and connectedness (Gilchrist, 2004; Orton, 2009). This implies that meeting around shared concerns and to create sustained cooperation will yield more positive and sustained outcomes than more superficial forms of socialising (Hole, 2011). In this context, working with and through community nodes (comprising people who may be charismatic and highly connected community activists) and generic anchor organisations (such as tenants' associations or parish halls) is an effective way of reaching more isolated people and spreading benefits across the whole community (Aiken et al, 2011; Dale and Sparkes, 2011).

Sentiments such as loyalty and solidarity shape the patterns of interaction within connected populations and produce powerful network effects (Christakis and Fowler, 2010). For community practice, knowledge of how the networks operate is useful because key players, the well-connected individuals and organisations, can be targeted as the people best placed to circulate ideas and information and to exert influence over collective decisions (Ormerod, 2010). There is growing interest in more distributed forms of leadership (Brafman and Beckstrom, 2006) and agency (Dale and Sparkes, 2011), with specialist functions located at different points in the network. In this model, leadership emerges to meet the requirements of the situation and this may become apparent only after a period of network formation through successive interaction and debate (Onyx and Leonard, 2011). For community practitioners, it may be useful to think of their role as 'hosting' these activities by creating opportunities for networking and trying to ensure that people meet on as equal a footing as possible.

Challenging power, tackling inequalities

The values and methods of community development offer valuable lessons for a networking approach to community practice. Essentially, community development aims to support community-led activities that address issues identified from direct experience and prioritised as ripe for change. Community development work creates and harnesses different forms of social identity and enhances the confidence of communities to speak and act on their own behalf (Gilchrist et al, 2010). This includes tackling some of the inequalities and divisions that make it difficult for communities to achieve a consensual view. In many deprived areas, this work is a necessary precursor to establishing community representation on partnerships.

Networking is often maligned as being manipulative, preserving the privileges associated with old boys' networks or involving only the 'usual suspects' within the voluntary sector. As the case study from Pakistan in Chapter Five illustrates, a balance may have to be struck between making sure that powerful people are 'on board' while attempting to design and deliver a project that challenges traditional power relations or upsets vested interests. Used, however, within the framework of values and commitments of community development, networking should promote equal opportunities, social inclusion and diversity (Gilchrist and Taylor, 2011). Community practice includes a range of positive action strategies, designed to ensure that the access requirements of potential participants are taken into account. This may require psychological, practical and political changes within communities, as well as challenging the institutional culture and procedures of various partners (Gilchrist, 2007).

Managing community diversity

Although policy documents often refer to 'the community' as if it was homogeneous and could speak with one voice, the term masks the complexity, diversity and sheer dynamism of the population living in a given area. There may exist communities of interest (eg around faith or culture), communities based on 'social identity' derived from a collective experience of oppression, such as being disabled or having a particular sexual orientation, and communities that organise themselves around an earlier displacement or origin, such as the African-Caribbean diaspora or economic migration. As we have seen, community representatives are often selected from a relatively privileged set of people, namely, those that have the time, the confidence and the charisma to gain leadership positions (Batty et al, 2010). They are not always the most appropriate or competent individuals to articulate the complex mosaic of ideas and opinion within the area, nor may they be given adequate resources and support to carry out this task properly. In order to ensure that marginalised voices and experiences have influence on decision-making, it can be helpful to have specific networks organised around particular themes or social identities. However, these should be fully linked into mainstream bodies such as wider local community engagement forums.

It is well-known that communities of black and minority ethnic people, including new migrants, refugees and asylum seekers, experience particular difficulties in being heard within partnership bodies, as do Gypsies and Travellers, young people, and children: a pattern of exclusion that prevails across most European countries (Geddes, 2000; Taylor, 2006; Blake et al, 2008; BTEG, 2010). These different experiences, perspectives and priorities do not easily form a coherent 'community view' that can be expressed by just one community representative. It is vital, therefore, that community practitioners work with different sections of the community to:

- overcome disadvantages;
- accommodate different needs and customs; and
- actively encourage minority or dissenting views to be heard.

Promoting social inclusion

An added complication arises because of the tendency to deliver government or local authority programmes on an area basis. Forums such as neighbourhood councils are expected to provide both the opportunities and infrastructure for residents to reach a considered and hopefully consensual view. This approach tends to neglect significant power differentials between various sections of the community, for example, around ethnicity, age or class. Community practice must therefore engage with communities of interest and identity, even where these transcend geographic or administrative boundaries.

The interests of such scattered communities need to be considered, especially when they are in a minority; otherwise, their requirements might be ignored or opposed by a dominant (and sometimes prejudiced) majority. In order for these communities to be heard, community practice aims to strengthen their voices through self-organisation, as well as helping them make constructive links with other sections of the population. In some areas, community practitioners have assisted minority communities to establish their own networks and associations. This should not be seen as creating segregated provision, or giving preferential treatment to some. It is about social justice and addressing the issues faced by socially excluded groups to ensure equality of opportunity. However, such strategies must be handled carefully if they are not to cause further divisions and grievance, especially when it comes to the allocation of funds or places on decision-making bodies.

Working across boundaries

An important aspect of community practice is assisting people to establish links with others that can then be sustained with minimal external support. The practitioner may set up or facilitate the initial connection (a process the author has elsewhere termed 'meta-networking'; see Gilchrist, 2009) but tries not to play the constant intermediary. Arranging events and meetings that bring people together across boundaries is a useful, if tangential, aspect of the networking role, including organising community-based activities or ensuring the inclusiveness of local communication strategies. Research indicates that networking can be effective in developing service-user or community-oriented partnerships in service delivery (Trevillion, 1999). Practitioners can be encouraged to develop links with people in various communities by allowing them time to do this and providing staff development support. Learning about other people's cultures and histories is an important aspect of the networking repertoire, enabling them to empathise with perspectives that are different from their own and to operate appropriately in different settings. Being aware of suspicions and assumptions that may exist across the community–institution boundary usually ensures that conflicts can be anticipated, clarified and resolved more amicably.

Community practitioners play an important, but often hidden, role in maintaining the web of relationships within communities and between organisations, creating circumstances in which people who might otherwise find it hard to communicate can connect and share ideas (Gilchrist, 2009). This is especially relevant in the development of temporary coalitions, where people from different sectors find themselves required to work together in unfamiliar surroundings. By talking informally to different partners, a community practitioner is in a position to understand where opinions are likely to diverge in the discussion and to pre-empt conflict by suggesting possible forms of negotiation or compromise. In this way, dissenting views might be accommodated by developing new forms of service delivery or finding ways around apparent obstacles to joint-working.

Community practice encompasses both capacity-building and engagement. This means considering what needs to change in the formal organisations involved in the partnership, and in relation to the communities they serve. Managers of community practice may have to face in more than one direction: helping their own organisation to adjust to more informal community-friendly styles of working, and supporting their practitioners in more nebulous ways to extend and consolidate local networking. These strands somehow have to be knitted together into a successful approach that includes working directly with community representatives and service users to support them while maintaining effective communication channels with the people they represent.

Regular and extensive networking within communities supports strong collective action and makes effective participation in partnerships more robust and sustainable. These activities are important, especially when they involve face-to-face interaction: the conversations, the greetings, the favours and shared values that are communicated when people meet and talk outside of formal meetings. Being able to interpret non-verbal signals is a useful skill within networks and partnerships because they create the basis for group loyalties and the identification of potential 'friends' and 'enemies'. Informal networks thread within and between organisations, shaping our experience of communities. They establish the basis of temporary alliances for collective action at local levels and galvanise enduring social movements that span the globe (Tarrow and della Porta, 2005; Katcher, 2010).

Negotiating the differences between formal and informal modes

Formal organisations are governed through legal structures and responsibilities, while communities are much more informal, coordinating their arrangements and activities through relationships, local customs and ad hoc voluntary associations. Organisations rely on negotiated, often explicit, regulations and protocols. Members of staff operate according to rules that designate the scope and limitations of their role. Lines of accountability generally operate through a hierarchical framework of job titles and fairly well-defined departmental responsibilities. Communities, on the other hand, function through interaction between individuals who have some basic level of acquaintance or association. The flow of emotions and influence through community networks depends on people's experiences of each other's behaviour and their values, attitudes and past associations. Usually, these convey mutual loyalty, shared commitments and trust; but interactions might be through antagonistic connections, reflecting prejudices, dislike, jealousy and fear.

Another difference between communities and formal organisations concerns representation versus participation as a means of influencing decisions. People participate in community activities because they want to. They tend to be motivated by personal or altruistic reasons (or both) rather than notions of civic duty or citizenship. Consequently, the views and commitments expressed are usually individual, rather than organisational. One of the aims of community capacity-building is to assist marginalised communities to engage in collective debate and negotiation, resulting in a shared perspective or agreed goals about what needs to be done to improve things. Working with groups that are disaffected or whose members have low confidence in the 'system' requires great sensitivity and persistence. It is more challenging for community practitioners than managers sometimes realise.

Managers and other professionals are sometimes reluctant to learn from the expertise, experience and emotion that communities bring to partnerships and other forms of participative decision-making. Community practitioners frequently find themselves on the 'front line', confronted by anger, cynicism or apparent apathy from the communities they are trying to engage and empower. The reality of community empowerment inevitably results in long-held views and practices being challenged. Managers are no longer 'in control' and their authority is threatened by forces and ideas from outside the organisation. Often, these will be conveyed by their own community practitioners, whose links with local communities have given them alternative perspectives and loyalties. However, their usually subordinate position in the organisation may make it difficult for their views to be heard, let alone have an impact. Reducing hierarchical or bureaucratic regulations will make their contribution more effective if they are encouraged to speak freely and to experiment with new approaches. Case study 5.2 in Chapter Five illustrates how one regeneration manager dealt with a situation of potentially conflicting accountabilities by enabling community members to meet semi-formally through a local forum.

Managing opportunities and tensions

This chapter has contended that networking works best through informal interaction – the conversations and mutual support that occur outside of, or on the periphery of, formal occasions, when people get to know each other, discover shared interests and build trust. It would be impossible to regulate or scrutinise this too closely, but there are issues that managers can help their workers to negotiate, or at least to be aware of. The first of these relates to roles and accountability. Networking relies on people stepping partially out of role, developing authentic relationships with others and operating beyond normal professional boundaries. We know from experience that rumour, gossip and opinion are very useful for gaining a sense of the emotional and political aspects of situations, but tend to be distorted by the individuals concerned. They are not usually a sound basis for action without further corroboration. Judgement needs to be exercised in appraising the validity of information gleaned from networking, before it influences formal decisions. Equal opportunities principles dictate that covert preferences and prejudices are removed as far as possible from organisational procedures and activities. The same applies to networking, but is more difficult to monitor.

Network models of organisation facilitate participation and learning. Dispersed and accessible information systems ensure that people across and beyond the agency's normal remit are able to compare different approaches, interpret their own experience and provide constructive feedback – the foundation of a flexible and innovative learning community (Senge et al, 2005; see also Chapter Four, this volume). Managers who encourage reflection and informal conversation across organisational boundaries are taking risks, but also establishing a culture of cooperation that ultimately yields benefits for both staff and communities. Community practice managers can model this in their own behaviour, by providing opportunities for colleagues to share ideas so that it becomes useful organisational intelligence. Community practice requires extending this openness beyond the bounds of the organisation, reaching out into communities, especially those that may initially appear most disaffected or oppositional.

Identifying outcomes, assessing impact

A key purpose of networking is to develop relationships based on trust and mutual respect, and it should be evaluated accordingly. Such intangible processes can be problematic for organisations accustomed to measuring progress in terms of specific outputs or performance criteria. The quality and diversity of connections within the practitioner's web are crucial, hence the importance of proper management of this aspect of community practice. Staff should regularly evaluate their contacts and conversations, and be encouraged to explain why they believe these might yield useful outcomes in the future. A manager should be confident that the worker is developing an array of connections that are representative of the communities within the organisation's remit and that they are using these to make progress towards agreed aims. Do they have good relationships with people across the age range? Are they familiar with all the ethnic groups active in the area? Are they comfortable talking with people with different belief systems to themselves? The tendency for people to network with those with whom they share certain characteristics and interests must be actively countered through good baseline information about the population and regular monitoring of contacts made or lost.

Managers should encourage community practitioners to be strategic in establishing links with key individuals and organisations across all sections of the community, and this may require additional training and support. Research suggests that good networkers are versatile, empathic, diplomatic and bold, and that for some practitioners, this may not come naturally (Gilchrist, 2009). There may be a gender bias to these skills and qualities which means that they are not always appreciated or financially rewarded. Good networkers need abilities in initiating and maintaining balanced relationships, understanding non-verbal communication, especially in groups, and the astute analysis of political and organisational relationships (Anklam, 2007).

Networking seems to thrive on intuition and imagination. There exists an underpinning expertise in perceiving the interpersonal dynamics of situations and identifying or creating new patterns of interaction. Managers should encourage those aptitudes and activities that make good networkers among their community practitioners. It may not be appropriate, however, to define specific targets or milestones, as it is vital that workers are free to take advantage of chance encounters and unexpected linkages. Serendipity is often the key that unlocks successful and innovative community initiatives, but networking in community practice should also be strategic in identifying possible collaborators and critical friends. Effective networking is far more than simply chatting and being helpful to others.

Breaking down barriers to people's participation in community life is often about quite practical changes to how things are done. The resultant web of relationships provides significant social capital, both for the agency and community members. It is a foundation for collective organising, through the bonds that enable people to trust the people they are working with, but also harnessing the bridging and linking connections, or 'weak ties' (Granovetter, 1973), that enable cross-sectoral partnerships to emerge (Dale and Sparkes, 2011). Recent developments in social network analysis, using computer programs that can present patterns of connections graphically as well as statistically, are being applied to measure the impact over time of various interventions, including community development (Ennis and West, 2010; Rowson et al, 2010).

The complexity of dynamic and diverse systems that characterise communities can make it well-nigh impossible to predict specific outputs, but, nonetheless, the evidence presented earlier indicates how strengthening informal networks benefits individuals and communities as well as improving service delivery and design. Networking creates a foundation from which other objectives can be realised, but there are dangers of 'abusing' network connections in ways that are manipulative or non-reciprocal. Relationships that feel exploitative or one-sided are not sustained and managers need to understand that community practitioners must invest in a variety of connections, not all of which will contribute to planned outcomes. This means that they have to give time, effort and attention to a number of linkages without necessarily knowing exactly which will benefit their work or the organisation.

Conclusion

Partnership-working is neither straightforward nor always the most appropriate way of empowering communities. It can be a cumbersome experience for all concerned. Meetings can be wasteful of activists' (unpaid) time and effort, getting embroiled in apparent bureaucratic niceties or overly technical discussions that could be dealt with elsewhere. Partnerships can be seen as a mechanism for managing rather than resolving conflict, usually in favour of the majority or most powerful interests. They tend to advance only on the basis of consensus, and this renders them risk-averse, detracting from the potential synergy that such combinations of expertise and experience should generate.

As we have seen, networks offer more flexible ways of promoting cooperation and improving coordination, providing mechanisms for delivering services and ensuring feedback from users. They allow (indeed, require) the development of trust, respect and cohesion within communities, facilitating voluntary association and building social capital. Informal networks strengthen the social fabric, weaving together different strands of community interests and initiative, thereby enhancing the basis for collective action, shared problem-solving, consensus and conflict mediation (Krebs and Holley, 2006; Holley, 2011). The lifeblood of communities flows through the capillaries of personal relationships and inter-organisational networks. Well-connected communities are vibrant and relatively autonomous of government agendas (Gilchrist, 2009). They have a resilience that preserves traditions of protest, self-help and solidarity, as well as building alliances that improve collective efficacy and partnership-working (Wilding, 2011).

Community practitioners need to understand and work with informal networks, encouraging members of networks to 'build bridges' across community boundaries and to use informal networking to select and support community representatives who can articulate a range of interests on partnerships. Networks enable community members to succeed in these roles, to build links with people operating in other sectors and to develop the confidence and status to challenge some of the power inequalities that exist between communities and statutory institutions, or within communities themselves. Managers of community practitioners are faced with a familiar tension between control, discretion and accountability. Partnership-working demands clarity of purpose, alongside a willingness to respond imaginatively to divergent interests, not least within local communities. Some of the recurring problems in managing community practice arise because of differences in the ways that communities operate, and the mismatch between their structures and processes and those of more formal institutions, for example, in relation to timescales and how meetings are conducted (for further discussion of tensions and dilemmas, see Chapter Five).

Managers of community practice must therefore adopt a delicate balancing act between partnership targets and encouraging independent community activity. Networking for community practice creates opportunities and builds relationships, but it also has to achieve meaningful outcomes. In the long term, these aims are bound to coincide, but only if there is a shared sense that some of the many difficulties encountered can be overcome through sensitive and empowering community practice.

References

Aiken, M., Cairns, B., Taylor, M. and Moran, R. (2011) *Community organisations controlling assets: a better understanding*, York: Joseph Rowntree Foundation.

Anklam, P. (2007) *Net work: a practical guide to creating and sustaining networks at work and in the world*, Oxford: Butterworth-Heinneman.

Barnes, M., Skelcher, C., Beirens, H., Dalziel, R., Jeffares, S. and Wilson, L. (2008) *Designing citizen-centred governance*, York: Joseph Rowntree Foundation.

Bashir, N., Batty, E., Cole, I., Crisp, R., Flint, J., Green, S., Hickman, P. and Robinson, D. (2011) *Living through change in challenging neighbourhoods: thematic analysis*, York: Joseph Rowntree Foundation.

Batty, E., Beatty, C., Foden, M., Lawless, P., Pearson, S. and Wilson, I. (2010) *Involving local people in regeneration: evidence from the New Deal for Communities Programme. The New Deal for Communities national evaluation: final report – volume 2*, London: Communities and Local Government.

Bevan, M. and Croucher, K. (2011) *Lifetime neighbourhoods*, London: Communities and Local Government.

Blake, G., Diamond, J., Foot, J., Gidley, B., Mayo, M., Shukra, K. and Yarnit, M. (2008) *Community engagement and community cohesion*, York: Joseph Rowntree Foundation.

Brafman, O. and Beckstrom, R.A. (2006) *The starfish and the spider – the unstoppable power of leaderless organisations*, New York, NY: Penguin.

Brodie, E., Hughes, T., Jochum, V., Miller, S., Ockenden, N. and Warburton, D. (2011) *Pathways to participation – what creates and sustains active citizenship*, London: NCVO.

BTEG (Black Training and Enterprise Group) (2010) *Getting involved in local strategic partnerships: a guide for black and minority ethnic groups in England*, London: BTEG.

Cacioppo, J.T. and Patrick, W. (2008) *Loneliness: human nature and the need for social connection*, New York, NY: W.W. Norton & Co.

Christakis, N. and Fowler, J. (2010) *Connected: the amazing power of social networks and how they shape our lives*, London: HarperRow.

CoIC (Commission on Integration and Cohesion) (2007) *Our shared future – final report of the Commission on Integration and Cohesion*, London: CoIC.

Cornwell, E. and Waite, L. (2009) 'Social disconnectedness, perceived isolation, and health among older adults', *Journal of Health and Social Behaviour*, vol 50, no 1, pp 31–48.

Csermely, P. (2009) *Weak links: the universal key to the stability of networks and complex systems* (2nd edn), Berlin: Springer-Verlag.

Dale, A. and Newman, L. (2010) 'Social capital: a necessary and sufficient condition for sustainable community development?', *Community Development Journal*, vol 45, no 1, pp 5–21.

Dale, A. and Sparkes, J. (2011) 'The "agency" of sustainable community development', *Community Development Journal*, vol 46, no 4, pp 476–92.

Ennis, G. and West, D. (2010) 'Exploring the potential of social network analysis in asset-based community development practice and research', *Australian Social Work* vol 63, no 4, pp 404–17.

Foot, J. (2009) *Citizen involvement in local governance*, York: Joseph Rowntree Foundation.

Foresight (2008) *Mental capital and well-being*, London: Business Innovation and Skills.

Foxton, F. and Jones, R. (2011) *Social capital indicators review*, London: Office for National Statistics. Available at: www.ons.gov.uk/ons/dcp171766_233738.pdf (accessed 7 December 2012).

Geddes, M. (2000) 'Tackling social exclusion in the European Union? The limits to the new orthodoxy of social partnership', *International Journal of Urban and Regional Research*, vol 24, pp 782–800.

Gilchrist, A. (2004) *Community cohesion and community development: bridges or barricades?*, London: Community Development Foundation.

Gilchrist, A. (2006) 'Partnership and participation: power in process', *Public Policy and Administration*, vol 21, pp 70–85.

Gilchrist, A. (2007) *Equalities and communities: challenge, choice and change*, London: Community Development Foundation.

Gilchrist, A. (2009) *The well-connected community: a networking approach to community development* (2nd edn), Bristol: The Policy Press.

Gilchrist, A., Bowles, M. and Wetherell, M.S. (2010) *Identities and social action connecting communities for a change*, Open University, Community Development Foundation. Available at: www.cdf.org.uk/wp-content/uploads/2012/07/Identities-and-social-action-Connecting-communities-for-a-change-A-Gilchrist-M-Wetherell-and-M-Bowles-08.09.10-for-web.pdf (accessed 7 December 2012).

Gilchrist, A. and Taylor, M. (2011) *A short guide to community development*, Bristol: The Policy Press.

Gow, A., Pattie, A., Whiteman, M., Whalley, L. and Deary, I. (2007) 'Social support and successful aging: investigating the relationships between lifetime cognitive change and life satisfaction', *Journal of Individual Differences*, vol 28, no 3, pp 103–15.

Granovetter, M. (1973) 'The strength of weak ties', *American Journal of Sociology*, no 78, pp 1360–80.

Halpern, D. (2005) *Social capital*, Cambridge: Polity Press.

Hampton, K. (2007) 'Neighborhoods in the network society: the e-Neighbors study', *Information, Communication, and Society*, vol 10, no 5, pp 714–48.

Hampton, K. and Wellman, B. (2003) 'Neighboring in Netville: how the Internet supports community and social capital in a wired suburb', *City and Community*, vol 2, no 4, pp 277–311.

Harris, K. and Flouch, H. (2010) 'Online neighbourhood networks study'. Available at: http://networkedneighbourhoods.com (accessed 28 February 2012).

Helliwell, J. and Putnam, R. (2005) 'The social context of well-being', in F. Huppert, N. Baylis and B. Keverne (eds) *The science of well-being*, Oxford: Oxford University Press, pp 435–59.

Henderson, P. and Vercseg, I. (2010) *Community development and civil society: making connections in the European context*, Bristol: The Policy Press.

Hole, K. (2011) *Loneliness compendium: examples from research and practice*, York: Joseph Rowntree Foundation.

Holley, J. (2011) 'Network weaver handbook'. Available at: www. networkweaver.com (accessed 28 February 2012).

Hothi, M., with Bacon, N., Brophy, M. and Mulgan, G. (2008) *Neighbourliness + empowerment = well-being: is there a formula for happy communities*, London: Young Foundation/Improvement and Development Agency.

Ipsos-Mori (2010) *Our nation's civic health – main report*, London: Department of Communities and Local Government.

Katcher, R. (2010) 'Unstill waters: the fluid role of networks in social movements', *The Non-profit Quarterly*, vol 17, no 2, pp 52–9.

Krebs, V. and Holley, J. (2006) 'Building smart communities through network weaving'. Available at: www.orgnet.com/BuildingNetworks. pdf (accessed 9 January 2012).

Livingstone, I. and Cotton, K. (2011) *Who's listening to the Big Society?*, Exeter: South West Forum.

Maguire, K. and Truscott, F. (2006) *Active governance: the value added by community involvement in governance through local strategic partnerships*, York: Joseph Rowntree Foundation.

Mayo, M. and Annette, J. (eds) (2010) *Taking part? Active learning for citizenship*, Leicester: NIACE.

Mayo, M. and Taylor, M. (2001) 'Partnership and power in community regeneration', in S. Balloch and M. Taylor (eds) *Partnership working*, Bristol: The Policy Press, pp 39–56.

MBF (Mentoring and Befriending Foundation) (2010) *Befriending works: building resilience in local communities*, London: MBF.

Onyx, J. and Leonard, R.J. (2011) 'Complex systems leadership in emergent community projects', *Community Development Journal*, vol 46, no 4, pp 93–510.

Ormerod, P. (2010) *N squared, public policy and the power of networks*, London: Royal Society of Arts.

Orton, A. (2009) *What works in enabling cross-community interactions? Perspectives on good policy and practice*, London: Communities and Local Government.

Phillimore, J. and McCabe, A., with Soteri-Proctor, A. and Taylor, R. (2010) *Understanding the distinctiveness of small scale, third sector activity: the role of local knowledge and networks in shaping below the radar actions*, Working Paper 33, Birmingham: Third Sector Research Centre.

Putnam, R. (2000) *Bowling alone: the collapse and revival of American community*, London: Simon and Shuster.

Ray, K., Hudson, M., Campbell-Barr, V. and Shutes, I. (2008) *Public officials and community involvement in local services*, York: Joseph Rowntree Foundation.

Rowson, J., Broome, S. and Jones, A. (2010) *Connected communities: How social networks power and sustain the Big Society*, London: RSA.

Searle, B. (2008) *Well-being: in search of a good life*, Bristol: The Policy Press.

Senge, P., Scharmer, C.O., Jaworski, J. and Flowers, B. (2005) *Presence: exploring profound change in people, organisations and society*, London: Nicholas Brealey.

Small, M.L. (2009) *Unanticipated gains: origins of network inequality in everyday life*, New York, NY: Oxford University Press.

Tarrow, S. and della Porta, D. (2005) *Transnational protest and global activism*, Lanham, MA: Rowman and Littlefield.

Taylor, M. (2006) 'Communities in partnership: developing a strategic voice', *Social Policy and Society*, vol 5, pp 269–79.

Taylor, M. (2011) *Public policy in the community* (2nd edn), Basingstoke: Palgrave Macmillan.

Thompson, G., Frances, J., Levacic, R. and Mitchell, J. (eds) (1991) *Markets, hierarchies and networks: the co-ordination of social life*, London: Sage.

Trevillion, S. (1999) *Networking and community partnership*, Farnham: Ashgate.

Umberson, D. and Montez, J.K. (2010) 'Social relationships and health; a flashpoint for health policy', *Journal of Health and Social Behavior*, vol 51, no 1, Supplement, pp S54–S66.

Wellman, B. and Frank, K.A. (2001) 'Network capital in a multilevel world', in N. Lin, R.S. Burt and K. Cook (eds) *Social capital*, Aldine De Gruyter: Hawthorne, pp 233–73.

Wilding, N. (2011) *Exploring community resilience in times of change*, Dunfermline: Carnegie UK Trust.

Woolcock, M. (2001) 'The place of social capital in understanding social and economic outcomes', *ISUMA Canadian Journal of Policy Research*, vol 2, no 1, pp 11–17.

SEVEN

The manager's role in community-led research

Murray Hawtin and Tony Herrmann

Introduction

This chapter explores the role of managers of community practice in supporting members of community groups and organisations in carrying out and implementing their own research. Earlier chapters in this book show how community practice needs to be underpinned by a comprehensive understanding of the resources, strengths, history, needs, weaknesses and aspirations of all community members. The starting point for this chapter is that effective community practice should also be supported by research that explores the causes, extent and impact of social issues and how these affect the lives of people in communities. We introduce the concept of 'community-led research' as particularly relevant to community practice, briefly locating this approach in relation to the larger literature on community-based, participatory and action research and exploring its practical application through the presentation and analysis of several case studies.

Managers responsible for community practice may find this chapter especially useful when considering how to enable and support practitioners, paid and unpaid, in community-led research – its design, implementation and the disseminating of evidence. A growing range of case studies of research in community settings can now be accessed in the literature and online, including descriptive accounts, evaluations and peer-reviewed discussions (eg Williamson and DeSouza, 2007; Goodson and Phillimore, 2012; SCARF, 2012; National Co-ordinating Centre for Public Engagement, www.publicengagement.ac.uk/how/case-studies).

However, some discernment is needed in deciding how different approaches to research, particularly those that engage and activate local people and members of identity and interest communities in the research and inquiry process, might be used in different settings and situations. To ground this discernment process, we have selected three case studies of research projects based in Dewsbury (in which one of the authors was a consultant), Torbay and Sheffield. The aim is to use these case studies to reflect critically on the key managerial roles played in the respective contexts.

Community-led research

We are using the term 'community-led research' to refer to research that is owned and undertaken by members of communities of place, identity or interest. This covers a range of possibilities in terms of how the research is initiated, managed, designed and conducted. Sometimes, the ideas for research come from within the community, while, on other occasions, research may be commissioned by another body and carried out by community researchers. Community-led research may also be designed and conducted in collaboration with other organisations or groups and/or supported though funding, training or mentoring by project managers or outside agencies. Furthermore, the capacity of members of communities to undertake research may develop over time as they undertake training and gain experience. Hence, there are degrees to which research is 'led' by communities. However, what all community-led research has in common is that the balance of power in the design and conduct of the research lies with community members. The role of managers is to support this process of community ownership and control.

Community-led research is an approach that is based on the key values and principles of community practice (see Chapter One). These include a commitment to: building collaborative links between practitioners, academics and communities; enabling participation of those being researched; empowering people individually and collectively in marginalised areas or from disempowered groups; and focusing on problem-solving, change and transformation.

The roots of community-led research

The origins of community-led research lie in a number of different traditions. One of the most influential in the field of community practice is the paradigm of 'participatory action research'. By this, we mean research that is initiated to solve an immediate problem or that comprises a reflective process of progressive problem-solving, which is led by individuals with others in teams or as part of a 'community of practice' to improve the way they address issues and solve problems. This may involve practitioner-researchers actively participating in organisational change. Thus, community practitioners, paid and unpaid, are both designers and stakeholders in the research, working with others to propose and implement a new course of action to help their communities improve their work practices, to change public policies or take other forms of action. Kurt Lewin (1948, pp 202–3) described action research as:

> comparative research on the conditions and effects of various forms of social action and research leading to social action [that uses a] spiral of steps, each of which is composed of a circle of planning, action and fact-finding about the result of the action.

Any contemporary discourse about individuals and groups in communities intrinsically engaged as actors in a research and community practice role has to take into account this early tradition and intelligence.

Action-oriented and participatory research involving individuals and community groups also owes much to the Brazilian educator Paulo Freire (1972), who developed a dialogical practice of conscientisation – creating knowledge for change based on the lived experiences of participants. This kind of approach is based on the belief that 'poor and exploited people can and should be enabled to conduct their own analysis of their own reality' (Chambers, 1992, p 5). The literature shows that from the early 1970s, community practitioners enacted and responded to the 'movement for change' generated by such approaches, advocating community research and its potential in the managing of community affairs. Materials supporting such practices have accumulated over the years. For example: Glampson et al (1975) produced a guide to the assessment of community needs and resources; Henderson and Thomas (1980) included an extensive community worker's perspective on 'community profiling'; Baldock (1974) and Twelvetrees (1991) encouraged 'neighbourhood analysis'; and Hawtin, Hughes and Percy-Smith (1994) wrote a definitive volume entitled *Community profiling* aimed at community groups and community practitioners wanting to use research in their work. Francis and Henderson (1992) and Derounian (1998) also explored the topic in a rural context.

Earlier chapters of this book have dealt with the history of community practice and the varying practice-oriented responses to government programmes and policy developments. Over the last two decades, there has been an explosion of community-based consultation and needs-assessment activity, based largely on developing more responsive public services. Alongside this, there has been a burgeoning of literature and online support aimed at practitioners wanting to adopt the skills and techniques of participatory research involving local people and groups – who are also becoming increasingly interested in the process (see Hawtin and Percy-Smith, 2007; Skinner and Wilson, 2002; NAVCA, 2006; Renewal.net, 2009; Whittet et al, 2010; Corti, 2012; IDeA, 2012; Open University Library, 2012). Not only has the internet enabled research models and techniques to be more accessible, but it has also facilitated community practitioners to have greater access to relevant and more complex information and resource materials as well as providing a means for gaining wider and more imaginative mechanisms for disseminating research findings. For example, access to transparent data is one of the fundamentals informing the development of a localism policy. Basic statistics for most local areas in the UK can now be accessed online in formats that are relatively easy to use. Smith (2012) has produced an excellent guide to get researchers started and the Audit Commission (2012) has also developed guidance to help users in this area. However, like much on the Internet, this material is inevitably repetitive, not always reliable and, more often than not, largely from the perspective of public service development and delivery – taking a consumerist, managerial or instrumental approach to deliver organisational aims and desired outcomes.

Reflecting back on the earlier discussion and the foundational pillars of Lewin and Freire, community practice and research driven and controlled by academics, service providers or community practitioners that does not engage members of communities contains the risk of focusing on problems and needs identified by 'outsiders'. Further, the risk is that the activity may not include achieving the fundamental changes desired or necessary to ensure the changes promote social justice. In a worst-case scenario, it may lead to a reinforcement of inequalities and the status quo. As Ledwith (2005, pp 50–1) notes:

> Any research into people's lives locates the voices of those people expressing their own experience at its core, as the beginning of a process of empowerment and change. This needs to be set within a critical analysis of the way that prejudice and discrimination target specific groups through poverty, making them more at risk than others, and creating a system of domination and subordination, locally, nationally and globally.

Case studies

The following case studies illustrate situations and contexts where some of the tensions and concerns outlined earlier were evident. They are not unique examples, but they have been chosen to help demonstrate what is possible where an effective community manager supports such initiatives.

Case study 7.1: Dewsbury Community Action Research Team

Dewsbury Neighbourhoods – part of Kirklees Metropolitan Council (KMC) – was established to regenerate part of Dewsbury, and its approach was firmly based on involving residents. The project manager appointed an independent-sector and a university consultant to recruit and develop a team of local residents. This involved offering training to enable residents to carry out research covering all aspects of the project's work. The training included research design, face-to-face surveying, establishing and running focus groups, establishing community-owned performance indicators, analysing data, evaluation techniques, and producing printed dissemination and other material. A local independent group, Dewsbury Community Action Research Team (CART), was formed with the following objectives:

- training and developing local people in research;
- enabling local people to act as 'residents' friends' in honest communication between all partners, including the council, other agencies, the private sector and local communities of geography and interest;
- ensuring that clear, open and honest messages were channelled (both ways) and avoiding unnecessary concerns caused by misinformation; and
- taking a key role in the development, delivery, monitoring and evaluation of all projects.

Planning consultants produced a 'master plan' using traditional consultative methods – although most residents did not know about or understand it. CART's initial task was to design research both to help 'translate' the options from regeneration jargon into language that residents could understand, and to identify residents' priorities and preferred timescales for the completion of every element of the master plan. The researchers devised a sophisticated questionnaire and successfully interviewed a representative sample of residents, including many who would never have attended a public meeting or otherwise been involved. A clear picture emerged, which informed the final master plan, and elements of it were implemented later. The manager acknowledged that:'Their [residents'] skills and local knowledge were a key asset in establishing priorities for the neighbourhood masterplans.... The vision for the wards would not be what it is without the assistance of the community researchers' (Dewsbury CART, 2011, p 2).

KMC then successfully secured approximately £10 million to deliver its regeneration programme and Dewsbury CART proceeded to carry out numerous projects, exemplifying its creative approach to community-led research. Some projects were commissioned by the community manager – often suggested by Dewsbury CART – while others were commissioned by different agencies. Projects included:

- a survey of views, needs and issues of local businesses and how the regeneration programme affected them;
- an audit of the waterways in Dewsbury from which the council and British Waterways put in place an action plan to improve them;
- evaluations of key regeneration schemes in the area;
- a consultation on public art installations;
- mapping local activity;
- a study on Asian women's health and their uptake of physical activity; and
- an overall evaluation of the three years of work of Dewsbury Neighbourhoods.

Although they did not claim to represent or speak for the community, Dewsbury CART members came from all its sections and age groups and were able to engage with many people that other organisations would struggle to reach and give them a voice of their own. The group enabled two-way communication, did not take sides and ensured that its activities were open and accessible to all in the community. There was no selection process for members, but researchers were expected to use their local contacts and knowledge to ensure openness and transparency. The project valued the local knowledge, expertise and resources, but recognised the dangers of exploiting local people as cheap labour. Researchers' time and skills were therefore acknowledged and they were paid as semi-professional lay workers, with members of focus groups given expenses for their time.

The research significantly influenced the design and implementation of much of the regeneration programme and the team developed a website, produced four newsletters and held a number of open days to collect further opinions and information, disseminate its findings and encourage discussion in the wider community. Throughout these activities, the scheme manager played a pivotal role in supporting and encouraging the team, building their confidence and ensuring their findings reached the appropriate audiences. As a politically sensitive area where the local press play a dangerous game, on several occasions, the manager was able to protect the community researchers from unnecessary interference and guide them through the maze of policies relevant to their research. She promoted Dewsbury CART to her colleagues and other agencies and through these contacts, the manager brought Dewsbury CART further related research work.

Case study 7.2: Torbay researchers

Residents in the most deprived neighbourhoods in the South West of England were given the opportunity to undertake community researcher training developed and delivered by South West Foundation, an independent charitable organisation initially backed by the National Empowerment Partnership. A six-week training programme gave residents the skills to design and undertake their own small-scale community research into the needs and aspirations of the community. Over three years (2009–12) the Foundation trained over 150 individuals in communities to design research projects, gather and analyse data from their communities, and finally to present that data to people with influence who could work with the researchers to bring about the change recommended by the research findings.

Participants were mainly people leading complex lives, who had never been in a position where those in power were prepared to listen to them. They shared a common aim of wanting to bring about improvements in their communities, and the changes they achieved included: establishing community shops and new play areas and skateparks; gaining support to improve services; and offering outings and activities.

Residents' groups from the Litchfield housing estate, Pendennis estate and the local church in Torbay came together to research the needs of their area. Among many findings, the research highlighted the need for play facilities for the Litchfield Estate. Faced with pressure from the local community, the council cabinet turned down a proposal to build houses on a community site. As the former Mayor of Torbay commented in an interview:

> "I listened to the local community ... it was a difficult decision as there is a desperate need for housing but the

thing is to get the community behind plans for the land ...
the community would like play facilities for children ...
it was my decision to turn the [housing] proposal down."

The group undertook further research and made a short film in which local residents spoke about how living on the estate was slowly improving. The film showed an interview with the local MP talking about the significant changes that local people, including the community researchers, had brought to the area. As the local MP commented (in correspondence with a local officer):

Pendennis has a got a lot better and the real key is people from the estate saying we want something better ... when people are identified as wanting to do things and get involved then the agencies come in behind it.

Working through the Windmill Action Group, the community researchers have since brought about new activities and facilities for the community, including accessing a £60,000 grant to build a new skatepark.

One of the essential ingredients in the success of the community researchers in Torbay was the ongoing development support provided by staff at Sanctuary Housing Association. The training empowers individuals to become active in their communities, and once the courses had finished, development workers on the ground used their expertise and knowledge to continue to support those who wanted to take further action. The scheme was managed and fully supported by the Community Development Manager in Sanctuary, with her team of practitioners including community development workers. Sanctuary provided important additional ongoing support and belief in the value of the community researcher approach, which has not only led to an additional course in Torbay, but has also encouraged other housing associations and local authorities to sign up to the Association's approach of involving community members in carrying out research into community needs.

In Torbay, where there had been a history of underfunding in the community, the power of presenting the research evidence was significant. Over £150,000 has been brought into the area in additional funding to improve facilities through the involvement of the community researchers. Councillors and officers responded quickly and positively, which gave the groups considerable confidence to carry on their activities.

However, the manager's role was central and provides many lessons for elsewhere, which we will explore in the following section. She facilitated her team in giving support to the community researchers after the training programme had finished, enabling the community members to move forward with their plans. Through the experience and skills gained in this example, the community manager also supported a course in another area where community researchers successfully explored local facilities for older people, activity needs for children under five years old and other issues, such as a lack of a bus service.

Case study 7.3: Children and Young People's Empowerment Project, Sheffield

Established in 2004, the Children and Young People's Empowerment Project (Chilypep) works with young people to: influence and improve their lives through empowerment and participation; help them to identify and address their own issues, concerns and priorities; bring them together to promote a positive image of all young people and develop understanding, awareness and greater tolerance; and help to ensure their needs, views and issues influence local decision-making and service provision. Following a city-wide consultation in which they had participated, Chilypep established the first Youth Council for Sheffield, which identified bullying as a key issue for vulnerable young people. The young people decided to undertake 'in-depth' peer research into this issue, using a range of different tools and techniques with different groups of vulnerable young people. Members of Chilypep's Learning Difficulties and Disabilities (LDD) Action Group were invited to take part in the research and they negotiated local authority funding to establish additional Lesbian, Gay, Bisexual and Transgender (LGBT), refugee and asylum seekers (RAS), and black and minority ethnic young women (BME) Action Groups. They also provided training following an established Peer Research and Consultation Training Programme. The manager of the Chilypep project had regular contact and positive relationships with the young people, encouraging them to develop negotiation skills and understand the political context so that they were more able to engage with decision-makers who might be resistant to listening to them. She offered advice about presenting their case in ways that might be received more positively and that showed the benefits to organisations as well as young people.

Once the research had been completed, the young people presented their findings to the Sheffield First Board, the Local Strategic Partnership, as well as to a range of service providers and policymakers at the local, regional and national levels. They made recommendations to address the issues identified, and worked alongside Chilypep and senior statutory-sector officers to take forward those actions. The outcomes included: the development of a Homophobic Anti Bullying Charter for Schools, developed by the young people in collaboration with Stonewall and the local authority; the piloting of the Circle of Friends anti-bullying model within a school for LDD children and predominantly BME/RAS children; and the inclusion of the young people's findings from the LDD research in the development of the City LDD Children and Young People's Strategy. The findings were also used by a range of organisations to support funding applications for further work to both statutory bodies and grant-givers, including successful grant applications amounting to over £450,000 for work with LGBT young people. Chilypep has also used the work as evidence of their expertise in youth empowerment and participation to work with other third-sector organisations to secure £1 million for work with young carers and £800,000 for work around young people's mental health.

The Managing Director of Chilypep worked at both the operational and strategic levels, managing the staff working with the young people (many of whom had joined the project as members of groups and been trained and supported to become qualified youth workers) and supporting the development of the groups and training packages. She ensured that staff members were trained and experienced in participatory research techniques and that the work would stand up to scrutiny in terms of its rigour and methodology. She also acted in an advisory capacity to the young people and staff, sharing her knowledge of local and national agendas and strategic priorities, and opportunities for influencing decision-makers and policymakers. Her role was exemplified when tensions arose due to young people identifying issues and priorities that conflicted with the agenda of statutory agencies, their officers and the political agenda of politicians from opposing parties. The manager was able to mediate between these by drawing attention to the commitment of politicians and service providers to listen and respond to young people through the city's Children and Young People's Participation Strategy. The manager had been heavily involved in producing and getting this strategy endorsed by the Children's Trust Board, of which she was a member in her role as a voluntary, community and faith (VCF) sector representative. As the Managing Director of Chilypep commented (in an interview):

> "Carrying out peer research was an incredibly effective way
> of empowering the young people, as they were able to speak

with confidence about the issues for young people not just from their own experience but based on solid evidence from a larger number of their peers. Often, adults who are resistant to listening to young people state that the young person's individual experience or issue is only theirs and doesn't represent the wider community."

Issues highlighted by the case studies

These studies serve to draw attention to a range of issues facing managers and others involved in research in partnership with community groups and individuals. The key issues relate to achieving rigorous standards of research and meeting the values of participation, achieving real change and enabling empowerment in the research process. This section reflects on some of those issues and explores how managers can use their role in addressing them.

Research practice

Research carried out by community groups and local activists is often criticised as being 'subjective', taking a predominantly qualitative approach, and sometimes its validity and reliability are questioned. Jones and Jones (2002, p 57) have pointed out that when local research has been carried out:

> it is extremely difficult to feed this information into the dominant group's thinking. Its validity is often questioned in terms of its scientific rigour, the representativeness of those involved, the size of the sample and its local 'unique' nature.

Such accusations may also be applied to qualitative research more generally, but are addressed by critical practitioners and researchers who value experiential knowledge over empirical 'facts' and who argue that community knowledge and experience are just as valid, if not better, ways of measuring the world as seen by the community (Neilsen, 1990). The managers in both Sheffield and Dewsbury argued that research driven and undertaken by local actors not only collects formal information, but also is rooted in people's direct experience. Therefore, insistence on 'impartiality' (as if objectivity is obtainable) downgrades those experiences and marginalises the validity of community knowledge, dismissing it in favour of another reality. A key activity in Dewsbury, supported by managers, was for Dewsbury

CART to discuss research findings from a position of the group's intimate knowledge of the area, its residents and the nature of feedback they received. These discussions then formed a further layer of analysis of the overall research.

Another criticism is that community researchers often lack the experience and expertise of trained academic 'experts', to which Titterton and Smart (2006, p 55) argue that 'part of the process should be a transfer of researchers' skills and knowledge to the community'. In all three case studies, managers believed that training researchers was essential not only to ensure a high standard of technical knowledge and skill and to validate the findings, but also because, as Reason (2008, p 208) explains, 'participative research is at its best a process that explicitly aims to educate those involved to develop their capacity for inquiry both individually and collectively'.

Cole (2006, p 65) identifies a further criticism relating to an inability to generalise from one area or issue: 'the implementation of an appraisal agenda often suffered because steering groups lacked legitimacy once the debate shifted beyond a narrow agenda that could be justified through reference to the appraisal report'. However, helping people to engage in local issues enables them to make links between those issues and broader ones. Chilypep covered a range of issues, working with various organisations, and in Dewsbury, the researchers also worked with a wide agenda – not just regeneration, but also issues around women's health and the local economy. Both groups developed a strong grounding in a range of concerns as well as the skills and knowledge to address other related community issues.

The values of community-led research

We have emphasised that empowerment is a central value in all community-led approaches. Ristock and Pennell (1996, p 2) have argued from a feminist perspective that 'empowerment as an approach to community research means thinking consciously about power relations, cultural context, and social action. It is an approach to building knowledge that seeks to change the conditions of people's lives, both individually and collectively'. Community-led research, therefore, aims for real changes in the community, raising the awareness of oppression and seeking empowerment through the research process itself.

Titterton and Smart (2006) have pointed out that there is a danger of raising community expectations of improved services and greater participation through community research. Indeed, any exercise that gratuitously promises what cannot be provided is at fault. However, areas such as Torbay and Dewsbury have had little provided, and it could be argued that their expectations and consciousness needed to be raised to encourage people to fight for additional resources. The three case studies illustrate some of the changes that community-led research can bring directly to communities, including improvements in services, the development of an anti-bullying charter and a neighbourhood agreement, and the provision of additional resources for poor communities. Research in the study areas also helped to change local policy in various ways. As a member of multi-agency strategic bodies such as the Children's Trust Board, the manager of Chilypep was able to influence the development of the Children and Young People's Participation Strategy for the city and ensure that the work that young people had done was built into the framework and strategy, and that they were able to directly influence it themselves by ensuring their views from the peer research were fed into the process. Community-led research can be used by critical community practitioners to bring about broader change by highlighting poverty, disadvantage and needs that are not being met as well as drawing attention to inequality in the allocation of resources and raising awareness of the impact of decisions taken by the state and other controlling interests on adults and young people. In all the case study areas, community-led research helped people to develop understanding, skills and confidence, for example, by exposing the role of master-planning and its use of language, and exploring with the community their sense of identity in Dewsbury.

Community-led research is also concerned about the way in which the research process itself empowers those involved directly in it, helping people who are marginalised to have a greater say in events and decisions that impinge on their lives through that research process. Some community-based social research has been criticised for the way it is structured, emphasising an inequality between the professional researcher, funders and the participants or those being researched. A broad spectrum of research approaches exist, which may leave those being researched feeling either disempowered or empowered. At one end of the spectrum, research 'experts' or practitioners are seen as 'in authority', undertaking quantitative research and analysis themselves (sometimes, purely desk-based). In the middle are research projects based on collaborations of professional and community researchers, practitioners, and community residents jointly directing and taking part. Finally, at the other end of the spectrum is 'emancipatory research', an approach pioneered by some feminist researchers and the disablement movement, which insists that the research is owned, designed, directed and undertaken by service users themselves (Nelson et al, 1998).

Without full participation of those being researched at every stage, most research in the community will be tokenistic, giving an illusion of consultation, and the findings will be impoverished, serving only to advance dominant interests, while community members will feel disassociated, if not alienated, from the whole process. All three case studies sought not only to make membership of the research group as open and representative as possible, but also to guarantee as wide a coverage of local people as possible through making the activities relevant and ensuring their importance to those being researched – whether it was renovations to their own property in Dewsbury, lack of play facilities in Torbay or bullying in Sheffield. Issues of lack of confidence and scepticism were addressed through individual and small group mentoring in Dewsbury and Chilypep, through early successes in Torbay and training in all areas. Training and individual support was also key in persuading people that their investment of time will have significance at a personal as well as community level.

When starting their empowerment research programme, Ristock and Pennell (1996, p 10) believed that 'empowerment must entail either eliminating power or redistributing it equally among researchers and research participants'. However, their notion of empowerment became complicated in practice when they realised that 'acting responsibly may sometimes mean keeping or taking on power in order to put in place measures to constrain abusers of power'. The Dewsbury manager used her position in a responsible way to ensure that community research findings were acted upon. From a similar perspective, Jones (2000, p 37) comments:

> Claims made about the achievement of empowerment within participatory research are difficult to substantiate and my view is that integrity lies elsewhere – in locating responsibility with the researcher to ensure that the process is neither experienced as disempowering nor has disempowering outcomes, and in seeking informant validation on the interpretation of data.

Khanlou and Peter (2005) raise the issue of the willingness of researchers to negotiate open agendas for the research process with communities from the start. Again, all three case studies felt that this was essential and although, like most cases in practice, it would be difficult to argue that they are ideal examples of fully emancipatory research, they were all aware of who makes decisions and the effects they are having on community members. The work of Chilypep was initially funded through external grants, regeneration funding and self-generated income, but the success of the work attracted support and funding from the local authority. However, officers began to exercise expectations on the project, which the young people felt was an attempt to exert ownership and control over the process. The organisation then diversified its income and the manager renegotiated the relationship with statutory services, enabling a more equal relationship.

Managers' roles in community-led research

Managers with insight into the richness and potential benefits of community-led research are in a strong position to support and champion such research initiatives within their own agency and with others, some of whom may not otherwise take it seriously. We have indicated some very real methodological issues, including a perceived lack of methodological rigour when 'lay' people conduct research. Managers with knowledge about research methods are in a key position to defend the research and highlight the training and quality checks that our case studies demonstrate community researchers undergo. In addition, the case studies illustrate a range of other ways managers may use their influence to support grassroots activity, support practitioners they work with and enable them to coordinate and link with other agencies.

Managers of community practice need to be in tune with the community and its 'lived' experiences, as disclosed through qualitative community research, and be responsive to the needs that research finds. Quite often, this reveals rivalry, misunderstanding, prejudices, tension and conflict within and between communities. A key role for the manager is to mediate between complex, competing interests by, for example, sitting around the table as a critical friend with community researchers, providing an affirming and unifying presence, and, where appropriate, giving participants responsibility and support to take key roles. Managers in the three case studies all had good working relationships with their community-led research groups, but were also aware of the dangers in adopting a hands-on approach or being drawn into over-colluding with the community on one hand, or the organisation that employed them on the other. Many residents in deprived areas question the motivation of agencies and are wary after experiencing tokenistic or manipulative forms of research that have not represented them fairly or been acted on. Managers can use their influence to motivate communities through confirming their agency's commitment and reassuring communities that managers do not have preconceived ideas about the outcomes of the research, as illustrated in the Dewsbury case study. Cole (2006, p 65) found that:

> although many appraisals had improved relations between the key agencies and the local community, this effect was marginal. In particular, agencies often lacked dedicated mechanisms to channel evidence from [community] appraisals into the decision-making process.

Managers have an important role in ensuring that community reports feed into agencies' strategic and action-planning, leading to development and better delivery of services. The role of the manager in Sheffield was crucial in this respect, as the Managing Director of Chilypep commented:

> "I was able to create a bridge for young people to access senior policy- and decision-makers, and ensure they had a platform to be able to present their peer research themselves, which was the most effective way of getting their voices heard."

Managers are also in a position to ensure that community groups who use the findings of community research for campaigning or bidding for funds are fully supported. In Torbay, management actively supported the audit and promised to address some of the recommendations, which resulted in increased resources to the community.

Although we recommend a hands-on involvement of managers in the community, it is important that this does not undermine the work of front-line practitioners or interfere directly with the work of practitioners or community members. On the contrary, their activities must be fully supported and protected. Community practitioners typically see research as central throughout the various stages in a project cycle, from building mutual trust and contact-making to evaluation. Therefore, support should include prioritising and enabling time for community-led research and ensuring that practitioners and others involved have sufficient skills, knowledge and resources to plan and carry out the activity. In Sheffield, the manager supported staff through supervision, when they could talk through their frustrations and issues, and identify ways forward that did not compromise their own or the organisation's values. The manager was also able to ensure that they received appropriate training and opportunities to develop their own understanding of the political framework. Practitioners and others can be intimidated by research. Cole (2006, p 65) found that 'many local politicians were wary of [community] appraisals and felt threatened by them'. In Dewsbury, the manager encouraged Dewsbury CART to undertake evaluations of her team's activities and acted as a bridge on several occasions between the work of Dewsbury CART and stakeholders such as local councillors, who could have felt threatened by it.

Collaboration as active and equitable involvement of all stakeholders is one of the key principles of community-led research and managers should bring together a range of different agencies, groups and individuals, allowing for mutual support and learning. The manager in Dewsbury organised regular inter-agency regeneration meetings, where key decisions were often made and at which Dewsbury CART played a pivotal role. Other agency staff unused to meeting residents often remarked how much they got from these meetings as did Dewsbury CART members themselves. Managers are in a key position to play a bridging role between different stakeholders such as the community, senior managers, committee members and other agencies. Indeed, managers can take a proactive approach to influence issues such as over-research in certain areas. In Sheffield, the manager encouraged staff to engage in networks and arenas where they were able to meet senior officers and decision-makers themselves and build relationships, respect and credibility, so that they and the work they were doing were recognised and valued. Through their contacts, managers are in a position to raise strategic issues with stakeholders – such as how a particular project should be undertaken or questions of administrative boundaries stipulated for a particular community-led initiative. Well-informed managers can also raise issues such as resource and policy implications and negotiate a more flexible and sensitive joint approach to community-led research initiatives. The managing Director of Chilypep was well placed to influence various strategic bodies, including a VCF infrastructure network, where she was able to establish the credibility of the research group

Conclusions

This chapter has made the point that 'research' in all its forms and guises is central to effective community practice, and community-led research fits well with the purposes, values and principles of community practice. Managers therefore need to consider the promotion and support of community-led research as constituting an important part of their mainstream activity in the same way that they consider financial and other key functions as being part of their work. Community-led research focuses on members of the community themselves owning and undertaking the research in collaboration with others, which arguably not only strengthens the quality and reliability of findings, but also reinforces grassroots understanding of both the research findings and the community practice. This necessitates a programme of learning basic research techniques that in turn helps to add to the confidence and capacity of individuals and groups. Community-led research is not a particular methodology or model; rather, it is a research approach based on key values and ethical principles, including: building collaborative links between practitioners, academics and communities; enabling the participation of those being researched; empowering people individually and collectively in marginalised areas or from disempowered groups; and focusing on problem-solving, change and transformation. For managers and practitioners seeking further guidance, it may be useful to consult a recently developed guide to ethical principles and practice in community-based participatory research in the UK (Centre for Social Justice and Community Action, Durham University and National Co-ordinating Centre for Public Engagement, 2012). Where community-based research is not underpinned by a strong commitment to ethical principles, community members are disempowered through tokenistic practices, and social inequalities and the status quo will be perpetuated. Ledwith (2005, p 31) argues that the role of this work is to 'create the context for questioning that helps local people to make critical connections between their lives and the structures of society that shape their world'.

With an understanding of research principles and practice, knowledge of data sources and means of disseminating findings, and some technical familiarity with the complexity of undertaking community-led research, managers of community practice play a fundamental role in supporting, developing, defending and promoting community-led research and ensuring that it is a coherent activity based on community values.

References

Audit Commission (2012) *Area profiles*, London: Audit Commission. Available at: www.audit-commission.gov.uk/performance-information/using-performance-information/Pages/area-profiles-people-and-place.aspx (accessed 13 June 2012).

Baldock, P. (1974) *Community work and social work*, London: Routledge & Kegan Paul.

Centre for Social Justice and Community Action, Durham University and National Co-ordinating Centre for Public Engagement (2012) 'Community-based participatory research: a guide to ethical principles and practice'. Available at: www.publicengagement.ac.uk or www.durham.ac.uk/beacon/socialjustice/ethics_consultation/

Chambers, R. (1992) *Rural appraisal: rapid, relaxed, and participatory*, Institute of Development Studies Discussion Paper 311, Brighton: IDS. Available at: http://opendocs.ids.ac.uk/opendocs/

Cole, M. (2006) 'Evaluating the impact of community appraisals: some lessons from South West England', *Policy and Politics*, vol 34, no 1, pp 51–68.

Corti, L. (2012) 'Virtual training suite', Economic and Social Data Service (ESDS), UK Data Archive, University of Essex. Available at: www.vts.intute.ac.uk/tutorial/social-research-methods (accessed 13 June 2012).

Derounian, J.G. (1998) *Effective working with rural communities*, Chichester: Packard Publishing Ltd.

Dewsbury CART (Dewsbury Community Action Research Team) (2011) *A community looks at itself*, COGS and Yorkshire and the Humber Forum, Leeds: Yorkshire and Humber Empowerment Network. Available at: www.dbamanagement.co.uk/assets/Community_Action_Research_Team_YHEP_Case_Study.pdf (accessed June 2012).

Francis, D. and Henderson, P. (1992) *Working with rural communities*, Basingstoke: Macmillan.

Freire, P. (1972) *Pedagogy of the oppressed*, Harmondsworth: Penguin.

Glampson, A., Scott, T. and Thomas, D.N. (1975) *A guide to the assessment of community needs and resources*, London: National Institute for Social Work.

Goodson, L. and Phillimore, J. (2012) *Community research for community participation: from theory to method*, Bristol: The Policy Press.

Hawtin, M. and Percy-Smith, J. (2007) *Community profiling: a practical guide*, Maidenhead: McGraw Hill and Open University Press.

Hawtin, M., Hughes, G. and Percy Smith, J. (1994) *Community profiling: auditing social needs*, Milton Keynes: Open University Press.

Henderson, P. and Thomas, D.N. (1980) *Skills in neighbourhood work* (1st edn), London: Routledge.

IDeA (Improvement and Development Agency) (2012) 'How strong is your neighbourhood? A mapping tool for communities'. Available at: www.idea.gov.uk/idk/core/page.do?pageId=17602393 (accessed 12 June 2012).

Jones, A. (2000) 'Exploring young people's experience of immigration controls: the search for an appropriate methodology', in B. Humphries (ed) *Research in social care and social welfare*, London: Jessica Kingsley, pp 31–47.

Jones, J. and Jones, L. (2002) 'Research and citizen participation', *Journal of Community Work and Development*, vol 1, no 3, pp 50–66.

Khanlou, N. and Peter, E. (2005) 'Participatory action research: considerations for ethical review', *Social Science and Medicine*, vol 60, pp 2333–40.

Ledwith, M. (2005) *Community development: a critical approach*, Bristol: The Policy Press.

Lewin, K. (1948) *Resolving social conflicts*, New York, NY: Harper Row.

NAVCA (National Association for Voluntary and Community Action) (2006) *Getting to know your local voluntary and community sector*, Sheffield: NAVCA. Available at: www.navca.org.uk/publications/vcsprofiles/vsprofilestoolkit (accessed 12 June 2012).

Neilsen, J. (ed) (1990) *Feminist research methods: exemplary readings in the social sciences*, Boulder, CO: Westview.

Nelson, G., Ochocka, J., Griffin, K. and Lord, J. (1998) 'Nothing about me without me: participatory action research with self-help/mutual aid organizations for psychiatric consumer/survivors', *American Community Psychology*, vol 26, pp 881–912.

Open University Library (2012) *Skills in accessing, finding and reviewing information (SAFARI)*, Milton Keynes: The Open University. Available at: www.open.ac.uk/safari (accessed June 2012).

Reason, P. (2008) 'Cooperative inquiry', in J.A. Smith (ed) *Qualitative psychology: a practical guide to methods*, London: Sage.

Renewal.net (now IDeA) (2009) 'How to carry out a Community Audit'. Available at: www.eauc.org.uk/sorted/renewalnet1 (accessed 13 June 2012).

Ristock, J.L. and Pennell, J. (1996) *Community research as empowerment: feminist links, postmodern interruptions*, New York, NY: Oxford University Press.

SCARF (Scottish Community Action Research Fund) (2012) 'Scottish Community Development Centre (SCDC)'. Available at: www.scdc.org.uk/what/community-led-action-research/scarf/past-projects (accessed 12 June 2012).

Skinner, S. and Wilson, M. (2002) *Assessing community strengths: a practical handbook for planning capacity building*, York: Joseph Rowntree Foundation, Community Development Foundation Publications. Available at: www.jrf.org.uk/publications/new-approach-assessing-community-strengths

Smith, M. (2012) 'Community profiling'. Available at: www.infed. org/community/community_profiling.htm (accessed June 2012).

Titterton, M. And Smart, H. (2006) 'Can participatory research be a route to empowerment? A case study of a disadvantaged Scottish community', *Community Development Journal*, vol 43, no 1, pp 52–64.

Twelvetrees, A. (1991) *Community work*, Basingstoke: Macmillan.

Whittet, A., McGreechin, A., Crooks, B. and Mouradian, J. (2010) 'The community research toolkit', Transformation Team and Mosaic Creative. Available at: www.transformationteam.org/uploads/ doc_15552009012012_CR_training_toolkit_intro.pdf (accessed 12 June 2012).

Williamson, A. and DeSouza, R. (eds) (2007) *Researching with communities: grounded perspectives on engaging communities in research*, London and Auckland: Muddy Creek Press.

EIGHT

Participative planning and evaluation skills

Alan Barr

Introduction

The demand for evidence-based practice is an often-repeated mantra. In recent years, it has been reflected in an increased requirement for performance management – especially in the public sector. Yet, systematic evidence-gathering seems commonly to be perceived by practitioners as representing an opportunity cost in terms of practical action and therefore as too onerous to justify a substantial investment of time and effort. As a consequence, minimal adherence to performance management obligations frequently eclipses evaluation that reflects on and explores the relationship between actions and outcomes. In so far as evaluation is given prominence, it therefore frequently responds primarily to the externally determined performance criteria of funders and managers rather than to the specific purposes of practice as perceived by the participants.

This is not to argue that funders and managers should not expect practice measurement against their criteria, but to challenge the notion that they are the only investors in community practice and that theirs are the only legitimate criteria for judgement. In an activity driven by voluntary commitment and energy, the primary form of capital underpinning community practice frequently comes from communities themselves. Their investment is predicated on the achievement of outcomes that address their needs and priorities. Any performance evaluation must therefore relate to their concerns. Equally, to honour the underpinning participatory principles of community practice, it must involve them as key judges of performance. Effective approaches to performance assessment in community practice must therefore adopt a stakeholder model that encompasses the interests and perspectives of all those who invest in it.

Implicitly, an approach that measures success against outcomes sought by key stakeholders is one that also engages them in planning and implementation. Participative planning enables the identification of the purposes and associated actions to achieve them that in turn set the criteria for the ultimate assessment of performance. Planning and evaluation are integrally linked.

Community practice, therefore, requires tools for participative planning and performance evaluation that reflect its operational principles. Unfortunately, however, performance management and assessment systems applied to practitioners by funders and managers are often based on the collection of quantitative data that bears little relationship to the underlying purposes of community practice. This chapter will explore approaches to planning and performance evaluation that are not only compatible with the principles of community practice, but also integral to its conduct. It will assert the view that while community practice managers and practitioners are accountable through hierarchical organisational power structures and contract compliance to which they must respond, they must recognise that community participants have a pre-ordinate interest in the quality of performance and, hence, should be viewed as primary stakeholders in the processes of planning and performance measurement.

Such an approach is entirely compatible with the following definition of performance management adopted by the Local Government Improvement and Development Agency (2011) in England: 'Taking action in response to actual performance to make outcomes for users and the public better than they would otherwise be.'

The critical question for community practice is who ultimately defines better outcomes. If it is not the communities themselves, performance measurement will fail to reflect the underpinning principles of community practice. But to assert this approach should not be seen as anything other than the logical conclusion of policies across the administrations of the UK that have come increasingly to emphasise localism and accountability to citizens.

The opening paragraphs of the English Department of Communities and Local Government web pages state: 'Decentralising government is at the heart of everything we do – transferring power from central government to local authorities and the communities and individuals they represent.... Decisions should be driven by people and communities locally' (available at: www.communities.gov.uk/localgovernment/about). Meanwhile, the English Localism Bill, now passed into legislation, was described by the government as setting out to: 'shift power from central government back into the hands of individuals, communities and councils' (available at: www.communities.gov.uk/localgovernment/decentralisation/localismbill).

Elsewhere in the UK, Scottish local authority and other statutory partners in community planning partnerships are required to engage communities in the development of their plans. Scottish Government guidance notes: 'Community engagement in this context must involve consultation, co-operation and participation' (Scottish Executive, 2004, p 7).

In Wales, the Welsh Assembly Government (2006) review of how public services will be delivered focused on 'citizen-centred' approaches, and in Northern Ireland, the Northern Ireland Assembly's (2010) 'Sustainable development strategy' stated that community engagement and participation in decision-making is essential for a truly sustainable community.

Such examples can be replicated across policy areas throughout the UK, and in many other countries. Policies of these kinds have not only promoted a participatory culture, but also encouraged communities to develop the skills and confidence to take more direct responsibility for addressing their own needs. Hence, they have given impetus to a growing social economy and reinforced a broader trend towards pluralism in the delivery of local services. Community organisations that have in the past primarily represented and promoted the interests of local groups have been encouraged to play a growing role, often contracted by the state, as service providers in relation to community needs.

In such policy contexts, participatory evaluation by community practitioners should be expected and supported by funders and management agencies. If it is not already the case, the challenge to community practice is therefore to bring its own practice up to date with imperatives of policy.

All of these introductory comments present managers and practitioners with some important challenges. How do they develop an approach to performance evaluation that reflects the participative, partnership and empowerment principles of community practice? How do they also ensure that their approach is sufficiently rigorous? How do they do this in a way that promotes continuous learning and improvement? How do they integrate and/or negotiate the perspectives of different stakeholders? How do they use these skills not only to fulfil the vision of a learning organisation within their own agencies, but also to move beyond this to a concept of complex partnerships as learning systems that are built on mutual accountability?

These are difficult, challenging questions. The aim and intention of this chapter is to critically reflect on and provide some pointers to good practice in both the management and operational procedures of community practice activity. It will do so with reference to the extensive work conducted by the Scottish Community Development Centre, which has developed and refined related tools to support participative planning and evaluation: *Achieving Better Community Development* (ABCD) (Barr and Hashagen, 2000); *Learning Evaluation and Planning* (LEAP) (Barr, 2000, 2007; Barr and Dailly, 2007; Scottish Community Development Centre, 2011); and a derivative of LEAP using the same framework but focusing solely on community engagement, called *Visioning Outcomes in Community Engagement* (VOiCE) (Scottish Government/Scottish Community Development Centre, 2010) (for further information, see: www.scdc.org.uk).

Background to the planning and evaluation frameworks

All three sets of tools (ABCD, LEAP and VOiCE) have been extensively applied in community development, community education and community engagement and, respectively, been the subjects of UK, Ireland and Scottish government-funded development and cascade training programmes. Their preparation reflected concern in the governments from which they were commissioned that different areas of community practice frequently failed to provide systematic evidence to demonstrate the changes that they claimed.

While governments were building community involvement into strategies for social inclusion, health equalities, neighbourhood regeneration, lifelong learning and active citizenship, among others, practitioners were under notice that evidence-based performance measurement would be a condition of sustained investment.

There can be no doubt that community practice is now expected to demonstrate these qualities. However, the manner in which they are demonstrated also needs to be consistent with the underlying principles of community practice. Thus, in developing the planning and evaluation frameworks, attention was paid to these principles and to existing literature that might provide pointers to good practice.

The frameworks owe a major debt to the underlying theory of community development and specifically to previous work on planning and evaluation in this context. The antecedents of these models are identifiable in the classic literature that has informed community development and participation. For example, the writings of Paulo Freire (1970), which have had a seminal influence on the participatory theory of community practice, emphasise that 'the oppressed must be their own example in the struggle for their redemption' (p 54). Their engagement in defining the nature of the problems to be tackled and the character of suitable solutions, planning how to achieve them and evaluating the success in doing so is therefore essential.

From another angle, these models of participatory planning and evaluation have been influenced by the principles of participatory action research. Kurt Lewin (1946, pp 34–5), who coined the term 'action research', referred to it as using 'a spiral of steps, each of which is composed of a circle of planning, action and fact finding about the results of action'. The models discussed here directly adopt this structure. They also reflect the development of participatory evaluation as a tool of rural development and related techniques like 'rapid rural appraisal' or 'appreciative enquiry'. As Jackson and Kassam (1998, p 3) have noted, there has been emphasis on the idea that 'evaluation should and can be used to empower the local citizens to analyze and solve their own problems'. This approach is central to community practice and the models described here owe much to the work of writers like Feurstein (1986) and Erskine and Brientenbach (1997), who give emphasis to the importance of a stakeholder approach and the ownership of the evaluation process lying with the participants rather than outside evaluators. In particular, they emphasise the importance of evaluating both the process and the outcomes of development work in a participatory manner. In a climate in which there often seems to be heavy emphasis on target- or goal-based planning, these influences are critically important.

While clear visions of the changes to be achieved in terms of impact on social or economic exclusion and its consequences are essential, if community practice is about empowering communities, performance must equally be measured by the participative manner in which such targets are identified and achieved. Similarly, it must pay attention not only to whether particular goals have been achieved, but also to the overall impact and effects of the action taken, recognising negative as well as positive results.

Exploring the ABCD, LEAP and VOiCE frameworks for planning and evaluation

The ABCD and LEAP frameworks share common underlying principles, several of which are considered in more detail later. The most important of these are that community practice must be:

- developed to address community needs and build on community strengths;

- planned on the basis of a shared vision between stakeholders of the intended outcomes of change;
- promoted with clear agreement on the inputs that each stakeholder will contribute, the joint process with which they will engage and the specific outputs they will deliver; and
- evaluated in a participative manner for the purpose of learning for more effective change.

At this stage, it may be helpful to clarify the use of the terms 'inputs', 'processes', 'outputs' and 'outcomes' and the relationship between them:

- *Inputs* – the resources used to formulate or execute a policy, programme or project: people, buildings, equipment, funding and so on.
- *Processes* – the manner in which the inputs are applied to achieve the intended outputs: how we go about it.
- *Outputs* – the specific products of the process activities involved in a programme or project: what we actually do.
- *Outcomes* – the effects of the outputs: the difference we make.

In the LEAP framework, the principles identified earlier are translated into a flow diagram (Figure 8.1), which sets out a series of steps for planning and evaluation. The diagram assumes that community needs have already been identified. Planning and evaluation are presented as integrated activities that operate in a cyclical manner.

Step 1

For planning and evaluation, it is the outcomes that are sought that should be considered first. They provide the vision of change for communities to which all other aspects of activity are directed. Hence, the first step is to identify the outcomes that it is hoped will be achieved. Since these are the reasons for doing the work, they become the critical focus for evaluation activity. It is very important to understand that it is outcome performance that is critical. Too often, evaluation focuses on output performance. This is pointless because outputs are instruments for achieving outcomes. They are not ends in themselves. Their usefulness can only be assessed in terms of whether they produce the desired effects.

Identifying the desired effects that community practice should have is the responsibility of all the participants, and particular priorities can only be distilled in the context of the specific conditions in a particular

Figure 8.1: Steps in a planning and evaluation framework

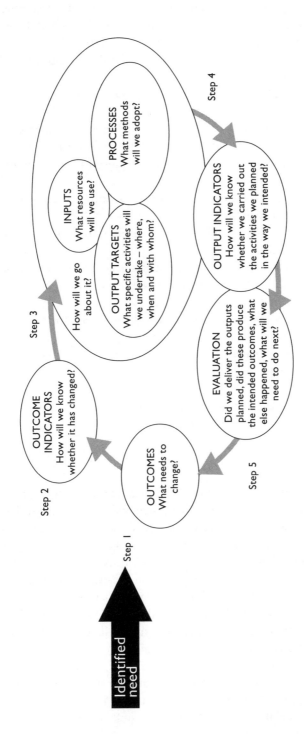

community (whether of geography, interest or identity). Extensive focus group investigation in the development of LEAP and ABCD indicates that, among community practitioners and community activists, there is nonetheless a broad consensus about the dimensions of quality of life in a healthy community.

In the ABCD framework, these are described as:

- *A learning community* – achieved through personal empowerment.
- *A fair and just community* – achieved through positive action.
- *An active and organised community* – achieved through community organisation and volunteer support.
- *An influential community* – achieved through participation and involvement structures.
- *A shared wealth* – achieved through community economic development.
- *A caring community* – achieved through social and service development.
- *A safe and healthy community* – achieved through community environmental and health action.
- *A creative community* – achieved through artistic and cultural development.
- *A citizen's community* – achieved through local governance and development.

Identifying what needs to change will involve exploration of needs in relation to one or more of these areas.

Step 2

Once community practitioners are clear what they are trying to change, the next step is to think about how they will know whether they have got there. In order to do this, it is necessary to be clear about where they started from – what are the baselines against which progress will be measured. This is important in order to benchmark progress. It is then necessary to be clear what sorts of measures and indicators will be used. A measure is a form of evidence that demonstrates a direct connection between what has been done and what has resulted from the action. An indicator is a form of evidence that can only suggest that there may be a connection. In community practice, people are generally more reliant on indicators than measures because there may be many influences that could have had a bearing on the outcomes observed. The evidence will become more persuasive as several indicators suggest a connection, but it may still not be possible to prove it.

Consider a neighbourhood campaign to improve personal safety involving initiatives such as self-defence training, improved street lighting, greater local police presence, a concierge system in high-rise flats and improved youth facilities. Here, those involved might look for changing levels of reported crime against people or property, perceived threat of crime, use of public facilities or engagement in community activities. All of these could suggest that safety has increased, but none of them is, in itself, proof. Even changes in the level of reported crime do not convey that crime has actually been reduced – people might simply have decided that there is little point in reporting it. Hence, a range of evidence is necessary to give confidence about the benefits of undertaking activities.

Setting out indicators and measures at the start directs attention towards the focused collection of relevant evidence. It also helps to cement the relationship between stakeholders as they reach agreement as to what will be seen as satisfactory indicators or measures of change, and who will be responsible for the collection of which aspects of the evidence.

Step 3

The third step has three parts. These are to identify the outputs, the processes to be adopted and the inputs that will be required in order to achieve the intended outcomes. Here, those involved will be concerned with how they will engage with individuals and community groups and the level of investment that will be made and by whom. Although, ultimately, community practice must be measured by its outcomes, it is necessary to know what the relationship is between the methods used, the investment made and the outcomes that result. The evaluation, therefore, needs to encompass assessment of the inputs, processes and outputs.

Decisions about inputs, processes and outputs are interactive. Action must respond to needs but also be realistic about the inputs that can actually be made available. Hence, in the diagram, these aspects of the cycle are encompassed within the large circle to signify that it will be necessary to find a balance between inputs, processes and output targets. Inputs, outputs and processes should be realistic, but they also have to be worthwhile and relevant to the intended outcomes. The process and work needs to be driven by a shared vision for change rather than the resources that are available, but it is possible at this stage to realise that overambitious outcomes have been set. In this case, it is essential to return to Step 1 and revisit the question: what needs to change?

Looking in more depth at inputs, it is important to stress the need for clarity about who will control them, what is actually available, from whom, over what period of time and with what conditions attached. It may be valuable to undertake a formal audit of the collective resources that are available from different contributors and, in particular, to identify any gaps that are apparent, for example, there might be the need for a crèche resource to support participation in a community conference on recreation and play. Such gaps will require consideration of where appropriate resources might come from and may necessitate the seeking out of new partners. If it is not possible to plug such gaps, interventions that are dependent on them are unlikely to succeed.

Thinking about the processes that will be adopted, these can be viewed at two levels. First, the overall approach of intervention can be highlighted: personal empowerment, positive action, community organising and volunteer development, participation and involvement structures, community economic development, social and service development, community environmental and health action, community arts and cultural development, local governance, and so on. Second, within each of these, there will be a wide variety of potential styles and methods of working that will often be used in combination, for example: promotion of dialogue and reflection, provision of information and advice, training, network development, action–research, personal support, mediation, advocacy, and so on.

It is crucially important for those who manage, and engage, in community practice to appreciate and understand that the way in which work is conducted reflects values. Too frequently, these remain implicit; indeed, sometimes, they may even be subconscious. Since the purposes of community practice encompass a clear set of values that is reflected in policies for social inclusion and justice, deciding the approach to intervention requires openness and explicitness. If this is not done, it may be found that the processes adopted contradict and undermine the intended outcomes of actions. It is not that attention to process becomes an end in itself (a not-uncommon criticism of community practitioners), but that it is needed to enhance the probability of successful outcomes.

Of course, it is what is actually done as much as the way that it is done that is critical. Actions or outputs are the instruments of change. Just as it is necessary to know who will contribute which inputs, so it is necessary to be clear who will be using these resources and in what ways. Outputs can be defined in quite precise terms. A community conference will be organised at a particular time and date with specification of its structure, content, participants and so on. An information pack can be planned with clarity about content, format and style, date of publication, print-run, or distribution. It is important to be explicit about the outputs that will be delivered.

If what has to be done is known, it is much easier for the participants to play their role in implementing these plans. If there is agreement as to what others will do, they can be held to account for delivering it. Mutual accountability is a key to effective practice partnerships. Measurable and timescaled outputs are the basis for completion of Step 4.

Step 4

The fourth step is to identify measures and indicators that will convey and indicate whether the planned activities have been carried out in the manner intended. The management of the process will incorporate the setting of specific targets for when, where and how the planned activities will be undertaken. The outputs will be designed and methods adopted that are most likely to achieve the desired outcomes. Unless it is known whether these are carried through, it will not be possible to judge whether any failure to achieve intended outcomes reflects deficiencies in the design and plan for achieving change, or in the way in which it was implemented, or external events.

Hence, these measures and indicators are needed to give information that helps to see whether targets have been met. It will also be necessary to know whether the preferred approach was efficient and equitable. Were more or less resources used than necessary? Was everyone who should have been involved enabled to participate?

Step 5

The fifth step is to draw together and evaluate the evidence of performance in relation to both outputs and outcomes. The practitioner will not only need to know whether they delivered their planned outputs, but also, equally, whether there is a connection between the specific investment made, the activities undertaken in the community and the outcomes that resulted. The evidence needs to be analysed not only to see whether the output was delivered as planned, but also, equally, to see whether it contributed to the intended outcome.

Also, in Step 5, it will be necessary to explore the range of outputs and outcomes that were set. Overall, this will enable consideration of what has happened and what relationship this has had to the role the practitioner has played. The answers to these questions provide important information for further planning, and a new cycle of planning and evaluation emerges. The community practitioner will then start the new cycle by posing the question: what now needs to change?

Stakeholder participation

It is of fundamental importance that those who manage community practice and engage in the process understand that the emphasis on a shared vision reflects the commitment of community practice to the promotion of community participation. The participative principle requires careful consideration, from the start, of who has a legitimate interest in any particular community practice activity and how they can exercise that interest in the process of both planning and evaluation.

In the introduction to this chapter, the term 'stakeholder' was used to acknowledge that there is a variety of participants who have a legitimate interest or stake in both what happens in communities and how it is done. These stakeholders will include: different community interest groups, which will have a wide range of levels of structure and organisation, from informal networks to well-resourced organisations; statutory, voluntary and private agencies working on (or with an interest in working on) relevant issues in the community; agencies that fund community activity; and formal representatives from political groupings. Such stakeholders have different contributions to make and benefits to gain from their participation. Engaging them effectively and collaboratively is a demanding task. Hence, unfortunately, lip service is frequently paid to the stakeholder participation principle.

Because policies have increasingly required user and community involvement, practitioners and managers have often felt obliged to show that they have done this. But without a value commitment to the principles involved, such promotion of participation is frequently little more than a token gesture. Participation may be manipulated to try to avoid controversy or conflict, restricted to engaging only with sympathetic voices, controlled in terms of the scope of the agenda and the range of information that is made available, and so on. Such approaches engender reciprocal distrust and lack of openness and honesty and far from resolving conflicts, tend in the long run to generate them.

The way in which stakeholders are engaged often determines the success or failure of community practice initiatives. It is vital, therefore, to try to get it right from the initial planning stage. It will be helpful for those involved in community practice to answer some key questions:

- Who has a legitimate interest in the needs that have been identified?
- How motivated are they to be involved in action to address the needs?
- Where does that motivation come from – what will they be looking for from their involvement?
- What barriers may affect their participation and what can be done to assist them to overcome these barriers?
- What conflicts of interest can be anticipated and how can these be constructively addressed?
- How can a common agenda be negotiated as the basis for shared action?

In applying the ABCD, LEAP and VOiCE planning and evaluation frameworks, it has been found to be helpful to bring the likely stakeholders together to address these questions in workshop-style events. The purpose of this is to enable the development of a dialogue between them and to negotiate the basis for joint action. It is important that each group appreciates the aspirations, motivations, roles, functions, constraints and opportunities of the others. Each group needs the opportunity to identify its own position and then to be able to compare this with others. It is likely that there will be common ground and some disagreement.

The common ground is the basis for generating partnership action but it should not be assumed that the latter is necessarily problematic. Partners may readily acknowledge that there may be goals that they do not share but that can be recognised as having legitimacy for another group while not damaging their own interests. Such goals can be accommodated. The only ones that require conflict resolution are those that are seen as being directly damaging to the interests of another stakeholder. Although these are often less frequent than is anticipated, it is essential that they are addressed from the start and that it is acknowledged that a partnership between the stakeholders will only cohere if they can reach agreement on what should be done and how. Trade-offs and compromise are often necessary.

Understanding who the stakeholders are, what their interests may be and how actively they may engage with the process of change is an essential component of competent practice. It will often be helpful to develop an analysis of the relationship between stakeholders that addresses:

- relative levels of power in the partnership;
- levels of activeness or passivity;

- strengths of motivation (positive and negative) to be involved in relation to different goals;
- capacity/skills to engage effectively; and
- opportunity to contribute.

The practitioner must have a mental map of the dynamics of the relationship between stakeholders and constantly assess changes that are occurring. The challenges of doing this are increased by the underlying commitments of community practice to an equalities agenda and, hence, to prioritising attention to opportunities for the participation of disadvantaged people. Analysis of the explanations for those disadvantages commonly leads to structural explanations rooted in the construction of opportunity and the perpetuation of privilege. It is important, therefore, to recognise that both the process of participatory planning and evaluation itself, and the issues that are addressed by it, are subject to the consequences of power differentials. As has already been acknowledged, those with power can potentially manipulate processes of participatory planning and evaluation to their own ends. Clearly, this is antithetical to the purposes and principles of community practice. Such blatant misuse of power is usually easy to spot but there may be more subtle and less conscious abuses of power differentials that need to be given attention.

Classically power has been viewed in terms of both position and personal characteristics (see, eg, French and Raven, 1959). When public agencies engage in partnerships with disadvantaged communities, those agencies inherently carry positional power based frequently on statute and political authority. It is important to acknowledge that such power is legitimate and in some instances non-negotiable. A planning authority or a child protection agency cannot, for example, act outside its statutory obligations. Nonetheless, such position is not infrequently abused with artificial boundary-setting that masquerades as necessary when in fact it does not truly represent the potential for doing things differently. In other words, while legitimate authority has to be acknowledged, it has to be used legitimately.

In developing their relationships with disadvantaged people, openness and honesty about the power that agencies carry is essential. It may well be that community participants would want to question the laws or regulations that may determine the boundaries of action they might wish to take. In such circumstances, the basis for participatory and partnership-based planning and evaluation may not exist. Such circumstances are not necessarily common, but when they occur, they will present irreconcilable problems for those community practitioners who are part of the power structure that is under challenge.

Personal power also needs to be considered in the context of participatory planning and evaluation. Among other factors, personal power can arise from developed expertise, control of information, recognised experience, past performance and associated reputation, ability to provide incentives or rewards for particular kinds of behaviour, personality traits, or connections to others regarded as powerful. In stakeholder-based participatory planning and evaluation in community practice, positional power is usually specific to particular people because of their role in an organisation. Personal power, on the other hand, can be relevant in analysing the role-playing of all participants (including the community practitioner). It can be both enabling and disabling depending on how it is used and how it is negotiated with other participants. Here, the underlying commitment of community practice to democratic principles provides a framework for analysis of the legitimacy of the way that participants may be using power. Used positively, it can provide leadership and direction; abused, it may undermine the whole process.

Integrated planning and evaluation

The phrase 'shared vision', which has been used to describe a key aspect of effective partnerships between stakeholders, also indicates that any discussion of evaluation must also be a discussion of planning. This integrated, symbiotic relationship reflects the reality that without clarity of purpose based on negotiated agreement between stakeholders, it will be impossible to identify appropriate criteria to judge progress.

It will also be impossible to develop evaluation as a tool for reflective learning about progress that enables more effective practice to be developed. This is not, however, to suggest that evaluation only needs to consider whether plans have been achieved, it will also be important to reflect on and learn from those things that were not anticipated. Information is required regarding what actually happened, not just whether what was undertaken was intended.

The closeness of the relationship between planning and evaluation can be illustrated by identifying the key questions that need to be answered to develop a coherent plan and those that should be addressed to provide effective evaluation. Table 8.1 sets out the questions that form part of the LEAP framework

Table 8.1: Questions in the LEAP framework

Planning	Evaluation
• What are the intended outcomes?	• Were the intended inputs made?
• From the perspective of all the partners, will the outcomes be desirable?	• Were the intended outputs delivered?
• In the context of the values and principles of community practice, will the outcomes be desirable?	• Did they lead to the intended outcomes?
	• What other outcomes resulted?
• What are the intended inputs?	• From the perspective of all the partners, were the outcomes desirable?
• What are the intended processes to be used?	• In the context of the values and principles of community practice, were the outcomes desirable?
• What are the intended outputs to be delivered?	• Were the outcomes achieved efficiently and effectively?
• Will these lead to the intended outcomes?	• What has been learned?
• Can the outcomes be achieved efficiently and effectively?	• How will the lessons influence, in future, the inputs that are made, the process that are adopted, the outputs that are provided and the outcomes that are sought?
• What other outcomes could result?	

Integrating planning and evaluation into everyday work

The emphasis that has been given to the integral relationship between planning and evaluation and to the centrality of stakeholder participation should indicate that planning and evaluation are necessarily integral to everyday practice. Both LEAP and ABCD are models that are designed to support this. However, while there is little contention about integrated planning, this is not necessarily so in relation to evaluation.

In developing the frameworks, extensive consultation was undertaken through focus groups with practitioners, managers and community representatives. This revealed a tendency for agencies to see evaluation as something that outsiders should do. Usually, this would be on a periodic snapshot basis rather than a continuous process of engagement with a project or programme.

The evaluations described also tended to be summative (reaching a final judgement about performance at the end of a funding period) rather than formative (offering insights into the ongoing process and outcomes of activity that can be fed back into practice development). Frequently, this seemed to reflect a view that evaluation was primarily about accountability to funding agencies for the use of their resources rather than about learning for future action.

Not surprisingly, therefore, many community representatives and front-line workers who had been subject to such external evaluation expressed substantial dissatisfaction about their experiences. First, they saw it as threatening because it was usually commissioned in order to make decisions about future funding. While they acknowledged a need to be accountable, they frequently felt that the criteria used did not reflect community perspectives; indeed, they were often undeclared. Second, and perhaps because the evaluation was for funders rather than the community, the results were frequently not shared with them. This elicited feelings of powerlessness, resulting from lack of opportunity to scrutinise or, if necessary, challenge methods adopted or evidence presented to justify conclusions. Even if the outcome of the evaluation was positive, the evidence was not available to inform future work. Third, the sense of powerlessness was reinforced by the fact that they frequently had no influence over who was selected to undertake the evaluation. It was often felt that it was conducted by people with little acquaintance with or commitment to the needs of communities.

For the evaluators, it appeared to be a technocratic task conducted by people with apparently little sense of the complexity of community practice or the demands it places on local people. Community representatives and workers, on the other hand, were frequently passionately committed to an activity driven by a value-based vision of a better community. Overall, therefore, as a result of these concerns, many community representatives and front-line workers have felt like victims rather than beneficiaries of evaluation. In some situations, managers were also uncertain as to how the evidence gathered would inform future work.

With these frustrations in mind, it might have been expected that there would have been a strong commitment to participative approaches and involvement in self-evaluation. However, this was not the case. It was frequently described as too time-consuming to be integrated into practice. Many simply saw it as boring or as a methodological mystery – they did not feel competent to do it. Another common concern was that a too close scrutiny of how things were going was likely to be a source of conflict between participants that would divert them from important activity.

Promoting a participatory and partnership-based self-evaluation model, therefore, met with resistance from different quarters. A conundrum emerged: some key stakeholders (particularly front-line agency workers and community organisations) were resistant to evaluation; others (particularly agency managers, funders and policy makers) were insisting on it, but only on their terms. The challenge for ABCD and LEAP has been to break down these tensions and persuade the stakeholders that all of their interests are best served by engaging in a shared commitment to partnership in planning and evaluation.

The best evidence of the benefits of this approach arises from the experience of practice. People who have applied either the ABCD or LEAP framework recognise the benefits of integrated planning and evaluation as a normal part of practice. Far from finding it boring, they discover that having evidence about the efficiency and effectiveness of their work is stimulating. Rather than fermenting conflict, it exposes conflicts that were in any case latent, and it enables differences of view to be addressed in a rational and informed manner. Indeed, exposing and addressing areas of conflict becomes a positive feature of progressive activity. Certainly, action-planning and evaluation require commitment of time and effort. However, this is more than repaid by the increased clarity that it provides to the understanding of what are effective, efficient and equitable ways of working.

The concerns about time are addressed most effectively when the systematic collection of relevant information is built into the normal process of work. For agencies, workers and community organisations, this may involve rethinking how and where they record activity. In particular, they can ensure that what they record is pertinent to the outcomes that they are trying to achieve and, wherever possible, build it into an activity that would have been undertaken anyway, for example, writing minutes of meetings.

To facilitate such integrated recording, LEAP and its derivative VOiCE have been developed into accessible online tools (for further information, see: www.scdc.org.uk). These enable practitioners to work with all other stakeholders through the key stages of planning and evaluation, recording, as they go forward, the nature of the needs, the dispositions of all the interest groups, the agreed outcomes and indicators, the actions and remedial actions taken, the results of the activity, and the judgements of the stakeholders of their efficacy and implications for future activity. The LEAP and VOiCE databases can be hosted locally or accessed online. They can hold thousands of records of projects, which can be reviewed by stakeholders separately or on an aggregate basis.

The experience of the ABCD, LEAP and VOiCE programmes is that once understood and tested, users generally find the principles of the approach to be straightforward and their confidence grows with their use. They find that it enhances their capacity for effective community practice.

Conclusions

This chapter has introduced a discussion of participative planning and evaluation with particular reference to three closely linked frameworks. It has indicated that attention to effective planning and evaluation is a necessity in the context of participatory policies. But the case for planning and evaluation does not rest on the need to meet policy obligations, but on the need to promote effective practice that is consistent with its purposes and underlying principles. The models described are predicated on principles that are widely reflected in discussions of evidence-based practice.

Four key principles to inform community practice managers and underpin practice activities can be highlighted:

1. *Participative planning and evaluation should be integral to practice.* Other writers on the topic acknowledge the centrality of this principle. For example, two writers reflecting on lessons from evaluation of a community initiative in Edinburgh state:

   Evaluation needs to be integrated into practice. There is a direct relationship between good practice that should involve evaluation, and the impact of project activity. Distinctions cannot be sustained between the impact of a project, how well it operates (quality) and the way in which it works (processes). Because of this, evaluation should be an integral part of the operation, not an externally imposed activity. (Erskine and Breitenbach, 1997, p 24)

2. *Participative planning and evaluation is the fundamental component to community empowerment and capacity-building.* 'Information is power' is a commonly used phrase. While it is obviously too simplistic, it nonetheless conveys an important dimension of the ingredients of community empowerment. The capacity of managers and community practitioners to analyse and learn from their situation for the purpose of planning appropriate responses depends on access to reliable information, not only to help define the problems to be tackled, but also to reveal the impact and, hence, capacity of their current and proposed actions. Such evaluation is also required for individual participants and community organisations. Information needs to be converted into understanding of oneself, one's organisation, their respective situations and the potential to influence them. In the context of community practice that works

with those who are likely to have experienced poverty, disadvantage, discrimination and exclusion, the benefits of an integrated evaluation that provides feedback of demonstrated capacity is a critical component in building self-confidence. Evaluating self-image and knowledge as an essential step in empowerment:

> Without some evaluation of people's image of their ability to act in their own interests, goals may be generated that are unrealistic because they have overlooked people's aptitude for solving problems. In this respect a major task is to revive people's confidence. (Rees, 1991, p 90)

3. *Participative planning and evaluation is the basis for effective learning organisations.* The empowering potential of participative evaluation for communities has its corollary in the context of more complex organisations such as community partnerships. The models described in this chapter share with many others the conviction that effective learning depends on clear analysis of both the problems and the competence with which they are addressed:

> Partnerships need to be learning organisations: not only about success and failure in regeneration strategy, by monitoring, but equally about the underlying attitudes and values, reflected in working practices that partners bring to the table. These are the indicators of organisational culture, which can be gradually and constructively shifted to embrace and reward partnership working. (Carley et al, 2000, p 22)

4. *Participative planning and evaluation is the basis for accountable and influential practice.* Accountability has been a theme of this chapter. The chapter began by highlighting the significance of participatory policy as introducing a dual view of accountability that is not only about hierarchical authority, but also about user and community rights and empowerment. Later, in discussing the relationship between stakeholders, it emphasised the idea of mutual accountability. Shared planning and evaluation is a necessary ingredient of a model of governance that embraces these ideas of partnership between governors and governed. Not least among the changes required is a capacity on the part of managers and community practitioners to listen to and work with communities to enable their voice to have real influence. If participative planning and evaluation genuinely

builds community capacity, it will build the strength of voices from below:

> Capacity building needs to be more than a process of enhancing skills and developing community structures: it is also about communities having an ability to influence and have a direct impact on decisions directly affecting them. (Skinner, 1997, p 4)

References

Barr, A. and Hashagen, S. (2000) *Achieving Better Community Development*, London: CDF Publications.

Barr, A. (2000) *Learning Evaluation and Planning (LEAP)*, Glasgow: Scottish Community Development Centre.

Barr, A. (2007) *Learning Evaluation and Planning (LEAP)* (revised edition Scotland), Edinburgh: Learning Connections, Scottish Government.

Barr, A. And Dailly, J. (2008) *Learning Evaluation and Planning (LEAP)* (revised edition UK), London: Community Development Foundation.

Carley, M., Chapman, M., Hasting, A., Kirk, K. and Young, R. (2000) *Urban regeneration through partnership: a study of nine urban regions in England, Scotland and Wales*, Bristol: The Policy Press.

Erskine, A. and Brientenbach, E. (1997) 'Evaluation in community development', *Scottish Journal of Community Work and Development*, vol 2, pp 17–24.

Feurstein, M.T. (1986) *Partners in education: evaluating development and community programmes with participants*, London: Macmillan.

Freire, P. (1970) *Pedagogy of the oppressed*, New York, NY: Herder and Herder.

French, J. and Raven, B. (1959) 'The bases of social power', in D. Cartwright (ed) *Studies of social power*, Ann Arbour, MI: Institute for Social Research, pp 150–67.

Jackson, E. and Kassam, Y. (1998) *Knowledge shared: participatory evaluation in development co-operation*, Ottawa: Ottawa International Development Research Centre.

Lewin, K. (1946) 'Action research and minority problems', *Journal of Social Issues*, vol 2, no 4, pp 34–46.

Local Government Improvement and Development Agency (2011) 'Performance management: introduction and background'. Available at: www.idea.gov.uk/idk/core/page.do?pageId=4405770 (accessed April 2012).

Northern Ireland Assembly (2010) 'Sustainable development strategy for the Northern Ireland Assembly Commission'. Available at: www.niassembly.gov.uk/Documents/Corporate/Sustainable%20 Development/Sustainable_Development_Strategy_April2010.pdf (accessed April 2012).

Rees, S. (1991) *Achieving power – practice and policy in social welfare*, Sydney: Allen and Unwin.

Scottish Community Development Centre (2011) *Learning Evaluation and Planning On-line Programme*, Glasgow: Scottish Community Development Centre. Available at: www.scdc.org.uk

Scottish Executive (2004) *The Local Government in Scotland Act 2003. Community planning: statutory guidance*, Edinburgh: Scottish Executive. Available at: www.scotland.gov.uk/ Publications/2004/04/19168/35271 (accessed April 2012).

Scottish Government/Scottish Community Development Centre (2011) 'Visioning Outcomes in Community Engagement (VOiCE)'. Available at: www.voicescotland.org.uk (accessed April 2012).

Skinner, S. (1997) *Building community strengths – resource book on capacity building*, London: CDF Publications.

Welsh Assembly Government (2006) *Beyond boundaries – citizen-centred services for Wales* (Beecham Review), Cardiff: Welsh Assembly Government. Available at: www.ukcolumn.org/sites/default/files/ Beyond%20Boundaries%20-%20Beecham.pdf (accessed April 2012).

NINE

Conclusion: sustaining community practice for the future

Andrew Orton

Introduction

The revised edition of this book discusses the evolution of forms of community practice and their continuing importance, as well as the enduring opportunities and dilemmas that remain for managers. Community practitioners and their managers face considerable challenges relating to organisational management, development, accountability and ethics, which interact in complex ways. The authors contributing to this volume explored many of these issues in the preceding chapters. This concluding chapter will consider how these issues can interact to form a combined challenge to the sustainability of community practice. Building on this understanding, this chapter explores how the continuing development of theory, research and practice in this field might improve the sustainability of community practice within constantly changing contexts. In order to do this, it begins by briefly reviewing some of the key challenges presented so far, in order to begin to draw out the potential links between them.

Key challenges for sustaining community practice

As noted in Chapter Two, the policy context within which community practice is operating has continued to evolve and change. This changing context brings new challenges, as well as the need for practitioners to learn from the tensions and dilemmas already experienced historically. Responding to this changing context presents particular problems for managing and sustaining community practice within an organisational context. These include aligning and adapting structures, cultures and processes so that they continue to support community practice, as discussed in Chapter Three. The enabling of learning at both individual and organisational levels, and the building of connections between these two levels of learning, thus becomes of central importance to achieving this alignment and realising the goals of community practice over time, as argued in Chapter Four. However, the contested nature of practice and its underpinning values and principles (as discussed in Chapter Five) means that community practice is always subject to ethical tensions, debates and dilemmas, which practitioners have to navigate and negotiate on a day-to-day basis. The relational nature of community practice means that networks and informal interactions also play a crucially important role in developing this work, and these often extend beyond formal organisational structures, as discussed in Chapter Six. However, the informal and often elusive nature of these networks can also operate in ways that can embed discrimination and limit equality of engagement. Chapters Seven and Eight highlight the central role of involving communities within forms of research, planning and evaluation, enabling community participants to direct practice as it evolves.

When considered together, these chapters demonstrate how the opportunities and challenges facing community practitioners arise across individual, organisational, structural and political levels of analysis and action. Indeed, the authors collectively argue that a reflective approach to community practice should consider each of these levels carefully. This would help to inform and develop community practice in a balanced and effective way over the longer term.

Moreover, the authors argue that these levels of analysis and action do not exist independently of each other. Instead, they are interrelated in complex ways. For example, everyday reflection and action by community practitioners at the individual level is frequently bounded by organisational policies and political decisions. At the same time, these practitioners may be facilitating processes by which groups may be challenging those same policies and decisions. Without recognising the interrelatedness of these levels, and the way that these relationships change over time, the capacity for understanding and undertaking effective community practice is necessarily constrained. As a result, the development of effective and sustainable forms of community practice depends on managers being able to understand the relationships between these levels. Having considered these relationships, managers then need to be able to make strategic links between different actions and combine responses at different levels to the challenges of changing contexts, doing so in a coordinated way.

New directions for research

Having considered the development of community practice so far, where does this leave the future development of community practice? In a rapidly changing world, it is impossible to predict with any degree of accuracy where this very adaptive field may head. Indeed, arguably, it is precisely the very adaptability of community practice that has enabled it to display considerable resilience in responding to the changing environment it has experienced, contributing towards its sustainability thus far. However, it may be possible to outline some key areas where continued theoretical development could help to address the ongoing challenges that have become increasingly apparent across the chequered history of this practice. It is also possible to highlight some promising directions for future research, which might help to contribute to improving its sustainability and effectiveness if developed further. This concluding chapter will explore just three of these areas in order to illustrate the dynamic potential of research to contribute to the practice and strategy of managers and practitioners in this field. All three of these areas involve managers of community practice making dynamic, ongoing links between individual, organisational, structural and political levels of analysis and action.

Exploring further the interplay between individual learning, organisational learning, organisational design and organisational management within broader changing socio-political contexts

Given the dynamic nature of community practice, the very idea of 'managing' it might be considered to carry within it inherent tensions. This is particularly the case if 'managing community practice' is understood to mean controlling it through planning and predetermining its outcomes. If forms of learning are central to this practice, as argued in earlier chapters, then it may be impossible to predict what might result from such practice at the outset, or exactly how it might develop. Such is the inherent unpredictability of learning. Indeed, if learning is central to community practice, an important potential indicator of success could be that some *new* learning takes place, or that certain aspects of practice are done differently, as a result of the community practice, compared with what was originally expected at the outset.

Nevertheless, what the previous chapters show is that organisational design and management still matter in community practice, even if the outcomes cannot be entirely controlled or predicted. However, we require alternative ways of understanding what this management entails.

These alternative conceptions of managing are less about controlling what might result from the outset in a predetermined way. Instead, they are more about creating and sustaining the kinds of supportive environments in which community practice and organisational learning are most likely to emerge, flourish and support each other. Some approaches to organisational design and management are more supportive than others in enabling this learning and development to take place, as Chapter Four begins to explore. Conversely, there are also aspects of organisational design and management that can hinder this learning and development, as well over 30 years of research into learning organisations has shown (eg Argyris and Schön, 1978; Senge, 1990).

There remain significant challenges for managers within this process – not least how they can create and maintain organisational spaces that are supportive of community practice *over the longer term*. Over time, such spaces may be closed off by those holding traditional forms of power within the organisation, especially when they begin to threaten the status quo of organisational operation by generating more collective forms of learning and change. Indeed, some learning organisation studies have suggested that this can remain the case even if change is necessary for organisational adaptation and survival (Argyris, 1999).

The process of encouraging the development of learning spaces within organisations and communities can also be particularly difficult given the complexity of settings within which community practice often operates. This is certainly the case within traditional organisations in the public sector, which have historically adopted hierarchical and fragmented bureaucratic structures while operating amid constantly shifting political landscapes. However, it is equally (if not more) true within the emerging hybrid types of organisations, which are blending aspects of public-, private- and third-sector organisational attributes (Billis, 2010). Community practice within such organisations brings with it the need to manage additional issues relating to accountability, marketisation and ownership arising from how these aspects are blended. These are only likely to get more pronounced if the current direction of neoliberal policy development continues.

Within such complex organisations, the role of community practitioners as boundary-crossers is crucial (Lewis, 2010), as they create bridges between different aspects of organisational operation. As explored elsewhere, teams of community practitioners can make important contributions to organisational development by taking on such roles (see Banks and Orton, 2007). When operating in these roles, the ways in which they are embedded in the structures of organisations become crucially important to their ability to sustain this work over the longer term. Making connections with both the senior leadership within the organisation and wider grassroots communities outside the organisation is crucial. This is because community practitioners need to have *both* intensely local connections with particular communities *and* strategic connections with decision-makers within organisations if they are to realise their goals, which involve bridging between the two.

Maintaining this boundary-spanning position can be a difficult balancing act for community practitioners and their managers. For community practice to sustain itself more effectively in the future, managers have to do much more than just get the basic design elements within their community practice right. These basic design elements are still important; for example, ensuring that the results of any public consultations are at the very least connected in some way with related organisational decision-making structures if they are intended to have any impact on them. However, managers of community practice also have other roles, including supporting their staff to resolve strategically some of the individual dilemmas that can result from their complex position (see Chapter Five). Furthermore, they also have to find ways to enable their wider organisations to recognise the double-binds that can result for practitioners and organisations when engaging in this activity. An example of this is when community practice generates organisationally mandated public engagement that criticises current aims and practices, threatening the organisational status quo (as discussed in Chapter Four). In such situations, practitioners are caught between (i) not enabling the public engagement that their organisations have mandated them to do, and (ii) doing it and being on the receiving end of negative organisational reactions. Regardless of what course of action is taken, the sustainability of their practice may be threatened, either because they are perceived as ineffective in carrying out their brief, or because they are seen as too disruptive in fulfilling it.

Indeed, many of the dilemmas faced by individual practitioners require collective action that engages a wider range of people within the learning and change process if the aims of community practice are to be achieved. Nevertheless, this process of generative collective action, which community practitioners stimulate, can often bring to a head pre-existing intra- and extra-organisational tensions. Because of this, it is easy for community practice itself to become the scapegoat for the much wider issues that gave it birth. For example, community practice can often find itself as the practical focus of wider criticisms of current policies designed to address perceived contemporary social problems. Illustrations of this include the way that community practice can itself become the focus of critiques relating to current government policies. Recent examples of such policies include those relating to active citizenship, localism and more responsive government, or, indeed, reduced state provision, resulting in demands for greater voluntary effort or private/third-sector contributions. These themes have been explored earlier in this book and also in the wider literature (see, for example, Alcock, 2010). When working at the interface between citizens and governmental bodies, community practitioners can be attacked from all sides, as people seek to resist the change that community practice brings for a range of different reasons. As a result, community practice can sometimes seem to generate conflict, and its role in doing so can undermine its own sustainability, as others may seek to manage this conflict by removing the practitioners who are its perceived source. This remains true despite the fact that it may be necessary for community practitioners to bring underlying conflicts to the surface in order to help people to work through them. Helping people to be more aware of these underlying issues, and helping them to engage in dialogue and learning together about them, may be central to the learning process that community practice seeks to engender. Indeed, it may be that seeming to generate short-term conflict is what is necessary for the aims of community practice to be realised in situations where such short-term conflict may help issues to become more resolved in the longer term as people learn more about the issues involved together. This means that community practitioners frequently find themselves in the midst of conflict, and may be blamed for it. Such double-binds constitute an indicative area where issues central to the future of community practice have strong resonances with the theories of learning organisations discussed in Chapter Four. Strengthening the engagement of senior leadership within the organisation with community practitioners can be one helpful avenue for addressing this, and Chapter Four considers others. However, the application of such approaches to community practice is an under-researched area. Applying learning organisation approaches might hold considerable promise in adding to practitioner reflections on how they can intervene to create new possibilities of resolving the dilemmas they face. A key part of applying these approaches is the involvement of a wider range of people within and outside their organisation in reframing the problem.

To involve this wider range of people also entails looking beyond individual and organisational issues to consider wider structural and political-level issues that may be influencing the dilemmas faced in everyday practice. Some of the editors of this volume have developed the concept of 'critical community practice' to refer to practice that takes into account these wider structural and political issues (see Butcher et al, 2007).

Critically exploring the relationship between localism and community empowerment

Making links between different levels of analysis and action is also at the heart of a second potential area for further research and practice development. This second area relates to the growing recognition that there are theoretical tensions in relationships between forms of localism and community empowerment that have both been widely promoted within policy discourses.[1] These tensions can have a profound impact on community practice undertaken by individual community practitioners in local contexts who have an awareness of the wider context of their work, as this section will explore.

There has been a widespread drive towards increased localism within policy frameworks in many countries, although this may take many different forms. Common forms of localism include the decentralisation of decision-making, the promotion of increased local autonomy, the application of principles of subsidiarity in terms of the level at which decisions are taken, or even just more emphasis on the local impact of policy decisions. Many policymakers have claimed that this increased policy focus on 'the local' will automatically increase the empowerment of local communities, as Chapter Two explored. If so, this would be a development that community practitioners might be expected to support. After all, forms of increased localism that bring decision-making closer to local communities might well be expected to make decision-making more accessible and amenable to involvement by active citizens in that locality, especially when supported by the work of community practitioners. All community practice necessarily takes place within a particular local context, and policy emphases that focus on these local contexts might be considered to create a supportive context for actions taken by community practitioners within them.

However, these claims warrant more critical scrutiny, particularly by managers of community practice, who are often in the vanguard of responding to new policy trends. While many might see the local as the most favourable scale of intervention for enabling community empowerment for the reasons stated earlier, there can be problems with such understandings, depending on what is meant by 'localism' and 'empowerment'. For example, Purcell (2006) challenges the assumption that localisation necessarily produces greater empowerment. He argues that decentralisation of decision-making is not necessarily required for democratisation, and that people can fall into a 'localist trap' of assuming that one necessarily leads to the other. Indeed, it is important to explore more critically the different understandings of what localism might entail within particular settings, as well as what its prerequisites and outcomes might be.

Understandings of the concept of empowerment are similarly contested, involving a range of interpretations about who might be empowered (from individualistic interpretations to those involving wider groups and communities) and what this might mean. There are also tensions inherent within the concept, even if the desire to empower is well-intentioned. If individuals or groups are dependent on another, more powerful person to 'empower' them, then might even the process of 'empowerment' itself and the way that it is targeted on particular groups form part of their relative lack of power? Might there be a risk that those seeking to 'empower' may subsequently withdraw their support if individuals or groups do not develop in the ways that the person seeking to empower them desires? If people remain dependent on this support, does it truly result in a gain in power by the subject of this process? As Cruickshank (1999, p 60) argues: the process of empowerment 'is a strategy for constituting and regulating the political subjectivities of the empowered.... Empowerment is itself a power relationship'. Such debates are important for community practitioners to consider when thinking critically about the nature of their work with individuals and groups.

Furthermore, at the heart of the debates about linking these two processes of localism and empowerment is an important question of whether there can ever be a purely localised solution through community practice for problems that have global dimensions. This is important because many of the issues that commonly form the focus of community practice within local communities involve problems that are at least partly constituted and maintained by forces operating at global levels. For example, complex social problems such as poverty, unemployment, difficult relationships between people in communities that are increasingly diverse due to migration, and the often-hostile reception received by refugees are all issues that have complex links at the individual, local, national and global levels.

The drive towards localist thinking can carry with it the peril of oversimplifying community relations, so that only relationships on the localised scale are recognised (Mohan and Stokke, 2000). In particular, there is a risk that localised community practice, focusing solely on the individual and organisational levels, might miss the vital importance of making wider connections outside the local area, including at national and transnational levels. Making these links and devising wider coordinated strategies across different localities will be vital if changes to systemic social and political problems are to be achieved (Mohan and Stokke, 2000). For example, community practice that leads to change on the individual and organisational levels can seek to be part of wider movements, as well as achieving localised gains. At the same time, such insights need to be balanced with the recognition that all actions necessarily take place within a local context and have to start from somewhere. Balancing these insights has proved crucial in many historical movements for social change, as exemplified in the feminist statement that 'the personal is political', and in many environmental campaigns that acknowledge the importance of local action in addressing global environmental problems. Exploring the dynamic and fluid nature of these power relationships between the individual, organisational, local, national and global levels is a helpful way of exploring the relationships between structural factors that affect people's lives and people's capacity to change them through individual and collective action (Dominelli, 2000).

However, even if the theoretical necessity of linking these different levels of potential action is accepted, the determination of the best practical ways of building such links remains highly controversial (Edwards, 2009). There are also important questions concerning how such levels of potential action might interact with communities of interest and identity as well as place. These are linked with the agendas and issues relating to co-production of community services and deliberative community engagement discussed in Chapter One. It is within these arenas that community practitioners could draw more extensively on the established international literature in the fields of community development and international development, which have been exploring responses that address such debates. However, these fields have also had their own related theoretical and practical challenges, so this is an area where further dialogue between those involved in community practice and related fields could mutually enhance their existing practice understandings. This leads to a third area in which the theory and practice of managing community practice could be further developed.

Developing strengthened communities of practice, members of which are better able to reflect together and learn from their past and current experiences

It is precisely because community practice involves working on issues that have individual, organisational, structural and political dimensions that community practitioners cannot develop their understandings of their practice in isolation. Authors of the chapters in this book have already pointed to various collective strategies that are used by practitioners and their managers to support a process of developing and learning about practice together. These include individual and team supervision and the development of underpinning networks. Arguably, the effectiveness of these types of collaborative learning strategies might be further improved with the development of more intentional 'communities of practice' (Wenger, 1998). These are groups of people informally bound together by shared expertise and their passion for a joint enterprise. Although sometimes difficult to establish and facilitate, communities of practice have the benefit of enabling members to support each other in reflecting together and learning from their past and current experiences. However, communities of practice do not necessarily just develop of their own accord; there is much that managers can do proactively to encourage their development (Wenger et al, 2002). Within such strengthened communities of practice, practitioners can support each other in developing essential skills such as negotiating dilemmatic space and handling authority relations (Hoggett et al, 2009). As Hoggett et al recognise, practitioners need to reflect on their own values, commitments and how these affect their practice as a crucial part of this process. For community practitioners, this often involves them going beyond the mistaken image of being considered 'neutral professionals' and instead involves them engaging directly with the highly political issues at the heart of their work. Managers of community practice can play a crucial role within this, both in supporting individual and collective forms of such reflection within teams of community practitioners, and in their work at the interface with the wider political issues as team managers. Indeed, the companion volume to this book, *Critical community practice* (Butcher et al, 2007), explores these issues in depth, including the values and understandings that might underpin critical and committed practice in this arena. Nevertheless, such understandings are necessarily always evolving, and do so within communities of practitioners who enact and discuss their responses to changing contexts together. This makes the further consideration of how best to encourage and develop such mutual reflection, sharing, collaboration and learning within communities of practice crucial.

Conclusion

When combined together, these directions for the future development of theory, research and practice within community practice could improve its sustainability, despite the many inherent and contextual challenges it faces. By reflecting together and learning from past and current experiences in a more collaborative way, new strategies for managing community practice can be devised by those involved within it. When such reflection is also informed by a critical awareness of previous attempts to devise such strategies, these previous strategies may be refined in ways that may help to overcome some of their historic limitations. As this volume demonstrates, such reflection and learning can be informed by a wide range of related theory and research, on which managers of community practice can helpfully draw in developing new ways forward.

At the same time, individual and collective reflection and learning also benefit from critical analysis of some of the underlying concepts and assumptions in common usage. Examples include the relationship between 'localism' and 'community empowerment' considered in this chapter, and discussions of the concept of 'community' in Chapter One. These discussions enable managers of community practice to be better able to explore how current understandings of this work can both help and hinder the ways that we develop it in practice.

In addition, it is crucial to extend these individual and collective reflections to include explorations of the interactions between the individual, organisational and wider socio-political levels of analysis and action. By doing this, managers of community practice can seek to improve their effectiveness by taking coordinated action that recognises the wide range of levels at which analysis and action can take place. This is essential given the complexity of the issues that managers of community practice are engaged in tackling. In the process, they can also raise awareness of the multilayered ways that community practice seeks to respond to these issues, and seek to make the environment more conducive at all levels to the realisation of the aims of community practice. By continuing this process of analysis, reflection, dialogue and action, managers of community practice can help sustain adaptable forms of community practice that further improve their effectiveness in the future.

Note

[1] This section draws on a literature review and critical synthesis carried out by Painter et al (2011) as part of a research project on 'Connected Communities', in which the author was involved. This scoping study was funded by the Arts and Humanities Research Council under the cross-council Connected Communities programme. A full copy, which includes a wider range of supporting sources than can be included here in this summary, is freely available at: http://dro.dur.ac.uk/9244/1/9244.pdf

References

Alcock, P. (2010) 'A strategic unity: defining the third sector in the UK', *Voluntary Sector Review*, vol 1, no 1, pp 5–24.

Argyris, C. (1999) *On organizational learning*, Oxford: Blackwell.

Argyris, C. and Schön, D.A. (1978) *Organizational learning: a theory of action perspective*, London: Addison-Wesley.

Banks, S. and Orton, A. (2007) '"The grit in the oyster": community development workers in a modernizing local authority', *Community Development Journal*, vol 42, no 1, pp 97–113.

Billis, D. (2010) 'Revisiting the key challenges: hybridity, ownership and change', in D. Billis (ed) *Hybrid organizations and the third sector: challenges for practice, theory and policy*, Basingstoke: Palgrave Macmillan, pp 240–62.

Butcher, H., Banks, S. and Henderson, P., with Robertson, J. (2007) *Critical community practice*, Bristol: The Policy Press.

Cruickshank, B. (1999) *The will to empower: democratic citizens and other subjects*, Ithaca, NY: Cornell University Press.

Dominelli, L. (2000) 'Empowerment: help or hindrance in professional relationships?', in D. Ford and P. Stepney (eds) *Social work models, methods and theories: a framework for practice*, Lyme Regis: Russell House Publishing.

Edwards, M. (2009) *Civil society*, Cambridge: Polity Press.

Hoggett, P., Mayo, M. and Miller, C. (2009) *The dilemmas of development work: ethical challenges in regeneration*, Bristol: The Policy Press.

Lewis, D. (2010) 'Encountering hybridity: lessons from individual experiences', in D. Billis (ed) *Hybrid organizations and the third sector: challenges for practice, theory and policy*, Basingstoke: Palgrave Macmillan, pp 219–39.

Mohan, G. and Stokke, K. (2000) 'Participatory development and empowerment: the dangers of localism', *Third World Quarterly*, vol 21, no 2, pp 247–68.

Painter, J., Orton, A., MacLeod, G., Dominelli, L. and Pande, R. (2011) *Connecting localism and community empowerment*, Durham: Durham University.

Purcell, M. (2006) 'Urban democracy and the local trap', *Urban Studies*, vol 43, no 11, pp 1921–41.

Senge, P.M. (1990) *The fifth discipline: the art and practice of the learning organization*, London: Random House.

Wenger, E. (1998) *Communities of practice*, Cambridge: Cambridge University Press.

Wenger, E., McDermott, R. and Snyder, W.M. (2002) *Cultivating communities of practice: a guide to managing knowledge*, Boston, MA: Harvard Business Press.

Index